# JUSTIFYING LAW

# JUSTIFYING LAW

*The Debate over Foundations, Goals, and Methods*

RAYMOND A. BELLIOTTI

TEMPLE UNIVERSITY PRESS

*Philadelphia*

Temple University Press, Philadelphia 19122
Copyright © 1992 by Temple University. All rights reserved
Published 1992
Printed in the United States of America

The paper used in this publication meets the minimum
requirements of American National Standard for Information
Sciences—Permanence of Paper for Printed Library Materials,
ANSI Z39.48-1984 ⊗

**Library of Congress Cataloging-in-Publication Data**

Belliotti, Raymond A., 1948–
    Justifying law : the debate over foundations, goals, and methods /
Raymond A. Belliotti.
        p.   cm.
    Includes bibliographical references and index.
    ISBN 0-87722-818-3 (alk. paper)
    1. Law—Philosophy.   2. Sociological jurisprudence.   3. Judicial
process.   4. Law and politics.   I. Title.
K230.B435J87   1992
340—dc20                                                    91-13988
                                                                CIP
                                                                Rev

For Marcia, Angelo, and Vittoria
*sangu du me sangu*

# CONTENTS

PART THREE
*Law's Aspirations and Philosophical Method:*
*Promises, Impasses, and New Directions*

# ACKNOWLEDGMENTS

THE SEEDS of this book were sown by the three men who are most responsible for my philosophical training: Leonard S. Carrier, Ramon M. Lemos, and James W. Rachels. Their influence endures.

I would also like to thank Richard D. Parker, Roberto M. Unger, and Lloyd L. Weinreb, whose law school courses were always most interesting and unsettling.

Jane Cullen, my editor, provided consistent encouragement, sound advice, and good humor. She understood that a book project can be taken seriously without taking its author too seriously.

Without the support of my wife, Marcia Dalby Belliotti, this book would not have been completed. She read the manuscript several times, counseled me about improvements, and never wavered in her conviction that my project was important. She invigorated me when I was timid, and she calmed me when I was foolhardy. Her love animated my passion.

Finally, I would like to thank the editors of the following journals for permission to adapt material from my articles: "Toward a Theory of Judicial Decisionmaking," 28 *The Catholic Lawyer* 215 (1983); "Essay Review: *Law and Revolution*," Harold J. Berman (Harvard University Press, 1983), 50 *Brooklyn Law Review* 351 (1984); "The Rule of Law and the Critical Legal Studies Movement," 24 *University of Western Ontario Law Review* 67 (1986); "Is Law a Sham?" 48 *Philosophy and Phenomenological Research* 25 (1987); "Critical Legal Studies: The Paradoxes of Indeterminancy and Nihilism," 13 *Philosophy and Social Criticism* 145 (1987); "Our Adversary System: In Search of a Foundation," 1 *Canadian Journal of Law and Jurisprudence* 19 (1988); "Marxism, Feminism, and Surrogate Motherhood," 14 *Social Theory and Practice* 389 (1988); "Radical Politics and Nonfoundational Morality," 29 *International Philosophical Quarterly* 33 (1989); "Beyond Capitalism and Communism: Roberto Unger's Superliberal Political Theory," 9 *Praxis International* 321 (1989); and "Marxist Jurisprudence," 4 *Canadian Journal of Law and Jurisprudence* 145 (1991).

# INTRODUCTION

## The Terms of the Debate
### *Legal Formalism and Legal Realism*

$J$*ustifying Law* presents a critical survey of a number of philosophical approaches to law and judicial decision making. In the context of classical and contemporary legal theories, it addresses the rationality and irrationality of law; the presence or absence of preexisting "right answers" to legal questions; the role, if any, of normative reasoning in judicial decision making; the actual effects of legal decisions on society; the appropriate roles for legal and extralegal materials in determining answers to legal questions; and the relationship between the Rule of Law and politics.

This book embodies a story, a historical dialogue with numerous layers of complexity. It is the straightforward tale of how theories of jurisprudence respond to and mirror concrete social reality and how various theorists at different historical periods have tried valiantly to sustain or unsettle the privileges of law. It also tracks the relentless philosophical struggle between objectivist and relativist accounts of value, knowledge, and reality and unmasks this struggle as symbiotic collusion rather than adversarial combat. Moreover, the book suggests a relationship between jurisprudential theory and political affiliation, and highlights the differences between those who pledge allegiance to the fundamental soundness of the current social order and those who stake their being on the need for massive social transformations. On another level this book tries to sharpen our understanding of subtle normative concepts such as legitimacy, rightful authority, and rational constraints. Furthermore, it is a self-conscious attempt to search for the truth about judicial decision making, insofar as truth is available to us. Finally, this book witnesses the intersection of the methods, findings, and internally competing visions of several disciplines: natural science, social science, humanities, and the arts. Although its story could be told and most of its various levels of complexity realized in numerous contexts, this work focuses on the judicial branch of our democratic republic, a judiciary whose power is often experienced as at once necessary yet arbitrary. As such, this book selects judicial decision making as its context to try to make sense of our conflicting experiences, often incompatible aspirations, and underlying fears when we confront life's existential puzzles.

I begin with a discussion of Legal Formalism and Legal Realism because these theories frame the terms of the debate. Classical philosophical discussions of judicial decision making invariably center on attempts to solidify or unsettle the claims of these two positions. Even most contemporary discussions focus on subtle attempts to refine formalism and realism and to resuscitate the primacy of one or the other. Thus, Legal Formalism and Legal Realism represent the poles that most legal theories tacitly assume exhaust the range of possibilities.

One of the missions of *Justifying Law* is to unmask and debunk that assumption. In Part One, I explain and criticize mainstream theories that form the core of law. In Part Two, I examine the leftist critique of law. In Part Three, I argue for a view that I call Critical Pragmatism. This position transcends the enfeebled polarities of formalism and realism, retains certain normative justifications for law's coercive power, and yet takes the leftist critique of law seriously.

## LEGAL FORMALISM

At its most uncompromising, this is the view that judicial decision making is a scientific, deductive process by which preexisting legal materials subsume particular legal cases under their domain, thus allowing judges to infer the antecedently existing right answer to the case at bar. Here judicial decision making is viewed as rational, constrained by preexisting, determinate norms and rules.[1]

Under this view, the law consists of a body of propositions with necessary normative elements. In our legal system, these propositions emanate from and constitute legislative enactments, lower-court opinions, United States Supreme Court decisions, and constitutional provisions. Thus, the law consists of a limited number of fundamental doctrines and principles, and legal growth occurs through the logical development of these materials. Judges have no discretion to appeal to extralegal materials when deciding cases, because sufficiently complex and bountiful legal systems are "gapless" and therefore contain antecedently existing right answers to all or virtually all legal questions. Judges discover the requirements of law through proper use of their cognitive faculties; they do not create these requirements through acts of will. Law is viewed as an intrinsic good, which constitutes its own ideal, rather than merely a human artifact designed to serve external ends.

Legal Formalism thus affirms the presence of a method of legal reasoning and justification that is uncontaminated by political and ideological dispute ("the rationality claim"); a distinctive rationality that is immanent in legal materials ("the immanence claim"); and a guiding normative vision, an intelligible moral order, that explains and justifies the bulk of received legal opinion but that has the capacity to criticize and stigmatize certain small pockets of doctrine as mistakes ("the normativity claim").[2]

The seductions of Legal Formalism may seem irresistible. If correct, the theory would strengthen adherence to the Rule of Law, underscore the prescriptive force of legal decision making by protecting law from the merely subjective preferences of judges and the arbitrariness of unbridled discretion, uphold the integrity and rationality of the legal system, and insulate judges from politics by illustrating the irrelevance of extralegal considerations in the decision-making process.

However, critics of Legal Formalism are numerous and strident. At a general level, Legal Formalism has been or can be criticized for its worship of lifeless abstractions and theoretical constructs, which results in a detachment from social reality; its treatment of legal categories and classifications as if they were natural kinds; its pretense that language embodied in legal rules is determinant; and its effect of artificially truncating the range of judicial interpretive choices.[3]

The rationality claim is demystified by the empirical observation that abstract, instrumental reasoning and open-endedness pervade the law. In legal decision making the evidence seems to underdetermine judicial conclusions. There can be no complete and determinant specification of normative concepts that might predetermine all future decisions. For example, in major constitutional cases phrases such as *due process, equal protection, cruel and unusual punishment, regulation of interstate commerce,* and *freedom of speech* hardly come prepackaged with determinate content.[4] Moreover, the competing specifications of general principles that emerge cannot be compelled by neutral logical legerdemain, but instead emanate, at least partially, from conflicting descriptive and prescriptive world visions.

The immanence claim seems redolent with vicious circularity. If normative legal principles are too general and abstract to admit full antecedent determination, then it is highly dubious that their coherent integration can gestate an internal ideal that is independent of extrinsic instrumentality. The immanence claim seems more like an attempt to shield law from scrutiny—to exonerate it from complicity in the social effects it harvests—than a convincing demonstration of an unassailable inner ideal. Formalists who embrace the immanence claim seem like desperate magicians who, after numerous failures to pull the rabbit out of the hat, are reduced to stuffing the bunny in the fedora.

Critics assail the normativity claim because of its dependence on an intelligible moral order.[5] Those who disbelieve that values are embedded in nature itself, or that normative concepts bear antecedent and determinate specification, are unlikely to evince passionate faith in the intrinsic goodness or inherent impartiality of law.

All the criticisms adumbrated above seem to lead to an inescapable conclusion: formalists mask the necessary and inevitably contestable political choices that judges make when selecting which general legal principles to apply to concrete cases and when determining how to apply them. Motivated by the desire to bring legal reasoning into the supposed realm of the natural sciences, thereby insulating judges from political conflict and sanctifying the Rule of Law, the formalists' vision seems to ignore the role of historical context and social reality in judicial decision making. Accordingly, this vision becomes susceptible to the charge radicals take to be most lethal: formalists have ignored and obscured social reality because they are mere apologists for the political status quo.

## LEGAL REALISM

This view, which emerged explicitly in the 1920s and reached its zenith in the 1930s and early 1940s, asserts that contradictory and conflicting decisions pervade the law.[6] Judicial decision making is not and cannot be fashioned from logical deduction. The realist claims that formalism must fail because of the limits of our language and logic and the indeterminacy of moral and normative concepts. Under this view, concepts are not embedded in nature but are merely conventions of social life. Any set of legal facts is, according to realists, classifiable in an indefinite number of ways. All legal classifications are merely conventions motivated by the interests of various classes or individuals possessing a relative power advantage that translates into privilege. Theory characterizes reality rather than reality being a given that humans discover in some non-theoretical fashion. Such an approach denies the existence of an ultimately objective or discoverable neutral meaning. In any nontrivial case, a judge can advance several plausible competing general principles, which generate conflicting conclusions. Because of all this, no interpretation or application of language can be logically required by the language itself. Words are created, defined, and applied by people saturated by their social conditions and historical context. Each act of judicial interpretation is therefore an act of social choice.[7]

Under this view, a judge's argument is merely a rationalization, and not the true explanation, of her decision. Judges necessarily manipulate precedent and other legal material after making decisions. That is, they cannot use past legal doctrine as a treasure chest within which they will discover the antecedent right answer to the instant case; rather, it is only after they arrive at a decision on other grounds that they can consult past doctrine for supporting material. Accordingly, a judge's private motives and values are fundamental to and necessary for understanding the legal conclusions she asserts. To understand judicial decision making we must look at the behavior of judges, not abstract legal argument.[8] Realists believe that considerations stemming from social needs and political conflict are more important to the development of law than are logical propositions. Moreover, realists believe that each fact pattern stands alone and, therefore, general principles cannot decide particular cases. Consequently, judges are constantly creating new law, not merely applying preexisting law.

It is important to note that realists generally do not suspect that their descriptive account of judicial decision making is the result of a plethora of insidious or dishonest judges; rather, judges decide as they do because of the limitations of our language, logic, and normative concepts. Therefore, realists reject even the possibility that officials in complex legal systems could substantially comply with most elements of the Rule of Law.

Legal Realists thus claim that law is in constant flux and is reshaped in the light of changing social reality; that judges, animated by private motives and values, constantly create new law through acts of will; that the personal element is paramount with judges, but is not entirely arbitrary because judges share the value standards of at least an important part of the community, as well as the common socialization of their profession; that abstract legal propositions do not and cannot provide predetermined answers to nontrivial legal questions; that the legal system is far from gapless, and antecedently existing right answers are present only for trivial questions; and that judicial decision making is thus riddled with discretionary and non-rational choices.[9]

In the face of this radical account, various realists offered three different prescriptive solutions: (1) some suggested that the proper response was extreme judicial deference to the expressed desires of legislatures. After all, at least elected legislators, unlike judges who are often mere political appointees, are directly accountable to the people.[10] (2) Others suggested that judges should be conscious of the strong discretion they inevitably possess and must reflect "up-to-date" values (translated: liberal or socialist values) in their decisions, while abrogating reliance on anachronistic laissez-faire capitalism.[11] (3) Still others concluded that judicial decision making should be based on empirical data gathered and analyzed by social scientists rather than on inherently malleable, artificial legal concepts. Such realists placed their faith in the emerging social sciences as the trainers of managerial elites and the discoverers of human behavior patterns. Administrative agencies were thought better equipped to perform such necessary tasks, and they were viewed as the appropriate instrument of social reform. Thus, such realists advocated a power shift from the judiciary to expert state agencies.[12]

There is a relationship between the adoption of a particular view of judicial decision making and the value judgment one makes about the political status quo. Most Legal Realists had reformist aspirations. They perceived the political status quo as reactionary, anti-democratic, and partially the result of looking at law from a formalist perspective. Conceiving the law instrumentally, they were overwhelmingly concerned with the results of judicial decisions rather than with analyzing abstract legal reasoning. Most believed that values had a historical context and were not capable of determinate, eternal resolutions. Moreover, questions of value were thought to arise, not from an intellectual vacuum, but from political struggle and commitment. Accordingly, realists conspired to achieve necessary political reform by taking an important preliminary step: the debunking of traditional formalist pretensions in judicial decision making.

Numerous criticisms have been or could be raised against Legal Realism. First, realism seems to accept and justify as inevitable a significant amount of judicial discretion in most legal cases, thereby signaling free rein to and overly broad powers for unelected officials. Second, such discretion is accompanied by the disintegration of even the possibility of achieving the aspirations embodied by the Rule of Law. Third, those realists who deny foundational justification for moral and legal reasoning invite the charge of self-refuting relativism. How can we advocate confidently the implementation of "up-to-date" values while we simultaneously explode the myth of nonsubjective moral justification? Fourth, the relentless and all-pervasive attack realists advance against formalist pretensions may result in an impotent, effete skepticism, which prohibits realists themselves from consistently developing a constructive program.

Fifth, realism replaces what it takes to be formalism's idolatry of logical abstraction with an equally pernicious worship: its blind obsession with and faith in the social sciences. It is unclear that psychological, economic, historical, and sociological analyses rest on any firmer foundation than moral theory and logical deduction. Sixth, realists may in fact be supraformalists in thin disguise. Like formalists, realists assume that the law is determinate and rational only if its identification and application are more or less mechanical. Thus, extreme realists share with extreme formalists the assumption that nondeductive reasoning is incapable of adequately establishing legal conclusions. Taken as a general claim, this suggests an extreme epistemological skepticism about the possibility of any substantive claim, for even the natural sciences produce conclusions that logically outstrip the evidence used to establish them.[13] Accordingly, it appears that realism debunks the pretensions of formalism by ironically assuming one of extreme formalism's main tenets and unwittingly degenerates into a rejection of the possibility of any substantive knowledge.

Finally, realism, despite its animating aspirations, ignores a certain aspect of legal reality: the rational constraint that judges report and experience when making their decisions.[14] Most judges believe and act on the assumption that the legal system is constituted by at least some of the virtues espoused by the Rule of Law, a reality which realists seem to ignore or deny. It is odd that realists implicitly hold the view that judicial decision making can be understood independently of the meaning and values that judges who participate in the process attribute to it.

## FORMALISM AND REALISM: ADVERSARIES OR SYMBIOTIC COLLABORATORS?

Extreme formalism and extreme realism are fueled by background theories that accept certain dichotomies about the nature of language, rationality, and normative reasoning.

*Language.* Formalism and realism accept the following dilemma: either language is constituted by fixed meanings that allow natural classifications, demarcated spheres, and principled line drawing, or language is merely conventional and its users are always and inevitably reflecting particular interests or ideologies.

Fixed meanings coalesce easily with the aspirations of the minions of deductive logic and facilitate the possibility of the Rule of Law. Moreover, fixed meanings can serve the human yearning for stability and order not merely in law but in life. As such, this formalist view of language, if correct, deserves a place of honor in the pantheon of classical liberal legal and political theory.

But linguistic conventionalists charge that such a view must rest on a belief similar to Plato's view of intelligible essences and thus confuses natural kinds with human artifacts.[15] They argue that no interpretation or application of language is logically required by language itself. There is no discoverable meaning built into the universe and no persuasive essentialistic explanation of the relationship between language and reality.[16] Absent a belief in a suprahuman entity, we must admit that language and meaning are human creations designed to advance certain human purposes and goals and to thwart other possible purposes and goals. The realist embrace of conventionalism underscores the human longing for social change and for the freedom to control and master nature. Accordingly, "social choice" becomes the slogan of conventionalists, choice that is permeated with and constituted by subjective political preferences.

Conventionalists, having accepted the truth of the language dichotomy, admit that their view of language explicitly calls into question the possibility of the Rule of Law. But they maintain that their view comports more closely with the phenomenology of discourse and deprives us of nothing we had not already lost; rather, it claims to liberate us from fantasy and illusion.[17]

*Rationality.* Extreme formalism and extreme realism accept the following dilemma: either legal rationality is a deductive process, whereby sound argument involves general propositions subsuming particulars and yielding true conclusions, or legal rationality is contaminated with subjective value preferences, and rationalizations based on such preferences masquerade as logical arguments.

Formalists embrace deduction because they harbor the suspicion that only a "scientific" rendering of legal rationality can redeem the Rule of Law. Any nondeductive method, whether it be inductive, analogical, or metaphorical, jeopardizes the traditional role of the judge as an applier and not creator of law. Moreover, the elements of the Rule of Law and adherence to the traditional judicial role are themselves necessary if our pledge of a "government of laws, not persons" is to be more than emotive, but empty, Independence Day rhetoric.

Realists, bearing a prior commitment to linguistic conventionalism, view the formalists' embrace of deduction as pretense of a most debilitating sort. Political opposition, according to realists, is silenced or muted by the bludgeon of a logic claiming to transcend human controversy. In this manner, through transcendentalism and mystification and with the connivance of the emotional rhetoric of the ideology of the Rule of Law, the political status quo is shielded from destabilization any more serious than marginal adjustment and incremental tinkering.

In truth, say the realists, our legal norms are necessarily broadly and vaguely stated and do not lead logically to particular results or specific rationales concerning substantive matters. As mere abstraction and form, legal doctrine begs for the content supplied only by judicial fiat. Hence, contradictory and conflicting decisions pervade the law, and there is no fully coherent body of legal doctrine. Moreover, there cannot be a coherent body of law absent complete uniformity of the political preferences of the judiciary over time, a miracle not even the co-opting and legitimating effects of centrist–capitalist ideology can accomplish.

Both extreme formalists and extreme realists accept the premise that if legal rationality is not deductive, then it is pretense and rationalization. The formalist, terrified by the prospect of the corrosion and desecration of the Rule of Law, denies that legal rationality is mere pretense and argues that it must therefore be deductive. The realist, truculently refusing to accept what she takes to be an illusion at variance with the phenomenology of legal decision making, denies that legal rationality is deductive and thus concludes that it must be mere rationalization that insidiously masks political motives and effects.

*Normative Reasoning.* Extreme formalists and extreme realists accept the following dilemma: either morality is justified foundationally by a metaphysical linchpin such as a normative order immanent in nature or a Supreme Being who embodies and defines goodness, or morality is yet another human artifact based on the conventions of culture, history, and contingent agreements.

Formalists invariably have been convinced that self-evident moral principles or privileged intuitions—immediate apprehensions of the essence of humans and the human good—are like scientific observations that indicate independent natural moral facts. Alternatively, they may espouse a literal rendering of the moral truths revealed by a Supreme Being. The law, under this model, is or should be linked with absolute, transcendent principles of morality that humans can discover but not create.

Realists deprecate the metaphysical assumptions of moral foundationalism as unworthy of belief. Based on faith and wish more than demonstrable proof, such beliefs appear to realists as the anachronistic psychological remnants of primitives desperate in the face of unexplained powers. Morality, for a realist, is explained instrumentally—as a compendium of customs and conventions perceived as necessary to social cooperation. Lacking any transcendental lives of their own, moral codes vary radically across cultures and are a human invention without independent or foundational justification.

*Objectivism and Relativism.* The versions of formalism and relativism described here are symbiotic collaborators more than adversarial combatants. They assume that the choices constituting the three dilemmas adumbrated above are exhaustive and thus define the range of possibilities. The acceptance of this fundamental assumption is what confers legitimacy and brio on the formalist–realist debate. Yet these three dilemmas are merely instantiations of a general dichotomy: objectivism versus relativism.

Objectivism champions the presence of an ultimate grounding, discoverable but not created by humans, that provides authoritative, ahistorical evaluation for all claims of truth. Relativism, abrogating the Metaphysical Realism that objectivists support, points out the incommensurability of and unremitting conflict among different paradigms, theories, and forms of life; absent a belief in the objectivists' metaphysical illusions, it claims that we lack the tools to postulate an overarching Archimedean framework and must acknowledge that we are limited to historical contexts and contingencies.

The debate between objectivists and relativists is a tired and disreputable discourse. Objectivists herald the broad areas of cross-cultural agreement and point out that the mere existence of other significant disagreements among paradigms, theories, and forms of life does not entail the absence of transcendental standards, because some of the conflicting postulates may simply be incorrect. Moreover, objectivists never claim that the existence of ahistorical standards guarantees that all cultures and historical periods will be able to grasp truths equally well. Finally, objectivists repeatedly play their trump card and warn of the nihilistic dangers of relativism, the only perceived alternative to objectivism, citing its inability to provide fundamental justification for its own claims, its invitation to chaos, and its implied message that power and the ability to assert one's will is more important than attention to foundational truths.

Relativists claim that the only broad areas of cross-cultural agreement concern highly general, abstract principles that lack the specification required for consensus over concrete issues. When specific policies are at stake, truisms such as "do good, avoid evil," "honor the dead," and "respect families" admit of too many contestable interpretations to support the thesis that there is a normative order embedded in nature. Moreover, according to relativists, objectivists assume incorrectly that the burden of persuasion rests on relativists to "prove a negative": the nonexistence of ethereal, admittedly transcendent standards that supposedly lie beyond our direct observations of the world we know. To relativists this seems too much like taking seriously a psychotic who believes in the existence of a six-foot pink rabbit named Vito, and who refuses to believe the insurmountable evidence against the existence of Vito and thus demands that nonbelievers have the epistemological burden to "prove" Vito's nonexistence. Relativists ask rhetorically, "Given the available evidence and the fact that we seemingly cannot prove the existence or nonexistence of such entities conclusively through rational demonstrations, which is more likely—that a supernatural being or other source confers a natural normative order on our world or that any perceived order is in fact a human invention subject to reimagination and re-creation?" Finally, relativists discharge their heaviest artillery: they claim that objectivism is an artificial device to ensure that traditionally received opinions gain a stature and legitimacy that make them immune to political destabilization.

Extreme formalism and extreme realism, which present themselves as adversaries locked in life-and-death struggle, are in fact (unknowing) collaborators in the perpetuation of the artificially truncated debate between objectivism and relativism. Both views disenfranchise enlightened critical analysis of fundamental moral, political, and legal beliefs. Extreme formalism disintegrates into a prissy, stagnant dogmatism that nourishes intellectual inertia and holds us hostage to the claims of the false necessity that the familiar is the inevitable. On the other hand, extreme realism despoils into an abject, radical cynicism that acrimoniously corrodes our unresolved souls.

The general debate between objectivism and relativism exudes gusto and vitality only if we share the antecedent commitment that these two poles define the range of possibilities. But it is precisely this commitment that much contemporary philosophy calls into question.[18] Such efforts aspire to expose the objective–relative, fixed meaning–conventionalism, deductive–nonrational, and Metaphysical Realism–radical historicism polarities as inadequate and transformable.

# PART ONE

The Core of Law
*Analytic Jurisprudence*

# CHAPTER 1

## The Immanent Moral Order and Law's Objectivity
### *Natural Law*

### THE ROOTS OF NATURAL LAW THEORY

Mᴏʀᴇ ᴛʜᴀɴ five centuries before the birth of Christ, the earliest recorded Western thinkers assumed that a natural order was immanent in the universe. They believed that this order was not created by humans but could be discovered by them through reason and careful attention to nature's messages. Moreover, the natural order was thought to be not merely descriptive and scientific but also normative and action-guiding.[1]

The presocratic philosophers (600–400 B.C.) took the universe to be self-generative and to embody the elements of change.[2] Conceived in such a fashion, the universe was itself a living organism that admitted of no distinctions between creator and created or between the material and the spiritual. These philosophers overwhelmingly supported the fusion of the descriptive and the normative: in spite of its considerable mystery, the order of the world was seen as not merely regular but also good.

Philosophical debates during this period centered on whether criteria of value were grounded in community conventions or in a higher reality.[3] Moreover, those who agreed that standards of value are conventional still disputed whether such an acknowledgment reduces morality to "might makes right." Meanwhile, those who subscribed to the view that only the permanent and unchanging is truly real aspired to a reaffirmation of the objectivity of morality grounded in the natural order of the universe.[4]

*Plato and Aristotle.* Plato (428–347 B.C.) abrogated merely conventionalist accounts of morality and instead championed a strong version of objectivism. He argued that concrete "Forms" or "Universals" existed in a suprasensible world that due to its unchanging and permanent nature constituted Reality.[5] The transient, sensible world of ordinary experience was merely an ersatz version of the organic unity comprised of the various Forms. The final expression of this unity is the Form of the Good, which explains the other Forms and the creative intelligence responsible for our world. Particular material objects in our world participate in and approximate their respective Forms, and finite human beings likewise approximate the creative intelligence. Under this view, the universe is guided by rational, moral principles and the human soul serves as a link between the world of Forms and our world. Accordingly, humans do not create morality but can discover it and direct themselves to it through reason. Moreover, earthly decrees and pretensions to justice are compelling only if they participate in and correspond to the objective reality constituted by the Forms. Clearly, through his metaphysical sophistication and elaborate ontology, Plato advances the early Greek presumption of a normative natural order.[6]

Aristotle's (384–322 B.C.) empiricism led him to the view that our material world is fully real. Although agreeing with Plato that change and movement must ultimately be explained by an unchanging, permanent entity, Aristotle did not rely on a suprasensible world of Forms. Rather, he posited a formal, unchanging aspect embedded in particular objects of our world.[7] Unlike Plato's Forms, such a "Universal" does not exist separately from particular objects, but it can be "abstracted in thought."[8] The formal element in all particulars is teleological: it is the function that a particular thing embodies by its nature. Our world—reality—is thus construed as a myriad of concrete particulars, each of which is unchanging in terms of its formal aspect and essential nature, but still subject to material changes and movement.

The origin of change itself, however, required additional explanation. Reasoning that the source and explanation of change must itself be unchanged lest an infinite regress occur, Aristotle concluded that there must exist an Unmoved Mover, an everlasting, unchanging source of all worldly movement.[9] Being unchangeable, the Unmoved Mover cannot contemplate or be concerned with transient worldly matters. Thus, the Unmoved Mover cannot originate change and movement through its own conscious deliberations. Accordingly, Aristotle argued, the Unmoved Mover must draw worldly objects to itself by being an "object of desire" and must have a nature of "Thought thinking Itself."[10]

Conceived in such a way, the Unmoved Mover is an impersonal, inaccessible entity who is the source and explanation of the tele-ological order of our world while being totally unaware of us. Aristotle makes no appeal here to a divine force that devises consciously a master plan for our universe or that ultimately rewards or punishes us in accord with our earthly deeds. Yet moral judgments are not relative or arbitrary for Aristotle because humans are by nature geared toward certain actions and ends.[11] He combines a healthy respect for community conventions with an insistence on the objective validity of moral principles.

*The Romans.* Starting from the presupposition that our material world is infused with Logos, a vital life force that is present in every part of the universe as well as in the universe taken as a whole, Stoics (third century B.C. through A.D. second century) contended that everything is one, that one is fully material, and that every part of the one is permeated by a rational creative energy that unifies and orders it.[12] Logos thus served as an immanent normative principle of order.

Although by reputation not an especially original philosopher, Cicero (106–43 B.C.) provided the clearest early statement of natural law through his impressive translations and compilations of Greek ideas into Latin terms. Cicero proclaimed straightaway that universal normative standards of behavior were embedded in human nature and could be discerned by reason. Such standards were the measure and not the mirror of human conduct. No friend of moral conventionalism, Cicero insisted that

> true law is right reason in agreement with nature; it is of universal application, unchanging, and everlasting. . . . We cannot be freed from its obligations by senate or people, and we need not look outside ourselves for an expounder or interpreter of it. . . . One eternal and unchangeable law will be valid for all nations and all times, and there will be one master and ruler, that is, God, over us all, for he is the author of this law, its promulgator, and its enforcing judge. . . . Whoever is disobedient [to the dictates of natural law] is fleeing from himself and denying his human nature.[13]

The Roman jurist Gaius (c. 160 A.D.) defined *ius civile* as the body of law applicable to a particular community.[14] In Rome, the *ius civile* was not applied to foreign subjects unless those subjects were otherwise subject to law of the same type. The *ius gentium*, a term which Cicero used to refer to natural law, eventually became the law that applied to both Roman citizens and foreigners. The *ius naturale* referred to universal principles of law agreeable to natural reason.[15]

The *ius naturale* highlighted the source and the *ius gentium* the practical application of the law of all nations. The two types of law are also distinguished by commentators in this way: the *ius naturale* was common to all humans, while the *ius gentium* tolerated slavery and was thus common to all free humans.[16] Another jurist, Ulpian, further distinguished in somewhat idiosyncratic fashion *ius naturale* from *ius gentium* by claiming that *ius naturale* applied to animals as well as to humans.[17]

In any event, the notion of a natural law grounded in an unchanging and universal reality, not created but merely discovered by humans, not merely reflecting but measuring actual state decrees, was clearly flourishing.

*Christianity.* The early Church identified natural law with the law of God as taught by Christ. The law of God, as embodied in the teachings and decrees of the Church, served as the ideal toward which actual state law should strive. This basic idea was later refined and systematized by the most influential proponent of the religious version of natural law, Saint Thomas Aquinas (c. 1224–1274).[18]

*Definition of Law.* Aquinas held that law has three components: it is (1) an ordinance of reason promulgated (2) for the common good (3) by the caretaker of the community. So conceived, law is a foundation for commitment and action, has the animating aspiration of unifying the parts (individual humans) to the whole (the perfect community), and must constitute a public (promulgated) measure of action. For Aquinas the law has two powers: the coercive power to command obedience from reasons of prudence (we obey the law because we fear the reprisals of state power) and the directive power to impose prescriptive obligations and to allow various propositions to exist as valid law (law embodies a moral dimension that should command our allegiance independent of our fear of state punishment).[19] Law's directive power stems from its ability to facilitate the ends of humans as social beings and members of a community. Law must aim at a common good, which is not merely the aggregation of all individual interests.

Lawmakers and citizens need to apprehend rationally the essence of humanity and the contours of human good: we are social animals, who live in common with others and who require cooperative endeavors to satisfy our needs, wants, and natural ends.[20] Moral principles are objective: they are binding on all societies and all people and are composed of self-evident propositions, and deductions and extrapolations of self-evident propositions. A proposition that conflicts with objective morality cannot be a "law" because it lacks the moral element necessary to confer directive power.

Critics of natural law theory have argued that this view is deficient because it cannot evaluate law. As all "law" under this theory is by definition morally good, no evaluation seems rational or permissible.[21] This semantic attack, however, is without force. The process of evaluation under natural law theory takes place before a proposition is bestowed the honorific title of "law." The reason natural law theory does not evaluate "law" is that the process has already taken place.

*Types of Law.* For Aquinas there are four kinds of law: first, eternal law that exists in the mind of God, fixes the essence of all things, orders human action to its appropriate ends, and is the origin of natural law. It governs the entire order of the universe and is dependent on divine reason for its existence and value. Because all creation is under the dominion of divine providence, all existing entities are inclined naturally toward their appropriate functions. Only humans, however, are self-conscious of their proper ends and can use reason to facilitate the attainment of them. Here Aquinas restates his strongly teleological assumption that all entities have an inherent essence that they are by nature inclined to fulfill. Humans, as God's greatest creatures, embody reason.[22]

Second, divine positive law, the law of God as revealed through Christ and the scriptures, resides in the infinite mind of God and is not directly accessible to finite human minds. Divine law helps to make eternal law explicit and available to humans. Moreover, divine law directs humans to their ultimate goal of eternal salvation and everlasting happiness with God.[23]

Third, natural law, founded on human nature and discovered by reason, is permanent and universal. Humans cannot subtract from it, and compliance with it is necessary if we are to attain our appropriate function. Thus, natural law guides humans to their earthly ends and is our "participation" in eternal law. The fundamental principles of natural law, however, do not require the use of elaborate deductive or inductive logical processes. Rather, the basic principles are self-evident, universal, and beyond rational demonstration: God has "instilled [the basic principles of natural law] into man's mind so as to be known by him naturally."[24]

In principle, all humans need and have sufficient knowledge and reasoning power to regulate their actions in accordance with natural law. The use of reason is essential to apply our natural inclinations to concrete, specific commitments and actions. Aquinas tells us that reason unassisted can discover the natural law, which is grounded ultimately in eternal law and divine reason itself, and can translate our inclinations into proper action.

Fourth, human positive law, comprised of legal statutes, decisions, and decrees of various governments, is valid—it can be described accurately as "law"—only if it is in accord with natural law. In fact, the proper role of human law is to make natural law explicit and applicable in particular situations. Human law is either arrived at deductively from the basic tenets of natural law, "That one must not kill may be derived as a conclusion from the [natural law] principle that one should do harm to no man";[25] or derived as a "determination," an instantiation, of a general principle: "[natural law] has it that an evildoer should be punished; but that he be punished in this or that way, is a determination of the [human positive law]."[26] Human law that has been derived deductively from natural law gains more directive power than that which is derived as a determination. But human law derived in either fashion is binding and is fully "law."

*Human Nature.* Unchanging human nature is perceived by Acquinas as exemplifying three basic inclinations: self-preservation, biological needs (reproduction, family life), and universal goods (orderly social life, concern for the interests of others, knowledge, avoidance of ignorance).[27] These human inclinations develop into the dictates of natural law as reason is allowed to extrapolate from them. Aquinas instructs us that the ground for all these inclinations is the first principle of natural law: "seek good, avoid evil."[28]

An important corollary is that Aquinas concedes straightaway that the specific translation of these general natural law principles to concrete cases will be controversial, contestable, and not a matter of logical necessity: "the more we descend to matters of detail the more frequently we encounter defects."[29] Disagreements will result because exceptional circumstances may make our generally derived rules inapplicable; humans differ in their respective abilities to discover moral truths, and in some cases "reason is perverted by passion, or evil habit, or an evil disposition."[30]

The religious natural law theorist's vision includes the apprehension of eternal human nature by human reason, drawing moral obligations from that human nature, obligations which demand that we bind our wills to those actions necessary for the flourishing of our natures and the attainment of our final ends. Thus conceived, the discovery of what the law is must be an a priori exercise, not an empirical investigation of particular legal systems.

Reliance on the existence and ultimate dominion of a Supreme Being, an unchanging human essence or nature, and objective standards of morality that are allegedly part of the "furniture of the universe"[31] seems mysterious and dubious to critics of natural law. They claim that either such entities have been proved not to exist or that they are in principle and practice impossible to prove or disprove.[32]

Natural law has traditionally aspired to translate physical and biological generalities into normative propositions. Betraying their rapture with the methods and the achievements of science, natural law theorists hope to discover similar laws of a moral nature embedded in nature. Unfortunately, most modern versions of this theory are wedded too closely with specific theologies, which even if correct may alienate those of different religious persuasions and thus fail to provide much common ground for normative reasoning. Moreover, even if an eternal human essence exists, how should we select which of its features reflect "natural law"? Neither the nature of the universe nor human nature sends us an unambiguous message about the world and our place within it. We must translate the universal descriptive elements, if any, that we perceive into prescriptions for human conduct, but if nature transmits contradictory messages then the advice "follow Nature" is itself logically incoherent. The journey out of this quagmire has included, in Aquinas for example, reliance on a unique human telos. But it is precisely this maneuver that forces natural law theorists to embrace specific theologies and additional metaphysical suppositions that expose them to further criticism.

Finally, the anthropological evidence is quite ambiguous regarding the existence of a timeless human nature: numerous variations in norms and customs are pervasive.[33] Furthermore, it is difficult to separate the innate inclinations of humans (our nature) from environmental influences (our nurture). Only by heightening the level of abstraction and generality to triviality and definitional truths can natural law theorists persuasively demonstrate the human commonality they allege.

*Hopes and Fears.* The aspirations of natural law theory include ensuring that the law is morally sound, providing evaluation of all particular legal systems, exalting the power of the Rule of Law, and realizing appropriate human potentials and ends. Aquinas carefully distinguishes rational and prescriptive imperatives of conduct from arbitrary expressions of human volition. He is not committed, however, to the view that any violation of natural law must be legislated against. Rather, only socially significant moral wrongs are the proper concern of human law and fall under its domain. Particular legal systems will differ to some extent according to social, economic, historical, and geographical circumstances. Aquinas concedes readily that in some legal systems there will be more or fewer rules than in others and that different legal systems will often display different adaptations of the same rule.[34] But two legal systems cannot with any validity embrace laws that are directly contradictory to one another. Under such circumstances, at least one of the statutes in question cannot truly be "law." Any proposition that does not conform to natural law is an imposter, and its enforcement is unjustified violence against the citizenry. Because it conflicts with natural law, such a proposition lacks directive force and is accordingly not binding.[35]

Aquinas underscores the importance of reason and the criterion of morality as the determinants of the existence of law. He stresses the enduring element of law—its timeless application beyond the practical needs of humans at a particular time. Although such application must adapt to variable, concrete social contexts, natural law has as its end that humans fulfill their function and achieve their essential purposes. Any variance from reason, morality, and law's enduring element denies a proposition the honorific title of "law." Thus, a proposition is not truly a law, regardless of its genesis and pedigree, if it is contrary to the common good, if its author is not the "caretaker" of the community, or if it opposes the divine good.

## CONTEMPORARY VERSIONS

*A Modern Reaffirmation.* John Finnis is probably the most influential and ingenious contemporary adherent of natural law theory. Finnis claims that empirical evidence reveals ten universal practical principles that indicate seven basic human values or basic human goods, one of which is "practical reasonableness."[36] Practical reasonableness itself presupposes nine methodological requirements that distinguish sound from unsound practical thinking.[37] Finally, reason applies those methodological requirements to the basic human goods and thereby generates a set of general, moral standards.[38] Thus, these elements of natural law justify the exercise of authority in a community. Finnis conceives the principles of natural law as explaining the obligatory force of human positive laws, even though such laws cannot be literally deduced from those principles.

Finnis insists that rather than our inferring moral principles from human nature, natural law is based on self-evident propositions, those that humans embrace without recourse to rational argument and logical proof.[39] Such propositions are not inferred from facts, thus they involve no illicit derivation of "ought" (prescriptive judgments) from "is" (descriptive claims). Nor are these propositions inferred from metaphysical claims about human nature, the nature of good and evil, or the appropriate function of humans. Rather, these propositions are apprehended by a simple, immediate act of noninferential understanding: we grasp that the object of our basic inclinations is an instance of a more general form of good. Finnis reiterates that the key to natural law is not merely that which is in conformity with human nature, but that which is reasonable.[40]

Natural law theorists are often accused of making illicit inferences from facts (descriptions about human nature, the function of humans, or the order of the universe) to values (prescriptions about what humans should do).[41] Presumably, such an inference is illicit in that no prescriptions follow logically from strictly descriptive premises. Prescriptions can be generated as conclusions under such circumstances only by smuggling in value judgments implicitly as premises. This criticism clearly misses the mark, at least when it is levied against theorists such as Aquinas and Finnis. They are careful to point out that rather than inferring basic prescriptions of natural law from descriptive premises, they regard certain universal principles and forms of good as self-evident, beyond rational demonstration.

But the notion of self-evidence itself is disturbing. Can natural law theorists truly identify the universal elements of morality? Is it not possible for equally rational humans, who are in good faith trying to apprehend natural law, to arrive at different, even contradictory, discoveries? Should not we be uncommonly suspicious of claims of "self-evidence" and "nondemonstrable truth"? Are not such claims the first refuge of charlatans and scoundrels who pretend to unveil timeless truths while they are in fact merely holding a mirror to their own projections, aspirations, and interests? In any event, are claims of self-evidence the best starting point when those claims result either in merely definitional (and thus trivial) truths or in radically contestable axioms?

*Universal Principles.* Finnis denies that cultures manifest preferences, motivations, and evaluations so disparate and unconnected that no values or practical principles can legitimately be said to be self-evident. He claims that anthropological research reveals the following ten universal practical principles that manifest human inclinations and values: (1) concern for human life (self-preservation is generally accepted as a proper motive for action, and killing others is permitted only under limited circumstances and with specified justification); (2) procreation of a new human life; (3) restriction of sexual activity (reflected in prohibitions against incest, promiscuity, and rape); (4) concern for truth; (5) values of cooperation (acknowledgment that the common good often trumps self-interest, that mutual obligations exist between individuals, and that some notion of justice holds within groups); (6) friendship; (7) some conception of title and property; (8) recognition of the value of play; (9) treatment of corpses of group members in some traditional and ritualistic fashion; and (10) concern for superhuman powers or principles.[42]

Although Finnis admits that none of these "universal practical principles have specificity"[43] sufficient to be regarded as moral rules, still he contends that the universality of such basic value judgments manifests the connection between basic human inclinations and corresponding human goods as well as displays the difference between merely pursuing an urge and rationally seeking a particular realization of a form of human good that cannot be fully "realized and exhausted by any one action, lifetime, or culture."[44]

Finnis does not believe that all human inclinations correspond to or reveal basic values. For example the urge to be greedy and the urge to inflict gratuitous harm are not inclinations reflecting self-evident human goods, but rather require explanation of a sort not required by the quest for knowledge and friendship.[45] Furthermore, Finnis denies that the ten basic values themselves can be reduced to any one form of human experience (such as pleasure).

*Basic Human Goods.* Finnis concludes from all this that the ten universal practical principles indicate the following seven, equally basic, forms of human good: (1) life, (2) knowledge, (3) play, (4) aesthetic experience, (5) sociability, (6) practical resonableness, and (7) religion.[46] He falls short of asserting, however, that these necessarily constitute an exhaustive list of human goods. Humans must promote these objective goods if their lives are to be truly meaningful. He believes, as do all natural law theorists, that a proper understanding of human well-being is necessary for moral and legal theory. The seven basic goods have no objective hierarchy of moral authority, and none can be reduced to any of the others.[47]

Finnis tells us that the intrinsic, objective value of his seven basic goods is self-evident. But to say that a principle is self-evident, says Finnis, does not mean that each of us has, as a matter of fact, formulated the principle; that we would all embrace the principle once it was formulated for us; that such a principle is known a priori, innately and without reference to experience; that such a principle is indubitable or known with certitude; or that such a principle can be derived from facts.[48] Finnis acknowledges all this in order to distance himself from past, unsuccessful attempts at understanding self-evidence and thereby to outflank the numerous historical skeptics of the concept. But what does this leave us as the positive meaning of "self-evident"?

Finnis adds two considerations: (1) self-evident values and principles will be acknowledged only by those who have experienced them and (2) self-evident values and principles are required to avoid an infinite regress of justification.[49] But (1) threatens to disintegrate into the viciously circular and useless "the intrinsic value of X is self-evident to only (some of?) those who have experienced X as intrinsically valuable" and (2) assumes that justification is possible only when incorrigible axioms serve as foundations. While the need to halt an infinite regress is real, such an assumption ignores the possibility of nonfoundational accounts of justification such as those found in coherence and pragmatic methodologies that accept no belief or principle as incorrigible and beyond revision. Surely an appeal to "self-evidentness" is not a necessary, and probably not the most persuasive, way to block the feared submersion into infinite regress.

We are left, then, with a rather empty notion of "self-evidentness": Finnis isolates the notion from direct critical attack by taking care to tell us what he does not mean when he uses it, but he provides neither a useful criterion of the concept's positive meaning nor a necessary reason for thinking we must appeal to it to salvage normative justification.

How did he get into such a predicament? Animated by a deep desire to avoid the traditional accusations lodged against natural law theorists—that they illicitly derive ought from is, that they lack an incontestable foundation for moral and legal theory, and that they rely too heavily on contestable substantive portrayals of the self— Finnis thinks he must sever all derivations of moral principles from claims about human nature.[50] But we have seen the price he must pay: although he may well elude most, if not all, of the classical objections to natural law theory, he makes a rather embarrassing appeal to "self-evidentness" and drains natural law of much of its practical significance for citizens and legal officials.

*Methodological Requirements.* According to Finnis, practical reasonableness, which involves the responsible exercise of human freedom, presupposes nine methodological requirements: (1) developing a rational plan of life encompassing effective commitments; (2) placing proper emphasis on the basic human goods ("no leaving out of account, or arbitrary discounting or exaggeration of, any of the basic human values");[51] (3) assuming an impartial perspective among moral agents; (4) detaching oneself enough from particular projects that failure in one area does not destroy the meaning of one's life; (5) taking seriously one's commitments and not abandoning them lightly; (6) striving to bring good into one's life and the lives of others; (7) avoiding actions that accomplish nothing but direct damage to a basic human good; (8) facilitating the common good of one's immediate communities; and (9) acting in accordance with conscience.[52]

One of the distinctive characteristics of natural law theorists is that they ultimately support their legal theory with their moral theory. Finnis, for example, tells us that there is no objective normative hierarchy of the seven basic goods and that none can be reduced to any of the others. Accordingly, consequentialist moral theories, which either assume that values are commensurable or that all value can be reduced to a single basic good, are from the outset fatally flawed. But given Finnis's analysis, how do we know what we ought to do? His answer may seem surprising given our usual image of a natural law theorist as an unbending and dogmatic objectivist. We are allowed to select, within the limits set by the methodological requirements of practical reasonableness, our own normative hierarchy of the seven basic goods.[53] While the second methodological requirement tells us that we must recognize all the seven basic goods and the seventh commands us not to do any act that does nothing but direct damage to a basic good, we have much latitude in developing our life's plan.

There are, however, at least three difficulties here:[54] (1) even if consequentialism is unsound because it assumes the commensurability or reducibility of basic goods, it may still be useful when we are confronted by different outcomes involving the same basic good. That is, nothing that Finnis has said undermines our commonsense intuition that, other things being equal, we should perform act X rather than act Y where X produces more of basic good G than the amount of G produced by Y and neither X nor Y violates any methodological requirements of practical reasonableness. Thus, Finnis has not eliminated consequentialist appeals after all. (2) The seventh methodological requirement may be too weak. We can imagine a case where Angelo advances a certain, relatively trivial, basic good, while ignoring the interests of Vittoria in another, certainly substantial, basic good, but where Angelo is morally permitted to do so under Finnis's theory because he does not violate the seventh requirement.

For example, while playing baseball, thereby acknowledging the basic good of play, Angelo sees that Vittoria is drowning in a shallow pond nearby. He reasons as follows: "Play and human life are both basic goods; there is no objective moral hierarchy; I can continue to play or stop playing and help the drowning girl, who I will probably be able to save easily; in either case I do not violate methodological requirement seven because in neither case would I be performing an action that does nothing but directly damage a basic good; I cannot perform consequentialist reasoning here because Finnis tells me that basic values are not commensurable; thus, I will continue playing baseball." We would think here, once more detailed circumstances are given, that Angelo did not do the proper act. Yet Finnis's account seems to permit his action morally. Even if a reader finds my specific example uncompelling, it would not be difficult to construct a different and more persuasive illustration that makes the same point.

(3) At other times, the seventh methodological requirement may be too strong. That is, it may block what we would normally think of as morally required action. Thus, William Wilcox writes,

> Suppose that I am too far from Sam [a deaf man] to save him [from being hit by a bus running a red light], but I can shout to Ralph [a nearby chess player], who could save him. Here [Ralph's] saving would be the result of a subsequent [and different] act [from the act of my shouting]. My act of shouting, of itself, does nothing but directly damage the basic value of play. Finnis should say that it would be impermissible for me to shout; yet surely this should be permissible.[55]

Perhaps Finnis can elude the force of (2) and (3) by claiming that one of the other methodological requirements solves the paradoxes, that he has a more subtle analysis of what constitutes a "single act," or that he employs a more refined notion of "direct" as opposed to "indirect" damage. But it remains unclear whether he can escape the power of these objections without resorting implicitly to two familiar maneuvers of moral theory that he officially abrogates: adherence to an objective moral hierarchy of basic values and appeals to consequentialist reasoning.

*Moral Mistakes.* While acknowledging the difficulty of applying moral reason in particular contexts, Finnis insists that incorrect moral judgments and the seeming diversity of moral opinion are mistakes that result from "too exclusive attention to some of the basic value(s) and/or some basic requirement(s), and inattention to others."[56] Such moral distortions are generated in turn by

> an uncritical, unintelligent spontaneity; sometimes, by reference to the bias and oversight induced by conventions of language, social structures, and social practice; and sometimes (and always, perhaps, most radically) by the bias of self-love or of other emotions and inclinations that resist the concern to be simply reasonable.[57]

Finnis admits that basic principles are not found unchanged in the law but contends that the framework of the basic human goods and methodological assumptions of practical reasonableness is embodied in the elaborate rules of a legal system. There are "central principles"[58] of law (e.g., prohibitions against murder and theft, enabling conditions for marriage and contract), Finnis instructs us, that are "straightforward applications of universally valid requirements of reasonableness."[59] However, the coherent rendering of such principles into an elaborate and complex legal system that provides answers to concrete cases demands numerous contestable determinations.

In the face of all this, critics press the following questions: Even if there exists a code of natural law, how do we discover it? More important, how do we know when we have discovered it? Because of its controversial and slippery character, and the high generality of its alleged prescriptions (e.g., "do good, avoid evil"), natural law may be of limited use to humans. Those searching for answers to concrete moral and legal questions will not find their purposes served by the abstract definitional truths of natural law. Even if "universal practical principles" and "universal forms of good" exist, they do not provide by themselves, or in concert with methodological principles of reason, any clear answers to the normative questions humans ask. Natural law seems too much like an apology for those who aspire to place moral reasoning on a plane similar to scientific reasoning—searching for and discovering truths that presumably exist antecedently—and too little like a method for arriving at specific right answers to questions of value. Finnis's basic goods, for example, reflect groups of human experiences and interactions commonly perceived as valuable, but they are described so generally that they preclude little or anything from falling under their rubric.[60] Virtually any desire that X be included as a basic good can be accommodated. Those who strive to discover the "right answer" to a moral or legal question will find only what they seek.

Given these considerations, as a guide to moral and legal decision making, natural law theory has at best limited usefulness. We cannot know our specific obligations in concrete contexts merely by acknowledging the platitudes of natural law and by pretending to apply human reason to highly abstract normative propositions. Given that judicial decision making is an explicitly practical enterprise—it aims at the resolution of specific disputes—the highly theoretical ontological assumptions and normative conclusions of natural law, regardless of their merits, seem radically inappropriate.

Interestingly, Finnis, in the context of criticizing Ronald Dworkin, tells us that "while there are many ways of going and doing wrong, there are also in most situations of personal and social life a variety of incompatible *right* options—that we should seek good answers, and eschew bad ones, but not dream of *best* ones" (emphasis in original).[61] In legal contexts Finnis admits straightaway that "no uniquely correct answer could be available in any case where there is identifiable a set of two or more options/answers which do not violate any rule binding on the judge or other chooser or interpreter."[62]

Such passages, and others found in Aquinas, leave the impression that perhaps critics are taking natural law theory to task in areas where natural law does not even purport to be applicable. Surely Aquinas did not take himself to be engaged in the primarily practical task of describing the principles of judicial decision making; rather, he was animated by the objectivist impulse that unless there are discernible determinate normative principles, our moral judgments and actions are ultimately groundless and without justification. His project was to validate the truth of objectivism by revealing the barest framework of the natural order he presumed exists in humans and the universe. Accordingly, his enemy was conventionalism and all forms of moral skepticism. Leaving aside for the moment whether his moral project was successful, we must note that he did not intend to demonstrate specific legal conclusions to concrete cases.[63] Those of us who are tempted to deride natural law theory for its inability to generate such legal conclusions are guilty of saddling natural law theorists with a task that they themselves were either unconcerned with or concerned with only peripherally.

But such a response still leaves a paramount question: If natural law cannot, and does not purport to, provide clear guidance for the specific content or application of law, then what practical significance does it possess?

Because its practical significance is indeterminate, natural law theory is whipsawed by both ends of the political spectrum. Radical leftists allege that natural law theory is an apology for the political status quo.[64] By mystifying and legitimating the present social order as fundamentally in accord with universal and timeless morality, natural law theory elevates and transforms the contingent present into the transcendental and eternal. This transformative process is dangerous because it results in a societal perception that the status quo is beyond reimagination and re-creation. Too often, it seems to such leftists, natural law theorists identify the natural and the prescriptive with that which is familiar, habitual, and established.

Political conservatives, on the other hand, charge that natural law is too unsettling to the received order.[65] By seeming to allow all citizens to judge for themselves whether the propositions commonly thought to be conventional are truly "law," and by permitting all citizens to act effectively as judges, natural law encourages individuals to destabilize the collective judgment of rightful authority and the community as a whole. Moreover, such an open invitation for civil disobedience jeopardizes the very possibility of nurturing the type of directive power of law that natural law theorists claim to prize.[66]

*Natural Law and the Interpretivist Turn.* Advancing what he calls a "natural law theory of interpretations,"[67] Michael Moore acknowledges that the law requires interpretation and concedes that legal reasoning, much like literary criticism, theology, and dream theory, depends on the antecedent existence of a text in need of such interpretation. In this way, Moore distances these "hermeneutical enterprises"[68] from the paradigm scientific projects of explaining phenomena. Concentrating on the reasoning engaged in by judges in deciding particular cases, Moore characterizes his view as a natural law theory because it affirms the following two propositions: there exists a moral reality from which we can generate right answers to normative questions (the content of this proposition will be referred to hereafter as "Metaphysical Realism"),[69] and the "interpretive premises necessary to decide any case can and should be derived in part by recourse to the dictates of that moral reality."[70] Thus, Moore denies that proper moral judgments emanate from conventional sources or shared values and affirms that moral judgments have a "necessary place in the interpretation of any legal text."[71]

*The Role of Interpretation.* Moore pinpoints the role of interpretation in judicial reasoning by claiming that "a full deductive justification for [a judicial decision] includes a statement of law, a statement of fact, and a statement interpreting the law so that it applies to the described facts."[72] A theory of interpretation in law instructs legal insiders in the derivation of interpretive statements. Once these three premises are in place, Moore contends that the proper legal conclusion can be deduced through the basic rules of propositional logic.[73]

Claims to "deductive justification" have historically been accompanied by whispers of "mechanical jurisprudence." It is important to note here that Moore does not fall prey to such seductions. In fact, the role of a theory of interpretation in deriving premises of the third sort is anything but mechanical application. Moreover, Moore does not claim that a theory of interpretation composes entirely the enterprise of judicial reasoning. In addition to a theory of interpretation, judges require "a theory of law proper,"[74] which tells how to derive statements of law ("the text"); a "theory about facts that determines which of an indefinitely large number of descriptions of 'what happened' should be used in deciding the case,"[75] this theory thereby generating statements of facts; and "a theory about logic and its place in legal reasoning."[76] Moore underscores that his is not a position that attempts to answer all the questions necessary for proper legal reasoning and judicial decision making; rather, he confines his project to one subactivity within the enterprise of legal reasoning: How should a judge derive the interpretive premises required to connect statements of law and statements of fact?[77]

*Metaphysical Realism.* Moore's answer to that question relies on the truth of Metaphysical Realism regarding meaning, value, and the nature of truth itself.

> Judges should guide their judgments about the ordinary meanings of words by the real nature of the things to which words refer and not by the conventions governing the ordinary usage of those words; judges should seek their own best theory of what a prior court did and not rely on what that court said it was doing; and judges should seek answers that are really correct when they rely on values in interpretation and should not feel obeisant to the conventional moral judgments of their society.[78]

Moore distinguishes his realist theory of meaning from conventionalist accounts on three grounds: (1) a realist account insists that the meaning of terms, rather than being fixed by societal conventions, is determined by "natural kinds of events that occur in the world."[79] Under such an account, "it may be arbitrary what symbol we assign to name this class of events, but it is not arbitrary that we have some symbol to name this thing."[80] Thus, we strive to apply properly a general term to an event that "really" instantiates it. We do this by "applying the best scientific theory we can muster about what [the natural kind] really is."[81] (2) A realist explanation of meaning contends that "fact will not outrun diction."[82] While it is a commonplace to observe that conventions can run out in extraordinary circumstances or difficult cases, realists claim that "our present scientific theory may be inadequate to resolve [whether a natural kind truly applies to a particular situation], but a realist will assert that there are relevant facts [that would resolve the issue] even if we presently lack the means to find them."[83] (3) Realist accounts of meaning "will not view a change in our conventions about when to apply a word as a change in its meaning."[84] Based on the presumption that natural kinds are the linchpin of meaning, realists believe that "our linguistic intentions are constant . . . even if our scientific theories change considerably."[85]

The power of a realist theory of meaning, according to Moore, is that it avoids the problems endemic to conventionalist accounts: their inability to include cross-temporal and cross-cultural genuine disagreements.[86] Moore is careful, however, to distance himself from any mechanical or literalist theory of interpretation such as the "plain-meaning" rule. The error of the plain-meaning rule is that it casts its lot entirely with ordinary meanings; that is, it insists that ordinary meanings are so clear that a decision maker need look to nothing else when interpreting. Moore, on the other hand, claims only that ordinary meanings are the place to begin when confronted by the interpretive task.[87]

Moore's positive argument in favor of realism relies on two observations: first, when contemplating and depicting our world we presuppose realism and, second, there is no perspective or vantage point from which we can deny legitimately those presuppositions and assert skepticism.[88] Moore is careful here to distinguish his Metaphysical Realism from coherence epistemology: "However much we are holistic, coherence theorists in our procedures for justifying particular judgments as true, we are nonetheless implicit correspondence theorists when it comes to the meaning of truth itself."[89] Finally, Moore contends that a realist account of meaning facilitates widely acknowledged Rule of Law virtues: separation of powers, equality, liberty, substantive fairness, procedural fairness, and utility.[90]

Sanford Levinson has questioned whether it truly matters whether we call ourselves metaphysical realists or conventionalists or pragmatists[91] and suggests that our jurisprudential self-description is unlikely to affect actual legal outcomes. We are necessarily engaged in disputation about the nature (or lack of inherent nature) of our world, and our metaepistemological or metaphysical suppositions are much more likely to resound in differences in the "rhetorical apparatus"[92] that we employ rather than significant differences in the particular ways legal cases are resolved. Levinson here quotes Ronald Dworkin favorably: "I have no arguments for the objectivity of moral judgments except moral arguments, no arguments for the objectivity of interpretive judgments except interpretive arguments, and so forth."[93]

The point seems to be that, in Levinson's judgment, the issues that most concern Moore—whether there is an important distinction between real and conventional values, whether judges do and must presuppose metaphysical realism when deciding cases, whether right answers to moral and legal questions can be generated from the structure of reality itself—are mainly or strictly theoretical exercises that do not translate into practical differences.

At a certain level, Levinson is unassailably correct. No serious thinker avows explicitly the self-refuting positions that "all moral/ legal conclusions are equally as good/bad" or "no position is any better than its competitors." Thus, even the most committed members of Legal Realism, after presumably debunking the objectivist pretensions of "liberal" thought, will go on to argue vociferously in favor of certain legal conclusions rather than others. None of us can truly live outside the arena of legitimate normative disputation. Once we are inside the enterprise of moral and legal decision making we must check the most virulent forms of skepticism at the gate.

But Moore would readily agree to all of this and use it to support his views about Metaphysical Realism. Moreover, he would deny that such theoretical issues are without practical significance. One underlying question is the justification of the judicial role itself. Moore has argued that Metaphysical Realists have a much easier task than conventionalists in providing a convincing defense of that role. This is an important claim because justifying judicial review has been a preoccupation of twentieth-century political thought. Furthermore, much of law's directive power is dependent on the theoretical support that can be legitimately mustered in favor of our legal and political systems.

Beyond that, Moore can claim that there are practical differences in the outlook of judges who describe themselves as "Metaphysical Realists," "pragmatists," or "conventionalists." Each will feel constrained, if at all, by different sources when interpreting texts and will be guided by different goals. The phenomenology of judicial decision making, and not merely its rhetorical apparatus, will be at least somewhat different depending on which self-description is internalized. While it is true that a school of conventionalists (or realists or pragmatists) is unlikely to reason and conclude in lock step, the process and goal of its deliberations will exhibit differences when compared with those of its competitors.

The respect in which Levinson's charge is accurate is on the whole rather trivial and could be accepted easily by Moore. When viewed more substantively, Levinson's charge even seems incorrect. There is, however, a version of Levinson's charge that has greater merit.

A more general methodological problem besetting Moore's account is that he falsely limits our choices by posing a suspicious dilemma between either accepting Metaphysical Realism or committing oneself to a crude conventionalism that identifies and equates popular preferences with normative soundness. As such, the versions of conventionalism that Moore entertains are either embarrassingly self-refuting or impossible to advocate with a straight face once one has entered into a normative enterprise in good faith. It is no wonder that Moore is able to pummel such a conventionalism silly with classical philosophical jabs and send it staggering around his neatly circumscribed ring. Moore then declares Metaphysical Realism, mainly on the basis of default, the winner of the contest and proclaims the resurrection of natural law theory.

When we step back from the dazzle of Moore's assault, however, we may well sense that the contest has been rigged in a way that would elicit the admiration of an Arnold Rothstein.[94] By selecting so unworthy an opponent, Moore does not honor Metaphysical Realism; rather, he cheapens the claims of victory. Under such circumstances it is not surprising that Moore can only reiterate that we linguistically presuppose a form of nonconventionalism. He does not establish the truth of Metaphysical Realism; he can only show that we are better off believing in its truth than we would be if we advocate crude conventionalism. That is correct as far as it goes. But much more is needed to convince us that a belief in Metaphysical Realism is correct and natural law theory has practical currency when applied to judicial decision making. At bottom, Moore reveals himself as yet another mainstream thinker who is a prisoner of the objectivist–relativist polarity discussed previously.

*Epistemological Problems.* Moore confronts the "underdetermination thesis," the view that there will be an indefinitely large number of theories describing judicial arguments that explain equally well a decided case or series of cases. A moderate realist who claims to be able to choose among such theories on the basis of their correlation or noncorrelation to moral or natural kinds must explain how our knowledge of general moral principles is firm enough to generate a proper selection. Moore acknowledges that the underdetermination thesis poses an epistemological difficulty for the moderate realist who, "no less than anyone else, is always working with a finite set of data with which a large number of theories will be compatible."[95] The moderate realist, from an epistemological vantage point, is in the same position as anyone else regarding whether his moral or scientific theory of the observed data is the "right theory."[96] But Moore is quick to note that none of this invalidates the realist's metaphysics: "Being uncertain that one has the right moral category—one that captures all and only the cases it ought to capture— is quite compatible with certainty that there is some such moral category."[97] Accordingly, Moore does not view the underdetermination thesis as fatal to his metaphysical position; rather, he sees the thesis as expressing certain epistemological difficulties that beset all interpreters regardless of their persuasion.

In sum, Moore underscores that a realist account facilitates best the Rule of Law values that animate the doctrine of precedent.

> To say what the holding of a case is or what weight it has is a matter on which moral knowledge is necessary if [Rule of Law values] are to be well served. Such knowledge, when combined with the historical knowledge of what earlier courts did with the facts of the cases before them, produces one ingredient in a theory of interpretation.[98]

The relationship between metaphysics and epistemology is more intimate than what Moore suggests, however. If we either cannot know moral reality or we can know it but never be aware of when we do, then the natural law enterprise as applied to judicial decision making is compromised seriously. Judges are engaged in the practical exercise of resolving the case at bar, and information about the presumed metaphysics of the world is of limited utility to them unless such information can be known and applied to dispute resolutions. Thus, if a self-proclaimed natural law theorist such as Moore is content to finesse most of the epistemological problems attending his position and is satisfied merely to point out what he takes to be our metaphysical presuppositions, then he is vulnerable to two classic charges: (1) that he has merely uncovered the uninteresting claim that there are few, if any, radical relativists engaged in practical normative enterprises and (2) that even if there is a moral reality to be discovered, its prescriptions are too abstract and general to be useful as determinate guides to judicial decision making. Such a natural law theorist wins a most hollow victory. It is a triumph of the flimsiest form, without substantive content and practical significance.[99]

*The Role of Values.* Moore points out that there are four kinds of questions demanding the judgments that constitute judicial interpretation properly conceived: (1) What are the ordinary meanings of the words of the text? (2) What interpretation of the text is indicated by prior holdings? (3) What is the underlying purpose of the text and how does that purpose weigh in relation to the ordinary meaning and the interpretation suggested by precedent? and (4) What, all things considered, is the best result in this case in relation to the ordinary meaning, precedent, and purpose judgments previously arrived at?[100] As an avowed natural law theorist, Moore unabashedly contends that value judgments are inexorably a part of judicial interpretation and, moreover, that judges must consult "real" as opposed to merely "conventional" values.[101]

*Real Values.* As with all natural law theorists, critics will squirm when confronted by Moore's incantation of real values. Moore defends the existence of real values by appealing to the presuppositions of our ordinary ways of speaking. He cites three indications that we all assume the presence of real, and not merely conventional, values: (1) we are confident that we can legitimately arrive at value judgments that disagree with the value judgments of the rest of our society; that is, when arriving at such judgments we are not merely engaged in or satisfied with anthropological discoveries of what our society already thinks, but we are striving for the right answer to the moral question posed.[102] (2) There is no logically necessary relation between normative statements ("bullfighting is wrong") and statements that describe a society's mental states of belief on normative statements ("most people in England think that bullfighting is wrong").[103] (3) "We have a linguistic device that we use when we wish to indicate that we are making a conventional moral judgment and not a real one" ("she is so 'good'").[104] Moore concedes that none of this establishes clearly the presence of objective values but concludes that such ways of speaking betray our presupposition that "we each think there is a difference between what is really good and what is 'good' according to some shared conception of goodness."[105]

Moore is satisfied that his readers will agree that judicial interpretation inevitably incorporates judgments of value. The question then becomes: Which kinds of values should judges consult? Moore offers several different justifications for his prescription that judges use real rather than conventional values. First, he reminds us that for those who believe that the truth of moral judgments is as firm as the truth of scientific judgments, the constraints of the imperative to "find the moral truth"[106] are every bit as powerful as those generated by the imperative to "decide cases on the basis of factual truths."[107] Thus, the allegation that judges who purport to use real values will in fact be abusing their powers and imposing their own views on litigants is misplaced. Such judges will, of course, be using their own "best judgments"[108] when confronting questions of moral truth; but that is no different whenever judges confront any factual question (including "social facts about conventions").[109] Absent a method of mechanical jurisprudence, judges must always judge. Second, there is no reason to suspect that judges who explicitly acknowledge real values must thereby undervalue the other ingredients in proper judicial interpretation: ordinary or statutory meanings, precedent, and the text's purpose.[110] This suspicion is not an argument in favor of using conventional values, says Moore, but only a reminder that judges must give sufficient weight to the values that fortify meanings, precedent, and purpose; that is, judges must note all four components of a natural law theory of interpretation and not distort the importance of any one element. Third, Moore has little use for the claim that judges should consult conventional values, a claim based on the belief that "shared values are most democratic because they represent what most people prefer on moral issues."[111] He stigmatizes this view as mere "preference utilitarianism"[112] and instructs us that "there are values higher than utility that everyone, including a court, should seek."[113] Finally, he concludes that

> there is a good reason on equality grounds to look to real values and not merely conventional ones: doing so promotes real equality and not merely the appearance of equality. Interpreting statutes by the right values ensures that cases that are truly alike are treated alike. Conventionalist interpretation will settle for less; for a conventionalist, it will be enough that cases that the public accepts as alike are treated as alike, even if a court can see a moral difference.[114]

In this manner, through adoption of Metaphysical Realism and denigration of conventionalism, Moore believes that he has presented "a practical thesis about the right way to go about interpreting legal texts"[115] (his four-part method) and a theoretical thesis based on our use of ordinary language that "our interpretive practices reveal us to be both metaphysical realists and . . . natural law-yers."[116] He is careful, however, to note that he takes no position on the classical natural law question of whether an unjust "law" can truly and validly be called a law.[117] Accordingly, his is a natural law theory of interpretation that intentionally avoids the issue of how legal texts gain the pedigree sufficient to confer authority.

*The Role of Lawyers.* Levinson alleges that Moore marginalizes and ultimately denigrates the role of lawyers. He says that "Moore's intellectual system reinforces a jurisprudence that I would describe as 'law without lawyers.' "[118] By portraying judges as concerned with justice and the pursuit of right answers, Moore subscribes to a view of the judge as a "seeker after knowledge of the good."[119] But law-yers find their experiences to be much different: "The task of the lawyer is that of the ancient Greek orator—the production of belief on the part of an audience, regardless of the merits of the belief. It is belief alone, and not knowledge, with which the lawyer is con-cerned."[120] Thus, Levinson sees a conflict between Moore's presenta-tion of the judicial role and the responsibilities of lawyers in our system.

Levinson's point here is that Moore's abstract and theoretical po-sition on interpretation, even if correct when applied to judges, fun-damentally indicts the professional role of lawyers, who make no pretense to be discoverers of truth and real values. Thus, Moore is caught on the horns of a dilemma: either his theory of legal inter-pretation is inaccurate or severely limited or it accurately describes what legal insiders should be doing and thereby underscores the moral bankruptcy of the professional role of lawyers.

Moore could, and Levinson explicitly recognizes this, try to navi-gate between the horns of the dilemma by providing a justification of the entire adversary system that prescribes carefully the different professional roles of various legal officials. Or Moore could accept unsqueamishly that his position on legal interpretation suggests needed changes in the professional role of lawyers. If he takes the first approach, he must show why lawyers are not and should not be interpreters of legal texts in the fullest sense of that expression; that is, he must provide a convincing justification for the lawyers' specific role within our system.[121] If he takes the second approach (which is more doubtful), he must conjure a role for lawyers more akin to the interpretive role played by judges. Such a conception would alter radically, and not merely marginally, our entire system of adversarial argumentation.

None of this, of course, shows any inherent flaws in Moore's account of judicial decision making. But Levinson's charge points out that those, like Moore, who concentrate almost exclusively on the process and justification of issues such as judicial review must also acknowledge the ramifications their theories have on other areas of concern within our adversary system of justice and within our general political models.

Moreover, Moore's invocation of "moral kinds" is sure to invite sharp responses. Stephen Munzer, for example, questions whether we truly "discover" moral kinds.[122] Given that Moore has conceded that moral terms do not name natural or physical properties and that they instead bear a "semantic depth" about which we must "articulate the best theory,"[123] Munzer is inclined to believe that we "construct" rather than discover moral kinds. Moreover, the notion of "semantic depth," which suggests that we have an incomplete understanding of moral words, strikes Munzer as inadequate to show that moral terms are "semantically determinate—[that a] uniquely correct answer exists as to whether [a moral term] applies to a particular state of affairs in reality."[124] Thus, even if there is a moral reality to be discovered, Munzer contends that the "instrument of discovery is unclear."[125] Furthermore, once the presumed likeness between moral reality and scientific reality is blurred because different methods of discovery are used in the two areas and because moral reality lacks natural–physical properties, the alleged analogy between moral and natural kinds becomes less convincing.

What are we to make of Munzer's attack? Moore has told us explicitly that he is less concerned with the problem of when and under what circumstances we can be said to have discovered the correct perception of moral reality and more concerned with establishing that we already presuppose the existence of such a reality. Accordingly, his thesis is intended to be more metaphysical than epistemological.

There is still something disturbing about all this. Moore is fond of reminding us that judges are concerned with getting the right answer to legal questions, that they presuppose Metaphysical Realism as part of their role, and thus that they do not merely consult conventional meanings and values when deciding cases. But this has to mean more than the trivial claim that judges do not subscribe to the most virulent forms of self-refuting skepticism, for we can all concede easily that once we enter fully the normative enterprise we leave such forms behind. Yet there are too many times when Moore, confronted with epistemological difficulties, seems to retreat to a position no more substantive than the trivial claim just described. Too often, his natural law theory of interpretation seems reducible to the position that judges are not radical relativists when performing their role, that they embrace no necessary connection between what a society thinks is right and what is right, and, thus, that they must be embracing, at least implicitly, moral realism.

Moore's separation of the metaphysical and epistemological issues surrounding realism is starkly apparent in his treatment of two common criticisms of natural law theory: that the prescriptions of the theory are either too abstract or if they are made concrete then they are implausible because they are not universally acknowledged.

Moore takes this to be a metaphysical attack—one that calls into question whether real values exist. He then softens the force of the criticism by insisting that the existence of real values is not dependent on their universal acknowledgment or their concreteness and particularity. Thus the critic's charges do not demonstrate the implausibility of metaphysical realism in values at all.[126]

Certainly Moore is correct in thinking that the existence of real values is separate from our universal agreement about their content. Given that natural law theorists view normative reasoning as involving discovery, there is no sound reason to think that all humans or all societies are equally good discoverers. Moreover, natural law theorists from Aquinas to the present have argued that the indictment of natural law's prescriptions as vague does not imply that real values do not exist.

But the critic's attack here is more properly taken as an epistemological critique of natural law. The critic could acknowledge straightaway that she has not demonstrated the falsity of Metaphysical Realism, and in fact could not do so, merely by pointing out the lack of universal agreement on value judgments. But she could insist that hers is an epistemological critique that is especially pertinent in a practical arena such as judicial decision making. Such a critic may argue that we can neither prove nor disprove conclusively whether real values truly exist, that virtually all those engaged in normative enterprises do not live and act as radical relativists, and yet that the applicability of natural law theory seems suspect given the epistemological difficulties besetting the practical quest for real values. Accordingly, this attack, so conceived, converges with some of the other criticisms presented above.

Natural law theory cogently points out that we abrogate whatever skeptical metaepistemological and metaphysical tendencies we nurture at the theoretical level once inside the enterprises of moral reasoning and legal decision making. Although most natural law theorists do not purport to be able to generate specific legal conclusions from their abstract, general moral propositions, and they ultimately resort to dubious appeals to self-evidence, they nevertheless perform a service by illustrating that the phenomenology of normative decision making seems to be in conflict with radical skepticism. Accordingly, natural law theory speaks to our objectivist impulse and challenges critics to reformulate normative justification in a way that is both true to our social practices but without foundationalist presuppositions.

# CHAPTER 2

# The Quest for Rigor
*Legal Positivism*

As a general movement, *positivism* designated the extension of the scientific method to other disciplines. Venerating the findings of the scientific method as the only legitimate knowledge and spurning the mushy conclusions of metaphysical inquiries, positivism reached its zenith in the Western world from the mid-nineteenth through early twentieth centuries. Speaking directly to our objectivist impulses and to our need for the security of firm epistemological foundations, positivism has retained much of its vitality as it has undergone contemporary refinements.

## JOHN AUSTIN (1790–1859)

The first modern positivist to advance a complex theory of law was John Austin.[1] Austin was concerned mainly with distinguishing the existence of law from the normative merit of law; that is, the existence of law—whether a certain proposition or rule is truly "law"—was thought by Austin to be an issue different from the moral evaluation of that proposition or rule. Exploration of the existence of law, according to Austin, is a purely descriptive process, a tracing of a proposition's pedigree, and does not require normative assessment. Accordingly, Austin insisted that one could utter the expression "morally deficient law" without doing violence to the concept of "law" and without committing self-contradiction.[2]

*Definition of Law.* For Austin, law is a "general command of the sovereign to govern the conduct of society's members" (henceforth referred to as the "imperative theory of law").[3] To understand Austin's imperative theory of law we must distinguish more carefully its constitutive terms.

The "sovereign" has two characteristics. First, it is the individual (monarch) or body of individuals (some determinate body) toward whom the bulk of society has a habit of obedience. The requisite habit of obedience, which is not dependent on an actual covenant, may arise from fear of the effects of violent revolution or from positive sentiments and attachments.[4] Second, this individual or body of individuals is not itself habitually obedient to anyone else.[5] In this concept of sovereignty, Austin recognizes explicitly a distinction between unconstitutional and illegal acts. Each society understands implicitly that there are certain constraints on the sovereign's power. Acts of the sovereign that conflict with these fundamental understandings are unconstitutional. If, however, such acts were made illegal because they violated the prohibitions of positive law, then the notion of sovereignty as "power unlimited by law" would be infringed.

A "command" has four characteristics. It is an indication of a desire that someone should act, or refrain from acting, in a certain way; it is backed by threat of sanction (punishment); it flows from those who possess the power and apparatus of punishment ("superiors"); and it implies an obligation of obedience on the people directed by it. A "general command" must be applicable to all alike—it must not include definite descriptions or proper names and must prohibit acts not merely on particular occasions but in a general way.[6] Finally, a political "society" must consist of a sovereign and subjects and must not be in a state of subjugation.[7]

*Austin's Critics.* Austin, although credited as the father of modern positivism, has been roundly and widely criticized. The most frequent and strident attack claims that he confused the concept of "obligation" with that of "being obliged."[8] That is to say, by placing so much emphasis on the power of the sovereign to enforce its will through threats of sanctions, the subjects of the law seem animated to obey only because of the law's coercive power. Thus, the law's directive power, its rightful authority, is relegated to a subordinate or nonexistent role, with citizens obeying essentially for reasons of prudence. As such, citizens seem merely to be obliged to obey the law for reasons of self-interest rather than being obligated to obey the law for reasons of morality or deference to rightful authority. H.L.A. Hart, himself a famous contemporary positivist, takes Austin to task on this issue and charges that by overestimating the coercive element of law the imperative theory sees the law as "a gunman writ large."[9] Just as a successful gunman may issue commands and be habitually obeyed, so too Austin's sovereign. But we would never conceive of a gunman as fashioning law merely because he has the power to elicit obedience to his commands; the edicts of our gunman are not only without but are probably directly contradictory to directive power. Accordingly, it seems that in his zeal to divorce questions about the existence of law from moral assessments and to acknowledge the role of political power in actual legal systems, Austin abrogated completely law's directive function.

Moreover, Austin's analysis seems geared uniquely for monarchical legal systems in that it does not seem under his analysis that the sovereign can command itself.[10] If that is true, then it is literally the case that the sovereign is above the law as a matter of conceptual necessity. Such a conception of law has limited utility in those legal systems that, at least in their official proclamations, claim that nobody, including state officials, is above the law. In those governments, such as federal democracies, where no clear instance of unlimited power can be identified, Austin's analysis misses the mark. Moreover, if the electorate of federal democracies holds ultimate political power, then it seems peculiar to conceive of an electorate as habitually obeying itself, and Austin's rubric of ruler–subjects must be refined.[11] In this vein, Hart disputes Austin's depiction of law as a "vertical relationship" such that law is handed down by commanders and habitually obeyed by subjects.[12]

Finally, political leftists view Legal Positivism as a sham, the instrument of the ruling class, which has a vested interest in maintaining the status quo and thus aspires to sanctify law. Positivism, through identification of law solely by pedigree and not by appeal to normative correctness, is charged with masking the workings of self-interest and the primacy of economic and social reality in legal decision making. In its quest to separate legal form from moral content, positivism is ahistorical—heedless of flux and the influences of ideology and theory on law. Positivism thereby encourages the mistaken view that law is politically neutral and, despite positivism's protestations to the contrary, fosters citizens' craven obedience to law. All this, it is claimed, heralds the tyranny of the descriptive (what the "law" is) over the prescriptive (what the law should be).

## H.L.A. HART (1907–    )

Although he distances himself from Austin's imperative theory of law, Hart is an unabashed advocate of Legal Positivism. He takes positivism to be characterized by at least four conditions: the existence of law is autonomous from morals, and thus valid law does not entail honorific moral status; laws are made by acts of human will, not discovered in moral reasoning by acts of cognition; rules and propositions have legal status because they belong to a legal system; and judicial decision making involves "rules plus discretion"—the vast majority of cases are resolved by routine application of rules and facts, but "hard cases" are resolved by judicial discretion, with judges looking to social policy and in effect reaching a legislative solution.[13]

*Rules and Laws.* Hart strives to replace Austin's notion of law as externally applied measures of conduct with a notion that acknowledges an inward dimension. This inward dimension, which tries to account for the phenomenon that Aquinas called law's directive power, recognizes the relationships and bonds existing between members of society. Hart takes the fundamental goal of positivism to be understanding the nature of (rightful) authority in a legal system and unraveling the real issues posed by morally deficient laws.[14] The most important elements in Hart's depiction of law are the rule of recognition, primary rules, secondary rules, and his notion of 'acceptance' and 'validity.'

*Validity and Acceptance.* For Hart, a legal system exists if "valid" laws are obeyed by the bulk of citizens and secondary rules are "accepted" by state officials.[15] A rule is accepted if and only if the standard set by the rule is perceived as imposing an obligation of obedience (internal acceptance)—deviation from it is taken generally as an indication of the deviant's culpability and a reason for criticism by others—and the standard does, as a matter of fact, meet with general compliance (external acceptance).[16]

Hart's notion of internal acceptance does not exclude but is not equivalent to either moral acceptance or (merely) prudential acceptance. Social rules that imply obligations have at least three characteristics: first, they generally demand social conformity and are accompanied by certain social pressures on violators; second, they are thought essential for the maintenance of social life; and third, they are not necessarily connected to the subjective desires of all those subject to them.[17] Hart gives a quaint example of the rule in England that gentlemen tip their hats when passing ladies on the street. There was internal acceptance of such a rule in the sense that those who violated the standard were thought to be rude or uncouth. Such criticism was based neither on moral grounds (a gentlemen who violated this rule was not thereby thought to be immoral) nor on prudential grounds (a violator of the rule had not thereby directly harmed his own self-interest).[18] For Hart the existence of a legal obligation is not necessarily connected to the likelihood of punishment nor to a citizen's subjective beliefs and motives. Thus, he distances himself from Legal Realist conceptions, which hold that legal obligations are mere predictions of what courts will do, and from Austin's imperative conception, which takes legal obligations to be essentially a function of external coercion.

Of course, not all rules that are accepted are laws. A primary rules exists as a rule if it is accepted; it exists as "valid" law if and only if it conforms to the rule of recognition.[19] A rule is "binding" if and only if it is either accepted or valid. It is possible for an extremely insular, stable, and closely knit society to be composed only of primary rules and avoid the institution of law entirely. But in virtually all circumstances such a society will exhibit three defects: uncertainty in citizens' expectations, inability to change and respond to historical trends, and general inefficiency.[20] The remedy for such defects, says Hart, is the development of secondary rules and the creation of a legal system.

There are three kinds of secondary rules: first, the *rule of recognition*, which remedies uncertainty and identifies and validates some primary rules. The existence of the rule of recognition is a matter of fact—the rule of recognition is not itself a valid law; rather, it confers the validity that makes some primary rules laws. The rule of recognition can take many different forms in different legal systems (e.g., what the monarch decrees, what the majority votes for, what is listed on the wall of the town square)[21] and can have different forms within a single legal system (e.g., what the highest court holds, what the federal legislature passes, what the chief executive decrees, what the constitution says). Second, the *rules of change* provide mechanisms by which primary rules can be changed, and they designate the agencies of that change.[22] Third, *rules of adjudication* authorize the procedures for determining—and designate the individuals who determine—when a primary rule has been violated. Rules of adjudication thus provide for the enforcement of primary rules.[23] The three secondary rules thus serve as "rules about rules," and Hart conceives of a legal system as greatly dependent on the union of primary rules, secondary rules, and judicial discretion.

Accordingly, Hart identifies the legal order in the development of societies. As primitive communities evolve they find that to survive and flourish they must go beyond primary rules.[24] Legal systems are not derived from general principles of sovereignty, as Austin believed, but rather develop from social life. Legal rules are maintained less by coercive external force and more by the ties and relationships that develop within societies.[25]

Several minor technical questions are raised against Hart: How does his general characterization of rules apply to secondary rules? How do secondary rules set up standards of conduct and an internal point of view? Moreover, who are the state officials? They cannot be merely those habitually obeyed, and that would signal a retreat into the imperative theory of law. They cannot be merely those who are empowered by secondary rules, because such rules exist as secondary rules because they are accepted by state officials. Neil MacCormick captures part of this point as follows:

> the rule of recognition presupposes the existence of "judges" whose official duties are regulated by the rule of recognition. And these are, per Hart, "judges" only if there are people empowered by a rule (or rules) of adjudication to make authoritative determinations of legal disputes. Are we to say that the rule of adjudication is a "valid" rule or not? It can be so only if it satisfies some criterion set in the rule of recognition. But the rule of recognition presupposes "judges" and "judges" presuppose a rule of adjudication.[26]

*The Problem of the Penumbra.* Some thinkers, says Hart, are led to accept natural law and reject positivism because they (mistakenly) believe that positivism must either approximate or degenerate into formalism. Hart views his version of positivism as an alternative to natural law theory and also strives to distance himself from formalism.

To illustrate the uniqueness of positivism, Hart asks us to consider the following law: "No vehicles are allowed in the public park."[27] Clearly, this law prohibits automobiles and airplanes from entering the park, but what does it demand of bicycles and roller skates, for example? Hart tells us that the term *vehicle* admits of a "gray area" of meaning, a "penumbra" of contestable cases in which the term does not obviously apply to various objects of transportation.[28]

According to Hart, there are at least three areas of indeterminacy in law. First, a statute, such as in the illustration above, may have unclear and contestable instances of application. Second, there may be difficulties in determining and formulating the appropriate precedents to apply in certain cases. Third, law is permeated with highly general standards, such as the standard of due care in negligence, the application of which often requires contestable judgments.[29]

Rather than lamenting the presence of indeterminacy in law, Hart accepts it as inevitable and desirable. Because of our need to make fresh choices, the flexibility of our current collective aims, and the impossibility of prior knowledge of future circumstances, a measure of legal indeterminacy has a salutary effect.[30] He tells us that formalists who aspire to eliminate indeterminacy fail to recognize the consequences of doing so.

> [To end indeterminacy in law] is to secure a measure of certainty or predictability at the cost of blindly prejudging what is to be done in the range of future cases, about whose composition we are ignorant. We shall thus indeed succeed in settling in advance, but also in the dark, issues which can only reasonably be settled when they arise and are identified. We shall be forced by this technique to include in the scope of a rule cases which we would wish to exclude in order to give effect to reasonable social aims, and which the open-textured terms of our language would have allowed us to exclude, had we left them less rigidly defined. The rigidity of our classification will thus war with our aims in having or maintaining the rule.[31]

Accordingly, questions of interpretation of meaning that arise in the penumbra—outside the settled core of paradigm instances—cannot be decided by logical deduction or any other alleged resort to formalism. Such questions, says Hart, must be resolved by the application of criteria purporting to support "what the law ought to be" on some social policy or purpose.[32] Laws often have gaps, and judges must exercise creative choices to answer some legal questions. These creative choices can still be rational, although "free." The choices are free in the sense that legal rules do not apply in a mechanical fashion, but rational in the sense that judicial decision making is constrained by numerous policies and principles that structure decisions by ruling out most rationales. Judges address penumbra cases by confronting the purposes of the relevant statute in light of the interests of the respective litigants. Often judges must weigh and balance conflicting factors in arriving at their decisions. In some such cases, this weighing and balancing may not produce a uniquely correct answer to the case at bar.[33] By this series of claims Hart distances himself from all strictly formalistic or mechanical methods of judicial decision making.

Yet, Hart insists, the problem of the penumbra should not seduce us to subscribe to natural law theory. Natural law theorists must maintain that the normative considerations to which judges appeal in penumbra cases are themselves antecedently existing parts of the law, that is, because natural law theorists identify law with moral soundness, they must claim that judges in penumbra cases draw out what is implicitly already part of the law. But the "ought" to which Hart refers does not necessarily reflect a moral standard; it merely presupposes, much like Hart's notion of internal acceptance, the presence of some standard of criticism.[34] Hence, judges may appeal to social purposes and goals that are not always accompanied by moral considerations. Accordingly, penumbra cases are resolved through the exercise of judicial discretion and the use of considerations that are at least sometimes extralegal.

Hart acknowledges willingly the "core of good sense" in natural law theory, its understanding that some degree of moral appropriateness must attend any legal system that endures. All legal systems purport to aim at justice, and law must embody at least a minimum content of morality; but Hart views this connection between law and morality as contingent, not conceptually necessary. He is careful to point out that positivism need not and should not be obsequious to law or a mere minion of the legal system. Although Hart does suggest that law is accompanied by a prima facie obligation of compliance, the existence of valid law without more is insufficient to establish a final moral obligation of obedience on the part of citizens.[35]

Hart points out that the truth of Legal Positivism is independent of the objectivity or nonobjectivity of moral judgments. Thus, it is incorrect to name the status of moral judgments as the main source of dispute between natural law theorists and positivists. Finally, Hart rejects the natural law slogan that "an unjust 'law' is no law at all." Hart tells us that those who embrace this slogan sacrifice conceptual clarity in the study and classification of law and disable their powers of moral assessment as well.[36]

Hart denies the existence of uniquely correct answers to many legal questions. He also suggests that judges understanding this should not act as if such answers were present in order to secure practical benefits.[37] Although we shall examine this issue more thoroughly in the discussion of Ronald Dworkin, I will note Michael Martin's response to Hart's position.

> It is possible that great benefits would result from operating with a presumption of a unique answer. Such a presumption might stimulate judges to seek common ground in the case of a disagreement and it might encourage more diligent legal scholarship and research to find legal standards that could serve as a basis of agreement. Furthermore, there might be great disadvantages in supposing that there is no one correct right answer. If judges made the law in hard cases, it might erode people's confidence in the objectivity of the judicial process. Indeed, it has been argued that, if the view that there is judicial discretion was widely held, it would be dangerous since it would undermine some of the most important practices in our legal system.[38]

Hart also seems saddled with a problematic relationship between the recognition that a primary rule is law and the obligation of citizens to obey that law. If a primary rule needs only to conform to the rule of recognition to gain confirmation as "valid law," it is not clear how the primary rule entails a (prima facie) obligation of obedience on citizens. Given that the rule of recognition is merely a "brute fact" and lacking the necessary moral imprimatur, the source of law's directive power remains, as it was under Austin's imperative theory of law, mysterious. Surely habit, custom, and routine obedience to authority are insufficient genesis for convincing prescriptive credentials. Moreover, the penumbra cases that Hart cites seem to undermine the positivists' more general aspiration of exalting Rule of Law values. To the extent that judges wield discretion (in a strong sense), the persuasiveness that we live under a regime of laws and not officials loses plausibility.

On the other hand, if the policy considerations that judges consult in penumbra cases are actually part of the law, when we construe law holistically, then it seems that much of the distinctiveness of positivism is lost. For under such an interpretation Hart's jurisprudence begins to converge with that of Ronald Dworkin (see Chapter 3).

*The Problem of Retroactive Law.* Hart must directly confront one of the classic recurring criticisms faced by positivists, that of retroactive law. The difficulty arises in situations where justice is clearly served by punishing someone for a particularly heinous act but where the perpetrator can plausibly claim that he or she followed existing valid law at the time of the act in question.

The classic scenario of the problem concerns acts committed during the Nazi regime, acts that were later punished by the victorious allies.[39] Assume that in 1944 a woman, who despises her husband, reports to the Nazi authorities that the man had disparaged Hitler. At that time there was a statute that prohibited, among other things, derogatory remarks about state officials. The woman was permitted legally, although not obligated, to report her husband's action. The man is subsequently arrested, convicted, and sentenced to either imprisonment or immediate action on the war front. He selects military service and is eventually killed in action.

In 1949 the woman is prosecuted under the subterfuge of an 1871 statute that prohibited the illegal deprivation of freedom. In fact, she is being prosecuted for using a blatantly immoral statute for her own purposes. The woman argues that the act she committed was legal at the time she committed it, while the prosecution argues that the statutes that allow her to make this claim were invalid because they clearly conflicted with basic morality. The objective of the prosecutors is to punish heinously immoral activity, and the explicit use of natural law theory offers that possibility.

The question becomes: What can a Legal Positivist say about all this? The positivist cannot say, as can the natural law advocate, that the law in effect in 1944 was not valid law. Hence, if positivists punish the woman, they are vulnerable to the charge that they are undermining the Rule of Law by employing retroactive legislation— they are in effect punishing her by means of a new law not in place when she committed her act; but if they do not punish her, it seems as if they are exposed as servile followers of law regardless of its moral content. The particular circumstances of this example are not paramount. Regardless of one's specific intuitions about the case of the malicious wife in the Nazi regime, it is not difficult to construct cases in which citizens perform clearly immoral actions that were permitted by (what must be conceded to be) valid law under a positivist analysis and that later pose uncomfortable dilemmas for adjudicators.

Hart holds that the Nazi decree under discussion was morally deficient, but law nonetheless. Clutching firmly the basic positivist separation between the existence and moral soundness of law, Hart concedes that there may be times when judges conclude that relevant settled law is too evil to be applied. In such extraordinary cases, the creation of retroactive law may well be a lesser evil than the application of the relevant legal rules. Judges ignoring settled law under these circumstances should candidly proclaim that they are setting aside preexisting law and compromising the ideal of fidelity to law in deference to other competing values.[40]

Hart's response to the problem has been criticized by Lon Fuller: "Surely moral confusion reaches its height when a court refuses to apply something it admits to be law."[41] For Fuller it seems odd for an avowed positivist to disregard law and compromise Rule of Law values after recognizing the courts' obligation to judge according to law in clear cases. Absent a showing that the instant case is in on the penumbra, it would seem that consistency demands that Hart bite the bullet and apply settled law.

Hart, however, is not defenseless here. Note that he is not arguing that a positivist judge must refuse to apply the relevant law in such circumstances but that a judge may so refuse when the law is especially immoral and the foreseeable consequences of the judge's action (including possible impairment of Rule of Law virtues and possible general undermining of the legal system) strike a clear balance in favor of ignoring that law.

In opposition to Fuller, Hart's position is neither internally inconsistent nor confused. He subscribes to the view that the identification of law is distinct from whether law ought to be obeyed or applied. Thus, he eludes the natural law criticism that positivism is committed to a "law-is-law" mentality and denies (as do most positivists) that the existence of law entails an absolute obligation of obedience. Given that law does not entail such obligations for Hart, there is nothing inconsistent in his maintaining that under certain carefully circumscribed situations judges are morally permitted to ignore what they acknowledge as relevant, and even settled, law. What would make this a confused and inconsistent position would be Hart's acceptance of the dictum that judges must apply all rules emanating from their legal system's rule of recognition. That would presuppose that the existence of law does imply absolute obligations of application or that there is something about the judicial role that demands that all law must be applied even if law itself does not imply obligations of application. But these presuppositions are exactly what Hart wishes to avoid because he believes that they upset the positivist project: they lead to a law-is-law mentality or rest on a belief that law is infused with a necessary moral component that creates absolute obligations of obedience.

Not only is Hart's position not internally inconsistent or confused, it is preferable to both formalism and natural law on the question of judicial application of immoral law. First, Hart's prescription is confined to a very small number of cases, those in which the law is grossly immoral. A judge following Hart's advice cannot disregard relevant settled law any time she believes it coalesces uneasily with her moral preferences or any time the balance of consequences favors ignoring the law.

Second, Hart need not be committed to the view that a judge's personal convictions alone come into play. He may claim that the relevant moral criteria that are being transgressed are society's own professed moral standards; that is, a judge may claim that the rule in question, although it is a "law" based on positivist tests for pedigree, is still logically and morally incompatible with the country's body of shared moral beliefs. Accordingly, a judge following Hart's prescription need not be using public power for private ends because the ends sought are not private purposes of the judge but rather serve the coherence of public purposes. Conceived in this way, the judicial action in question is not an arbitrary exercise of power, nor must it rest on a cognitive theory of ethics.

Third, unless one is a deontologist of a most radical Kantian sort, there is no good reason to contend that "fidelity to law" is a sacred, absolute value. As Hart's common sense allows him to recognize, there are competing values that can at least sometimes trump fidelity to law. To admit this does not reduce us to crude instrumentalism but only allows judges to acknowledge honestly what virtually all of us admit in our lives: at least sometimes the consequences of compliance with a generally acceptable rule or value are so socially disastrous that compliance with the rule is irrational. There is no "moral confusion" here, as Fuller contends, unless one thinks that positivist (and any other) judges must acknowledge one and only one value and must do so "come hell or high water." But to accept that proposition is to beg the question against Hart from the outset. Moreover, Fuller cannot brandish the slogan "judges are required to uphold the law" with quite the confidence he seems to imagine. Hart's point is either that, in extreme cases, judges' duty to advance justice trumps their duty to uphold the law or, alternatively, that in extreme cases, ignoring certain legal rules is consistent with a more general duty to uphold the law—a duty that is upheld when we conceive the law more holistically. (I would guess that the former is closer to Hart's position.) The point here is that the judicial duty "to uphold the law" may not be quite as self-executing an expression as Fuller imagines.

The reasonableness of Hart's position can be seen in worst-case scenarios: if an otherwise morally acceptable legal system has a relevant rule of recognition that identifies all orders of the queen as law, and the queen orders that the first-born of all her subjects be put to death under threat of the penalty of death to themselves, then that decree is "law" according to positivism.[42] What is a positivist judge to do when deciding a case in which a mother has refused to put her firstborn to death? Should the judge proclaim piously that he must uphold the relevant law "come hell or high water"? Or does the gravity of the situation and the gross immorality of the law permit him to ignore the queen's decree even while recognizing that it has the proper pedigree to be declared "law"?

The fact is that any theory of judicial decision making is uncomfortable when confronting the Nazi case under discussion. Although I am generally unsympathetic to legal positivism, I think Hart's answer is stronger than both formalism's restrictive view ("judges

must apply the law come hell or high water") and natural law's disingenuous posturing ("regardless of its pedigree this 'law' is not
truly law so there is no judicial duty to apply it").

## HANS KELSEN (1881–1973)

*A Pure Theory of Law.* Kelsen advances what he
calls a "pure theory" of law, a general account that purports to eliminate all extralegal references and to describe the law only.[43] Prizing
the alleged autonomy of law, Kelsen aspired to isolate positive law
from moral evaluation. He thought that its coercive dimension was
the law's distinctive social aspect. Thus, the moral content of law—
whether a particular law is morally good or bad—is not a significant
question for Kelsen's pure theory. Kelsen goes beyond Hart here.
Where Hart admits enthusiastically the core of good sense in natural
law theory and finds a place for normative or quasi-normative notions such as internal acceptance and obligation, Kelsen dismisses all
such concepts to the scrapheap of "nonjuridical" questions relating
only to the effects, not the nature, of law.[44] Animated by a strong
need for stability and certainty in law and reacting to the chaos of
pre–World War II Europe, Kelsen placed his faith in analytic examination of the logical form of law.

As a positivist, Kelsen extols the separation of factual claims from
value claims. But he again goes much further than Hart when he
opposes all objectivist theories of value.[45] Because he is a subjectivist
in value theory who contends that there are no objective, rationally
derived, moral truths, Kelsen says that a pure and scientific theory
of law cannot resolve value disputes because such disputes are not
amenable to scientific analysis.

Kelsen distinguishes carefully between "truths about statements
concerning reality," where truth is established if and only if a proposition corresponds to reality, and "establishing the truth of a norm,"
where the norm is either valid or invalid, rather than true or false.[46]
The validity and invalidity of norms are dependent on a more general norm. Ultimately, the validation of the various levels of general
norms is dependent on a basic norm, the *Grundnorm*, which is itself
valid because it is self-evident.[47] The *Grundnorm* carries directive
power and establishes various authority, including the power to create other norms.

> The basic norm [*grundnorm*] is that norm which is presupposed when
> the custom through which the constitution has come into existence, or

the constitution-creating act consciously performed by certain human beings, is objectively interpreted as a norm-creating fact. . . . The basic norm determines the basic fact of law creation and may in this respect be described as the constitution in a logical sense of that word. . . . The basic norm is the presupposed starting point of a procedure: the procedure of positive law creation. It is itself not a norm created by custom or by act of a legal organ; it is not a positive but a presupposed norm.[48]

Different series of norms stem from acts of will, not acts of discovery, by those individuals and institutions who have by higher norms been delegated the power to create. Thus, Kelsen's "pure theory" understands law as a logically consistent and internally sufficient system of norms. In the legal system, the *Grundnorm* is often the first constitution that establishes an efficacious order. If a particular legal system is no longer effective on balance, the *Grundnorm* is amenable to the formation of a new legal order. Accordingly, the autonomy of law is conceived as a logical progression of norms.[49]

A norm is a valid legal norm if and only if it has originated in the way appropriate to the legal order to which it belongs and it has not been annulled—either in the way established by that legal order, by way of atrophy or disuse, or through a more general ineffectiveness of the entire legal system.[50] Although law cannot exist unless backed by threats of coercion and law's effectiveness must be real, Kelsen insists that "power" and "law" are not equivalent. Law is, according to the pure theory, a specific order, classification, and structure of power. Thus, legal norms claim to regulate human conduct through their coercive power.

Kelsen finds himself in the typical positivist quagmire: hoping to release his analysis of law from mushy, unscientific judgments of value yet admitting on some level that law cannot simply be the raw manifestation of power and coercion. The more a positivist purifies his theory of law, the more he is vulnerable to charges that only the coercive power of law remains. Yet when a positivist later decries the identification of might with legal right and affirms the obligatory force of his "*Grundnorm*" or "rule of recognition" or "brute fact conferring legal validity," he seems to walk unsteadily with a wink and a nod back into an embrace with contaminated and nonrational moral reasoning. The problem for Kelsen is magnified because he holds an explicitly subjectivist account of value judgments and betrays a certain disdain for any rational analysis of moral reasoning.

Moreover, the nature of Kelsen's *Grundnorm* remains a bit mysterious. The invocation of "self-evidentness" to which he resorts is often the first and last refuge of desperate theoreticians who sense quickly that their questioning of and justification for legal–moral phenomena must cease somewhere. Infatuated as Kelsen is with correspondence theories of truth, his analysis is relentless and linear. But the appeal to self-evidentness leaves us only with a fundamental "Norm of all Norms" that cannot distinguish itself from a gunman who is habitually obeyed. The directive power of law must emanate from the social bonds between citizens and institutional authorities. Citizens will be most likely to internalize law's dictates when they comprehend and participate in the rationale underlying law's demand for obedience. Much of this is lost in Kelsen's dispassionate logical analysis. Thus, the quest for a theory of law uncontaminated by judgments of value ends with whimpers of "self-evidentness," "brute facts backed by coercive sanctions," and thin, disingenuous reassurances that "law and power are not equivalent."

Furthermore, there are some technical misgivings that can legitimately be raised against the pure theory of law. First, its insistence on viewing institutional relations in a strictly hierarchical fashion tends to subordinate judicial power to legislative forces and thereby obscures the reality that the judiciary often shares power equally with the legislature or even surpasses it in the process of judicial review. Second, there will be occasions when two different legal norms are equally valid but mutually incompatible. In other words, it may well be that the pure theory will declare, from the perspective of cognition, the validity of both of these norms but is precluded, from the standpoint of evaluation, from adjudicating between them to determine which of the two norms should control the case at bar. The choice between the two would be an act of (strong) discretion completely unguided by law as conceived of by the pure theory. More important, Kelsen seems to construe legal interpretation here as a two-stage process: the cognition of legal norms, followed (in the case of equally valid but conflicting norms) by extralegal and unguided choice. But many—those who believe that in such instances judges cannot merely give effect to their volitions but must instead attend to the purposes and policies underlying legislative efforts—contend that Kelsen's analysis distorts judicial interpretation.[51]

Finally, we may dispute one of the basic assumptions animating Kelsen's project: the radical subjectivity and relativity of values. Driven by a fear of the rampage of unverifiable and nonrational value judgments, Kelsen takes refuge in the logical pretensions of the pure theory. But, as we have seen previously, the claims of relativism that engendered Kelsen's fear and nurtured the retreat to the safety of logical analysis are neither as persuasive nor as threatening as he imagined.

## JOSEPH RAZ

*Positivism Defined*. Raz lists what he takes to be the three main areas of dispute between Logal Positivists and natural law theorists: the proper identification of law ("the social thesis"), the moral value of law ("the moral thesis"), and the meaning of the law's paramount terms ("the semantic thesis").[52] As a social thesis, positivism contends that the identification of law is a question of social fact. As a moral thesis, positivism maintains that the moral value of particular laws and the legal system in general is a contingent matter that depends on various societal contexts at different times and in different places. As a semantic thesis, positivism insists that paramount terms such as "right" and "duties" bear different meanings in legal contexts from those borne in moral contexts.[53] Raz takes the social thesis to be the one that most clearly differentiates positivism, and he does not think that the social thesis necessarily entails the moral or semantic theses.[54]

*The Weak Social Thesis*. Raz explains but does not endorse positivism's weak social thesis, which accepts that law and morality can be connected in certain ways: for example, a legal system's rule of recognition might contain moral tests for legal validity, and thus, at least occasionally, a law's validity might not be determined solely by the fact and manner of its adoption.[55] The weak social thesis still avows that the validity of law is not necessarily dependent on its moral merit, but, acknowledging that moral tests for law have been recognized explicitly by some legal systems, allows for the contingent possibility that the identification of a particular law might well depend on moral arguments and considerations. Thus, the weak social thesis is distinct from a full-blown natural law theory in that the weak social thesis takes moral arguments and considerations to be relevant only insofar as they are antecedently recognized by the legal system in question.[56]

*The Strong Social Thesis*. Abrogating reliance on the weak social thesis, Raz instead endorses what he calls positivism's "strong social thesis," which maintains that a jurisprudential theory is acceptable only if its test for identifying the existence of law depends exclusively on whether that law had the appropriate legislative, judicial, or other social source, while the content of law is properly determined by facts of human behavior that can be described entirely in value-neutral terms and without reference to moral reasoning.[57] Thus, a rule's legal validity is necessarily a function solely of its social sources or pedigree. The strong social thesis is constituted by four presuppositions: (1) a theory of law must include tests for determining whether particular propositions are "law" and for identifying the content of those propositions that are law; (2) our vocabulary of value-neutral terms is rich and complex; (3) value-neutrality does not entail a crude behaviorism that dismisses human intentions, motivations, and moral priorities; and (4) a rule is a legal rule if and only if it meets the social conditions specified by the tests in (1) that identify the existence and content of law.[58]

Raz is not denying that legislation is often animated by regard for moral principles and values, or that judges sometimes employ moral argument when adjudicating legal disputes, or that law often embodies moral concepts. Rather, his claim concerns the proper contours of law: once the relevant institutional and social facts have been identified they delineate the extant law. Any further examination of "justness," "fairness," or substantive "moral value" involve extralegal appeals that transcend the extant law and may result in the creation of new law.

Raz tells us that the strong social thesis is justified because legal systems are social institutions involving efficacy, institutional character, and sources. Efficacy requires that we identify a legal system in part by the fact that large segments of citizens generally adhere to the law's demands and internalize its requirements. This condition distinguishes defunct or aspiring legal systems from actual ones. Thus, efficacy characterizes effective but not noneffective law, although it does not separate legal from nonlegal systems.[59]

The institutional character of law involves the concept of a legal system as a structure of guidance and adjudication that stakes out supreme authority within particular societies. Legal systems have limits because of their institutionalized character—they contain only those standards and rules that are linked in certain ways to the functioning of the relevant adjudicative institutions. Thus, the law does not encompass all moral and nonmoral standards of justification or all social rules and conventions.[60] The law comprises only that subset of standards of justification, rules, and conventions that has the proper institutional connection.

*The Sources Thesis.* While positivism's weak social thesis also underscores the efficacy and institutional character of law, the strong social thesis is distinguished by its emphasis on the sources thesis. The sources thesis states that the existence and content of law are fully determined by social sources.[61] A law has such a source if its existence and content can be explained without reference to moral arguments. Thus, the sources of law are those social facts that confer validity and that identify content. Raz gives us two reasons for accepting the sources thesis. First, he claims that as a descriptive matter the sources thesis both explains and mirrors our current conception of law. Second, he insists that as a prescriptive matter there are powerful reasons to continue to adhere to that conception of law.[62]

As an example of how the sources thesis reflects our current conception of law, Raz asks us to consider those characteristics we find desirable in judges. One class of qualities would include knowledge of and skill in interpreting the law, demonstrated legal experience, and facility with the argumentative strategies of our adversary system.[63] Another class of qualities would include wisdom, understanding of human nature, moral sensibilities, and general empathy.[64] Raz instructs us that while both classes of qualities are important for qualified judges to possess, only the first class of qualities captures the (strictly) legal qualifications of judges. The second class captures a judge's moral character, which, although not irrelevant to the judicial role, is independent of (strictly) legal skill.

Moreover, Raz declares that the sources thesis captures well the distinction we acknowledge between settled and unsettled law. When applying settled law, the judge's task is a routine and quasi-mechanical use of his strictly legal skills; but when the law is unsettled, a judge is thought to develop and invoke extralegal arguments that include moral and social policy considerations.[65] The sources thesis, says Raz, explains why these distinctions are part of our current conception of law: questions are resolved by settled law when legally binding sources provide solutions to the case at bar. If a question cannot be resolved by materials derived from legal sources, then it does not have a legal answer and the law on such a question is unsettled. In deciding unsettled law the court must necessarily "break new legal ground" and develop the law through use of extralegal considerations.[66]

Furthermore, Raz believes that the sources thesis captures and justifies another basic insight into the function of law. We all acknowledge that social life requires various kinds of cooperation, forbearance, and coordination among large segments of citizens. One of law's functions is to draw the boundaries between strictly private action and action that is binding on all members of society regardless of their disagreement with such action. Society must draw these boundaries in public, ascertainable ways that serve to guide and regulate its members. Declaring a rule or proposition to be "legally binding" is distinguishing it as authoritative.[67] All societies distinguish mere expressions of view or informal requests from authoritative rulings. Law is one kind of authoritative ruling that signifies that one of society's institutions claims dominion over citizens: law declares that citizens are required to comply with certain standards simply because those standards were designated by the proper authority. Raz takes this declaration to be independent of whether the standards are justifiable on other (extralegal) grounds. If the very heart of law's authority is that its rulings and declarations are binding independent of other justifications, then those rulings and declarations can be identified without reference to (extralegal) justificatory arguments.[68] The sources thesis, Raz reminds us, captures this aspect of our current conception of law.

In this vein, Raz terms "dependent reasons"[69] those considerations for action that apply to litigants and over which there is dispute. Adjudication involves the "preempting"[70] of these dependent reasons by an authoritative legal judgment. The authoritative nature of law thus requires that the identification of law must be made without reference to the dependent reasons on which the legal official resolved the dispute.

Given that positivist adherents of the weak social thesis such as Hart, natural law advocates, and Ronald Dworkin's disciples all claim that it is not always possible to identify law without reference to dependent reasons, their theories must be renounced as inconsistent with the authoritative nature of law.[71] The strong social thesis, on the other hand, identifies law exclusively with "the three common sources of . . . legislation, judicial decision, and custom,"[72] without relying on dependent reasons and considerations. Thus, for Raz, only the strong social thesis is consistent with the authoritative nature of law. Raz denies, however, that citizens have a general obligation to obey the law. Such an obligation would apply "to all the law's subjects and to all the laws on all the occasions on which they apply."[73] Raz maintains the distinction between laws and morals by asserting that reasons for obeying law must be considered case by case.

It should be apparent that Raz's explicit intention is to demonstrate why the positivist's strong social thesis is uniquely able to explain and justify law as we know it. Whether he has succeeded is much less apparent.

His claims about the institutional character of law, for example, may succeed in casting doubt on the most radical forms of natural law theory, but they are less successful against a positivism based on the weak social thesis, Dworkin's view, and most other jurisprudential theories. The weak social thesis and Dworkin's view can agree quickly that not all justifiable standards are embodied by law and can acknowledge that law and morality are not identical. Proponents of the weak social thesis admit that moral considerations are important for identifying law only to the extent that such considerations are antecedently recognized by the legal system. Dworkin never concludes that law and morality are identical, only that law is inevitably connected with political morality. This claim, although going far beyond what the strong social thesis asserts, does not go so far as to sanctify all justifiable standards as "law."[74]

Raz's determination to maintain the distinctions between settled and unsettled law, legal skills and moral character of judges, and easy and hard cases also has currency in contrasting theories. The advocate of the weak social thesis recognizes all these distinctions, as does Dworkin. The precise boundaries of the distinctions may be interpreted differently by these other theories, but clearly the distinctions are not obliterated. The weak social thesis demands that judges be able to discern the moral considerations, if any, antecedently recognized by their legal systems; and Dworkin demands that judges be able to use the constructive method of legal reasoning in a coherent fashion. But neither states that moral considerations are identical to law or that moral standards may be used in just any way judges see fit. Both theories circumscribe carefully the times and extent to which normative evaluation is permitted. Even Dworkin allows direct appeals to background morality on only a few carefully specified occasions.[75]

Raz's real point here might be that only the strong social thesis draws the boundaries of these distinctions where they ought to be drawn. Here he seems to be relying on what he takes to be prevalent or common-sense perceptions of the proper judicial role. But we may question the power and accuracy of such perceptions, if they indeed comport with the strong social thesis. It is, after all, exactly such common-sense perceptions that other jurisprudential theories are calling into question. These other theorists could well argue that Raz has begun as an avowed apologist for the very vision of judicial practice they find fatally flawed. Moreover, someone like Dworkin could argue that his theory, not Raz's, explains and justifies certain elements of current judicial practice where judges take themselves to be using their "legal skills": reference to highly contestable principles of political morality when resolving the legal rights of litigants; viewing such appeals not as creating new law but as sustaining preexisting rights; and the judicial experience of such appeals as rationally constrained by legal doctrine, not as an exercise of judicial discretion.[76]

Advocates of the weak social thesis, on the other hand, would contest Dworkin's claim that positivism cannot account for the cited aspects of judicial practice, but they would also dispute the claim that proponents of the strong social thesis have drawn the boundaries of the aforementioned distinctions better. The strong social thesis, they would argue, overvalues the necessity of a certain conception of the boundaries of those distinctions, one in which one side of the boundary is purged of moral references. But this denies an important empirical phenomenon: the fact that at least some rule of recognitions explicitly include certain moral standards and thereby include carefully circumscribed appeals to morality as part of identifying "settled law" and as aspects of the "legal skills" of judges.[77] Thus, it is not so clear that the strong social thesis draws the boundary lines of the important distinctions where they must or should be drawn.

Raz, however, does not obviously beg the question against his jurisprudential opponents. He also stresses the ability of the strong social thesis to uphold Rule of Law aspirations—that the law provide adequate notice of its requirements and public, ascertainable standards such that "members of the society are held to be bound so that they cannot excuse non-conformity by challenging the justification of the standards."[78] Here Dworkin would repeat his earlier claims about the phenomenon of judicial appeal to contestable principles of political morality, rational constraint, and experience of applying preexisting rights, not creating new law. Dworkin might attack proponents of the strong social thesis for embracing an excessively broad notion of judicial discretion that ultimately tends to corrode the very Rule of Law aspirations that they claim to support.

Advocates of the weak social thesis, on the other hand, would argue that the strong social thesis overinflates the Rule of Law values of determinacy, predictability, and clear notice to the point that they become the paramount, or even sole, function of law. In this regard, W. J. Waluchow writes in support of the weak social thesis:

> Consider, for example, Hart's insistence that the law should sometimes remain flexible in its application. He argues . . . that the possibility of blindly committing ourselves to undesirable results in unanticipated cases is often a sufficient reason for framing legal standards in loose, open-textured terms as "fair," "reasonable" and "foreseeable." We thereby allow considerable room for maneuvering when these standards come to be applied in actual cases. We no doubt also pay a high price in terms of predictability and the like when this route is taken. But clearly this is sometimes a price worth paying.[79]

Moreover, both Dworkin and advocates of the weak social thesis can point out that Raz assumes without argument a stark contrast between predictability and notice, which allegedly flow from law based on the strong social thesis, and indeterminacy and uncertainty, which allegedly flow from law that includes appeals to moral considerations. Yet massive controversy can attend the proper interpretation and application of certain rules whose institutional pedigrees and status as "law" are not in dispute; and appeals to moral considerations, at least on some occasions, can facilitate rather than hinder predictability and notice.[80]

Raz places great faith in his argument that only the strong social thesis honors the way law preempts dependent reasons and direct moral assessment. But it is not clear that the only or main function of law is to resolve disputes about dependent reasons, or that appeals to morality necessarily hinder dispute resolution, or that the litigants necessarily are in conflict over all the relevant dependent reasons, or that appeals to morality always implicate the dependent reasons a law was intended to settle. Again, Raz seems preoccupied with one function of law and obsessed with the need for predictability and certainty. While it is true that the strong social thesis is the jurisprudential theory that most stridently exalts those themes, that quest may ignore the ways that certain moral criteria for the identification and application of law are recognized by some legal systems and may undervalue other functions of law.

Accordingly, although Raz does a fine job of restating and refining many of the classic weaknesses of radical versions of natural law theory, it is less clear that he has exposed fatal flaws in Dworkin's view or in positivism's weak social thesis.

## BEYOND LEGAL POSITIVISM AND NATURAL LAW: PHILIP SOPER

Accounting for law's directive power is a paramount difficulty for positivists. They must advance reasons for obeying law that are different from fear of law's coercive force yet that permit law's (conceptual) independence from morality.

In his *Theory of Law*, Philip Soper strives to generate a nonpositivist definition of law that links legal and political theory. Disillusioned by the excessive abstractness of much legal theory, Soper insists that the point of legal philosophy must include answering the practical questions, What ought one to do? and What is law that I should obey it? Soper assumes that law necessarily entails a prima facie obligation of obedience: "The phenomenon of prima facie obligation is universally associated with the institution of law."[81]

Soper claims that contemporary Legal Positivists fail at the same task at which Austin failed: to identify law so that its imperatives command our allegiance in a way different from that commanded by mere coercive force. Moreover, while natural law theory can highlight law's directive power, it cannot "identify law apart from the substantive moral inquiry into justice."[82] The price paid here, according to Soper, is that natural law theory fails to give currency to our deeply felt belief that there is a prima facie obligation to obey law even when a particular decree is substantively unjust.

*Obligations of Obedience to Law.* To remedy this, Soper says: "Instead of defining law to ensure that it always obligates, one [should seek] an account that explains why it has any tendency to obligate at all. In this way an independent concept of law is preserved, distinct from that of morality."[83] Soper's agenda is then set: to advance a theory of law that can distinguish law from the mere exercise of coercive power and thus account for law's directive power, which Soper takes to be its ability to necessarily generate prima facie moral obligations of obedience, yet one which does not require a substantive moral inquiry into justice.

The issue of the existence of the requisite prima facie obligation, Soper tells us, is not one that can be resolved merely by observing the behavior of state authorities, by asking legal insiders such as lawyers, or by appealing to citizens.[84] More is needed here. Soper's conclusion is that two conditions are necessary and jointly sufficient to generate prima facie moral obligations of obedience to law:

> [The] features [that are necessary and jointly sufficient to generate prima facie moral obligations of obedience to law] are (1) the fact that the enterprise of law in general—including the particular system, defective though it may be, that confronts an individual—is better than no law at all; and (2) a good faith effort by those in charge to govern in the interests of the entire community, including the dissenting individual. . . . Legal systems are essentially characterized by the belief in value, the claim in good faith by those who rule that they do so in the interest of all. It is this claim of justice, rather than justice in fact, that one links conceptually with the idea of law.[85]

The first condition rests on the traditional view that "coercive systems do not obligate if they do not provide a measurable advance in security over the [Hobbesian] state of nature."[86] The second condition ignores the (substantive moral) content of an official's decree and highlights the official's good faith effort to serve the common good: "The entire approach . . . makes the sincerity of [an official's] belief rather than its [substantive moral] accuracy the critical ingredient in generating respect and obligation."[87] By acting in good faith to promote the common good in the essential arena of government, state officials, even when they fail from a substantive moral perspective, do not violate citizens' natural rights and thus uphold their end of the common enterprise. Soper places primacy on the power of such efforts to help generate moral obligations because an official acting in good faith for the community merits her citizens' respect; that respect constitutes a reason for citizens to comply with what the official believes citizens ought to do, and officials believe that citizens should obey the imperatives of law.[88]

The two conditions of the analysis are thought by Soper to presuppose certain "natural rights," without which the conditions themselves would go unsatisfied. Hence, natural rights are "rights against the state which can be invaded or ignored only at the cost of losing the title of law."[89] The first condition is supported by a "right to security,"[90] which is constituted in part by the requirements necessary for (at least) the minimum safety of citizens and certain Rule of Law values: a measure of settled expectations is nurtured when judicial decisions are enforced and like cases are decided alike. The second condition is also supported by the Rule of Law values of general and consistent application of law, as well as a "right to discourse":[91] the right to discuss political and legal issues with state authorities as the way of testing the sincerity of those authorities. This right to discourse is not absolute; rather, its requirements are fulfilled when citizens confront their officials and make the normative arguments that officials must respond to in order to establish the sincerity of the officials' normative beliefs. Accordingly, any social order or particular legal system that fails to provide its citizens (at least) minimum security or that denies its citizens the opportunity to engage in normative discourse with state authorities lacks the prerequisites for "legality."[92]

Soper trusts that this analysis, unlike crude positivism, allows him to distinguish the imperatives of law from those of mere coercive force. Thus, a gunman, even if she believes sincerely that her actions serve her victim and the common good, cannot command the requisite directive force of law because she is not sovereign and she represents no monopoly of force or any other essential component of a legal order. Moreover, unlike natural law theory, Soper's analysis does not require a substantive moral inquiry into justice or the content of specific laws: law creates prima facie obligations of obedience when Soper's two conditions are in place. Finally, Soper's analysis does not require blind or sycophantic obedience to law: the moral obligation created by law is prima facie and thus may be over-ridden in contexts where the substantive moral content of a law is particularly pernicious.

Soper's two conditions of legality may strike us as insufficient, at least in some cases, to generate prima facie obligations of obedience on the part of citizens. Discrete and insular minorities (e.g., blacks in the antebellum United States, Jews in Europe during the 1930s and 1940s, blacks in South Africa under apartheid) who labor under oppressive and discriminatory social conditions might well prefer such a context rather than the all-out chaos and radical insecurity of a Hobbesian state of nature; moreover, the rulers of such regimes may well believe sincerely that the laws that enforce such social or-ders serve the entire community, including the minorities them-selves. It would seem that Soper is committed to saying that these minority groups thereby have prima facie obligations of obedience to the very decrees that ensure their continued subjugation.[93] This seems more than a bit strange.

In fact, Soper is aware of the availability of such a criticism:

> Officials who accept the beliefs that underlie such moral judgments [e.g., that policies that embrace slavery or apartheid are morally justified and in the best interests of all] are acting in the interests of justice and fairness as they see it, and in that sense in the interests of all (including the disadvantaged group. . . ). Thus, tempting though it may be to de-rive a substantive constraint from a theory that requires acting in the interests of all, the constraint is empty, as formal equality always is.[94]

Soper, then, seems prepared to admit as legal systems social or-ders that include laws such as apartheid, provided that the rulers believe in good faith that those who are disadvantaged under such an order do not thereby suffer injustice. He is careful to point out, however, that social orders that practice genocide are not legal sys-tems because they violate completely the security of their victims and thus fail to provide the minimum safety required of legal sys-tems. Here Soper gains the ability to call a regime such as that in South Africa a "legal system," which distances him from several nat-ural law theorists, and thus he may be taken to have strengthened the definition of what is "law."[95] But in doing so we may question whether he has weakened the plausibility of his thesis that law nec-essarily entails prima facie obligations of obedience on the part of citizens.

We might rejoin on behalf of Soper that the obligations are only prima facie and can thus be overridden under circumstances such as these. What seems strange, then, is that these minorities would have a "final" or "all-things-considered" obligation of obedience to the decrees that condemn them to subordinate status. But Soper's analysis is certainly not committed to such a moral monstrosity.

Such a rejoinder is not without force. But we must remember that the presence of even a prima facie obligation of obedience is disturbing. Those moral theorists who make use of prima facie obligations take them to be serious moral constraints that can be overridden only by an even stronger obligation or set of obligations. Not just any (good moral) reason we might advance for doing or refraining from an action translates into a prima facie obligation (e.g., even strong considerations of utility are not thought to trump a prima facie obligation). While it is no doubt true that Soper's analysis does not necessarily impute an all-things-considered obligation of obedience to the minorities in question, it is still discomforting to say to these minorities, "Look here, you have a prima facie obligation of obedience to the very decrees that ensure your present status. If you want to contend that you should not obey these decrees, you have the burden of persuasion and must now advance weightier obligations (and not just good moral reasons) that might outweigh that prima facie obligation of obedience." The point is this: although this criticism against Soper is not conclusive, it does point out the squeamishness we might feel at imputing even the thinnest prima facie obligation of obedience under the given circumstances. Accordingly, we may question whether the two conditions of Soper's analysis, both of which are fulfilled in this illustration, are truly sufficient to generate prima facie obligations of obedience.

In certain respects, Soper leaves unclear the relationship between the fulfillment of his second condition and the generation of prima facie obligations of obedience. He tells us that state authorities who make good faith efforts to act justly and serve the entire community deserve respect from citizens, and that respect provides a reason to comply with the wishes of such authorities. But a critic might argue that the mere presence of respect for someone does not, without more ballast, translate into a reason to obey that person.[96] Moreover, it is not at all clear that officials, who make good faith efforts to act justly and serve the entire community, deserve, on that basis alone, respect from citizens. Does the obdurate, insensitive, uninformed ruler who believes in good faith that blacks should be enslaved for their own good or that Jews should not be allowed to emigrate because by doing so the common good is impaired, merit respect? If we think, along with Soper, that good faith efforts to serve justice are sufficient for meriting respect from citizens, then we will, in cases such as those mentioned, place a premium on ignorance and callousness. Thus, we find that there may be a stiff price to pay when we sever the substantive moral content of an official's beliefs from the sincerity with which those beliefs are held.

Moreover, John Fischer points out an ambiguity that accompanies Soper's second condition: Must officials sincerely believe that their decrees are "morally justifiable" ("the weak formulation" of the second condition), or must they sincerely believe that their decrees serve "the common good or the interests of all"[97] ("the strong formulation" of the second condition)? Fischer claims that Soper vacillates between these two formulations and that neither formulation is adequate.

The weak formulation is inadequate because it produces paradoxical conclusions when we compare two rulers who effect the same policies but under different beliefs about their moral justifiability.

> Consider a ruler who pursues self-interested policies and indeed regards them as not morally justified. Call him Ruler I. Suppose that Ruler II pursues exactly the same self- interested policies but does so believing in their moral justifiability (but not in virtue of their serving the common good). Let us further say that Ruler II realizes that his policies are severely harmful to the interests of some groups (even in the long-term). Under the weak [formulation of Soper's second condition], Ruler II's regime classifies as a legal system (given that the regime achieves minimal security) but Ruler I's does not. The distinction between law and coercion derives not from the content of the policies but merely from their official justification. . . . Why exactly should the difference in attitudes between Rulers I and II make only Ruler II's society legal?[98]

Fischer then notes that the only way to distinguish the two regimes significantly is to suppose that one of them "obligates" but the other does not. Fischer, however, finds this unpersuasive and echoes versions of the criticisms raised above against Soper.

> Suppose I am a black person and both societies have apartheid. Now why should the fact that Ruler II has a belief in the moral correctness of apartheid generate an obligation for me to obey him, whereas I would have no obligation to obey Ruler I? After all, the policy is equally objectionable (and against my interests) in both cases, and both rulers sincerely realize this.[99]

If we examine the strong formulation of Soper's second condition, Fischer tells us, we will find that it fares no better than the weak formulation. The strong formulation requires that a ruler believe sincerely that his directives benefit the common good, the "interests of all."[100] Fischer argues that the strong formulation is not necessary for law because "it seems too much to demand that rulers believe that their directives benefit all classes (or serve the 'common good') for a system to qualify as legal."[101] Fischer's point here is that many directives are in fact morally justified and given their genesis merit the honorific title "law," yet do not benefit the interests of all subjects. As a matter of pure description, there would be few, if any, legal systems or particular laws in existence today if the strong formulation were taken seriously. Moreover, it seems clear that laws should not, as a matter of conceptual necessity, be required to serve all classes or individuals. There are times when it is proper to require some citizens to make sacrifices in order to serve the interests of other citizens.

Fischer concludes that appeal to the weak formulation renders Soper's analysis incapable of providing sufficient conditions for legality[102] while appeal to the strong formulation renders his analysis incapable of providing the necessary conditions for legality.[103] We might rejoin on Soper's behalf that it is not necessary that officials believe sincerely that every directive serves the common good but only that the law, taken as a whole, serves the interests of all. Thus, an official can recognize that a particular directive does not serve the interests of all because it may require some citizens to make sacrifices for others, but can still evince a good faith belief in the moral justifiability of the legal system. Under such a view, the good faith beliefs of officials would still be necessary for the existence of a legal system.

But this response creates another problem. Once an official acknowledges that a particular decree is morally suspect, it is unclear why citizens have even a prima facie obligation of obedience to that law. We may concede for argument's sake that citizens have a prima facie obligation of obedience to a (morally justifiable) legal system taken as a whole but still wonder why that obligation implies obedience to a decree explicitly recognized by officials as not in the interests of all.[104] The point is this: to require officials to believe sincerely (and with a straight face) that every decree serves the interests of every citizen or class of citizens is much too strong, but if we acknowledge that officials know this and if we thereby require only that officials believe sincerely that the system as a whole serves the interests of all, then we merely restate, rather than answer, the question, Why do we have an obligation to obey this law?

Soper seems to understand clearly the problem: whatever general justification one advances for a legal system as a whole, there will be particular decrees for which that justification is inapplicable. In those cases it is difficult to claim that citizens have a prima facie obligation of obedience. Furthermore, Soper narrows the solutions available to him to those that show that prima facie obligations flow from the conceptual nature of law. In grounding his solution in notions of respect to rulers trying to do their best, however substantively feeble their efforts may be, Soper may be taken to confuse the respect often, but not invariably, owed to persons trying their best to do necessary societal work with respect as a necessary conceptual element of law that entails prima facie obligations of obedience.[105] We may well owe respect to officials as persons who are in good faith doing their best, but that does not imply that we owe respect to the substantively unjust laws they create. Accordingly, it is more likely that Soper has restated the question, Why should I obey this law? rather than provided an answer grounded in the very nature of law.

Finally, it is not even clear that officials' good faith beliefs or moral justifiability are necessary components of a legal system as a whole. As Thomas Morawetz points out, "The good faith of legislators and judges usually is observed and presumed, but it is too easy to imagine an alternative legal system in which the citizens are cynical about the good faith of officials and in which that cynicism is warranted. This is not, or not yet, a description of naked coercion, and I am unpersuaded that it is clearly not a description of law."[106]

*The Judicial Role.* Soper denies that an individual judge justifies her decisions through her own political and moral theory. Instead, a judge must use her normative theories when deciding whether the secondary rules (in Hart's terminology) require her to apply certain rules of obligation (laws) to citizens.[107] Such a judge might follow a particular rule of obligation, even if she thinks that it is substantively unjust, because she believes she is obligated to do so by secondary rules that she believes are themselves just. Here Soper tells us that judges' good faith claims of justice reflect a "pure process theory of justification":[108] the secondary rules that define the procedures of law creation and application are just "even though the process of following those [secondary] rules may occasionally generate unhappy results."[109]

Soper's conception of the judicial role serves as a specific illustration of his general problem with the good faith requirement of condition two. First, if we take that requirement as a demand that judges must have a good faith belief in the moral justifiability of their particular decisions, then that requirement seems too strong: many claim that the proper judicial role includes applying and upholding the law even when judges suspect that doing so has unfortunate results in the instant cases.[110] Second, if we take the good faith requirement as a demand that judges must have "only" a good faith belief in the secondary rules that compel particular decisions but they need not have a good faith belief in the moral justifiability of every application of these secondary rules, then that requirement still seems too strong: judges are not, as a matter of fact, required to swear their (moral) allegiance to every secondary rule of their legal systems; they are required only to interpret and apply those secondary rules in appropriate circumstances.[111] Consider the case of a judge who believes that some, perhaps many, of the secondary rules of her legal system should be reformed but who nevertheless interprets and applies those rules because she does not take the judiciary to be the proper agency of change. Such a judge is still a judge and the secondary rules in question still have the force of "law," even though that judge lacks the requisite good faith belief in the moral justifiability of those secondary rules. Third, we may take the good faith requirement as a demand that judges must have only a general good faith belief in the legal system as a whole. This, too, seems too strong. While, as a matter of fact, most judges (at least those in "democratic" regimes) undoubtedly do have such a belief, it is unclear whether a judge who lacked that belief is thereby not a judge or that the rules of obligation she applies are not "law."[112] Finally, even if all judges as a matter of conceptual necessity must possess this general and diffuse good faith belief in the moral justifiability of the legal system as a whole, it is still unclear how their collective good faith beliefs imply a prima facie obligation on the part of citizens to obey all law.

Legal Positivism has strong appeal because it seems to combine formalism's veneration of Rule of Law virtues with realism's commonsense skepticism. However, it makes no appeal to absolute obedience to law nor does it degenerate into radical cynicism about law's authority. Unfortunately, it is not clear that Legal Positivism can liberate itself from appeals to rules of recognition or *Grundnorms* that tend to reinstate an imperative account of law. Accordingly, Legal Positivism cannot explain adequately law's directive power.

And although Soper's ingenious attempt to derive a new theory of law points us in the correct direction, it depends too heavily on the subjective beliefs of those with power. Using the earlier theories as our points of departure, we now turn to Ronald Dworkin's complicated and sophisticated view of "law as integrity."

# CHAPTER 3

## The Right Answer Thesis
*Ronald Dworkin's Legal Idealism*

THE MOST PROMINENT contemporary philosopher of law is Ronald Dworkin. In his first influential work, *Taking Rights Seriously*, Dworkin admits the inexorable political elements in judicial decision making but still maintains that judges lack discretion (in a strong sense), insists that antecedent right answers to all or virtually all legal cases exist, and exalts the presence of rationality in law and judicial decision making.

*The Nature of Law.* For Dworkin the validity of law is relative to particular legal systems, and law consists not only of rules but also of principles and policies. Discovering what is the law is an empirical matter: there is no single ultimate test for law. We must instead examine particular legal systems at particular times. The law, however, is not separate from morality, because the best underlying explanatory theory of law includes the morally best justification of the settled constitution, judicial decisions, legislative enactments, and legal practices.[1]

Dworkin draws a crucial distinction between principles and policies. Arguments from principle are said to justify political decisions that benefit some person or group by showing that the beneficiary has a right to the benefit. Arguments from policy justify such decisions by showing that the benefit advances a collective goal of the political association. According to Dworkin, judges may rely only on arguments from principle when deciding cases, while legislators may include policy considerations as support for statutory enactments.[2]

To illustrate how the law is not merely constituted by explicit rules and statutes and how judges use the principles embedded in law, Dworkin invokes two cases: *Riggs v. Palmer* (1889) and *Henningsen v. Bloomfield Motors* (1960).[3] In the *Riggs* case a grandson, who was the heir named in his grandfather's will, murdered his grandfather. The question for the court was whether a convicted murderer can inherit from the estate of his victim. Although no legal statute prohibited an inheritance under these circumstances, the court held that a fundamental principle controlled its decision: "No person may profit by his own wrong." Although this principle was not stated explicitly in legal doctrine, presumably it was part of the best theory underlying the law. Accordingly, the grandson was barred from inheritance.[4]

In the *Henningsen* case a man purchased an automobile and signed a contract in which he agreed that the manufacturer's liability for product defects was limited to "making good" the defective parts. The man was subsequently involved in an auto accident apparently caused by product defects. Although he could not advance a statute that explicitly supported his legal position, the plaintiff argued that the manufacturer should be liable for medical and other expenses of the persons injured in the crash. In deciding the question, Can a manufacturer limit its own liability even if its product is radically defective? the court appealed to the following principles: "In the absence of fraud the person who signs a contract is still bound by its terms even if he chose not to read the contract"; "in a society in which the automobile is common and necessary, a manufacturer is under a special obligation in connection with its construction, promotion, and so on"; and "a court should not enforce an agreement in which one of the parties is unjustifiably taken advantage of because of economic necessity." Swayed more by the unequal bargaining power between the parties and the unfairness of adhesion agreements than it was moved by the principle of freedom of contract, the court found the manufacturer liable despite the clear wording of the contract.[5]

Dworkin categorizes rights as being either background or institutional.[6] The former are moral rights that are independent of the existence or authority of political institutions. They largely constitute the background morality that serves as the evaluator of political and legal norms. Institutional rights are concrete entitlements embedded in the constitutions, legislative enactments, and judicial decisions of the political structure. Because Dworkin maintains that the most important moral rights are already institutionalized in American law, an American judge has less need to appeal to background morality than does a judge in a more corrupt political system. Thus, Dworkin endorses the notion of institutional autonomy, which restricts direct appeals by judges to background rights in all cases but those in which the standard legal materials provide uncertain guidance.[7]

*Judicial Reasoning.* The duty of a judge is to discover the antecedent right answer and enforce the preexisting rights of litigants, not to legislate or create a new solution.[8] This concedes "discretion" to the judge, but only in the unassailable and weak sense that it calls on her to exercise judgment. Dworkin denies explicitly that judges have discretion in the strong sense that they are free to make decisions without a prior duty to decide in one way rather than another. Accordingly, for Dworkin, judges are rationally constrained by preexisting legal materials.[9] One of the unique aspects of Dworkin's position is the sophisticated reasoning he believes judges must employ to discover the constraints on their decisions.

Judges must construct a scheme of abstract and concrete principles that provides a coherent justification for all common law precedents and for constitutional and statutory provisions. His scheme, as applied to the United States, is ordered vertically into four levels: constitutional provisions, decisions by the United States Supreme Court, legislative enactments, and lower-court decisions.[10] The justification for lower-level principles must be consistent with the principles providing justification for higher-level materials. The scheme is also ordered horizontally in that the principles that justify a decision or act on one level must be consistent with the justification offered for other decisions and acts at that level. The resulting judicial theory, Dworkin assures us, will reflect only what the Constitution, common law precedents, and statutes themselves require, and ignore the judge's independent personal convictions about morality and optimum policy.

At each vertical level of justification the judge's task is somewhat different. At the constitutional level she must develop a comprehensive theory of principles and policies that justifies the constitution as a whole. She does this by generating possible explanatory theories that justify different aspects of the scheme, testing the resulting theories against the nature of more general political institutions, and, upon exhaustion of the effectiveness of that test, elaborating the successful theory's contested concepts.[11] At the statutory level, judges must decide which arguments from principle and policy could properly have convinced the legislature to enact particular statutes. Judges here are not trying to discern the "actual intent of the framers"; rather, they are trying to discover the best justification of settled doctrine.[12] The actual intentions of the legislature are relevant only when necessary to choose between equally appropriate theories. At the common law level, judges must recognize that earlier decisions exert a "gravitational force" on later decisions insofar as arguments from principle justify such decisions. Roughly, if prior decisions D are justified by principles P that act as reasons for D, and P dictates a certain conclusion C in the instant case I, and P has neither been "recanted nor institutionally regretted,"[13] then C.

This comprehensive scheme incorporates a theory of mistakes. That is, the scheme must limit the number and nature of events that can be stigmatized as mistakes and adumbrate for future decision making why such events are mistakes. To disparage an event as a mistake is to deny its continued gravitational force—its authority for future judicial decision making—but not its specific institutional authority—its authority to effect the particular institutional consequences the event encompasses.[14] A mistake will be "embedded" when the event's specific institutional authority is situated firmly and outlives the loss of its gravitational force. A mistake will be "corrigible" when the event's specific institutional authority depends on its continued gravitational force.[15]

The best justificatory theory for existing law must furnish a more consistent fit with legal materials and must provide a more compelling moral justification in light of background morality than those accounts provided by competing theories.[16] Suppose, however, that theory X stigmatizes fewer aspects of legal doctrine as mistakes and thus provides the more consistent fit, whereas opposing theory Y better meets the requirements and aspirations of background morality. Dworkin apparently suggests the following as a plausible, but probably too crude, answer: the consistent fit criterion is the threshold requirement; once two or more competing theories equally fulfill this requirement, background morality becomes the adjudicating criterion.[17]

Dworkin concedes straightaway that individual judges constituted by different backgrounds will construct different, mutually inconsistent theories. Moreover, it will often be impossible to demonstrate that only one of those theories is uniquely correct. Nevertheless, a judge must believe that there is some single correct justificatory theory that announces a single solution for each case. Dworkin rejects the notion that the truth of a proposition of law must be demonstrated on the basis of both physical facts and facts about human behavior. In his view, the presence of controversy among reasonable legal insiders acting reasonably is not logically sufficient to yield the inference that antecedent right answers do not exist.[18]

*The Constructive Model of Reasoning.* An important element of Dworkin's theory is his often misunderstood account of moral reasoning that forms an analogue to his portrayal of judicial reasoning. He espouses a constructive model of reasoning in which moral intuitions and past doctrine are stipulated features of the general jurisprudential theory each judge must construct, and such materials are not described as scientific observations that point to their correlative objective facts.[19] Judicial decisions bear the constraint that they may not exceed the explanatory powers of a judge's theory. Far from assuming relativism or nihilism, this model remains neutral with respect to the objectivity of moral intuitions and beliefs. The constructive model stands in opposition to the natural model of reasoning, which presupposes the existence of an objective moral reality.

The advantage of the constructive model lies in its independence from the metaphysical assumptions underlying the natural model: the existence of a supreme being, or a fixed human nature, or immanent normative rationality embedded in the universe. Its adherents are at a disadvantage, however, because none can claim that her theory is the best possible and imaginable justification for moral and legal reasoning. Advocates of the constructive model, because they stipulate the existing legal materials and prevalent moral convictions of their society as features of the legal theory they construct, may claim only to discover the best explanatory and justificatory theory of law or morality for their society as it is presently situated. Thus, Dworkin's theory does not bridge the gap between the descriptive account of law in a particular society and objectively sound moral principles against which the quality of all existing laws may be evaluated.

This difficulty, however, is not so problematic as many critics have suggested.[20] The aforementioned gap will be present in every jurisprudential theory except an extreme version of natural law theory. Dworkin does not claim that he has closed this gap but merely that legal questions are basically issues of moral principles (based on the constructive model) and not issues of legal facts, as has been often supposed.

In sum, Legal Idealism pronounces that theory gives rational structure and determinate content to what appear to be open-ended legal principles and policies, that virtually all legal questions have antecedently existing right answers, that complex legal systems are gapless and thus judges do not have discretion in a strong sense, and that the constructive model of moral reasoning is best used in legal contexts.

*Right Answer Thesis.* Much criticism has surrounded Dworkin's right answer thesis: his assertion that there exists a single right answer to the questions posed by hard legal cases. Some critics find this claim indefensible unless it can be demonstrated that there exists one right answer to questions of morality and social welfare.[21] Others protest that the thesis involves a contradiction because on the one hand Dworkin's constructive model leaves open the question of whether moral judgments have objective truth value, while on the other hand the right answer thesis suggests reliance on the natural model of reasoning that is supported by the belief in moral foundationalism.[22]

This criticism, however is unwarranted. Dworkin appeals to background morality only in those situations where standard legal materials yield uncertain guidance regarding the legal rights of citizens or where competing justifications of legal materials seem equally coherent with those materials. Dworkin assigns it adjudicatory force only in providing the correct answers to legal questions posed in those situations. Moreover, the notions of background morality employed derive from the constructive model. The right answer thesis, therefore, does not depend on the existence of one objectively sound answer to questions of background morality but rather on the presence of one answer, whether objective or intersubjective, that meets the criteria of the constructive model. Accordingly, Dworkin should not be charged with a contradictory dependence on both models.

This resolution of the criticism, however, fashions the grounds for a more telling criticism of the right answer thesis. If this thesis depends on the existence of a single right answer to questions of background morality based on the constructive model, two questions remain: Do single right answers that meet the criteria of the constructive model exist for questions of morality? and, if they do exist, Is their discovery any more certain than the discovery of the right legal answer to a hard case absent any appeal to background morality?

The nature of the constructive model suggests that more than one moral code will emerge and, thus, references to background morality cannot supply single right answers to questions of morality or law. Even if right answers do emerge from the constructive model, their identification will prove so uncertain that references to background morality will cease to provide single answers in difficult cases. Because there is good reason to suspect that the most difficult cases in law are just those in which moral principles are most uncertain and because a judge's appeal to background morality may only increase the uncertainty of the legal disposition in such cases, it is not easy to perceive how references to background morality can serve the function for which they are intended. Moreover, there may be no objective way to choose between two or more self-consistent mutually incompatible sets of values, particularly if one remains agnostic about the existence of objective moral facts. It may be that judgments about the rational or moral superiority of a given system merely beg the question in favor of that system.

This attack on the right answer thesis does not demonstrate that morality is not objective or that right answers to difficult legal questions do not exist. The criticism is designed to call into question the plausibility and practical justifiability of embracing the thesis. The critic cannot prove conclusively that right answers are always or often unavailable, and neither can Dworkin prove conclusively that right answers are always present. Thus, the question becomes one of the meaning of and justification for the right answer thesis. Is the thesis merely a methodological assumption that Dworkin employs to convince the judiciary that it labors under prior constraints? Or is it meant as a fact about the nature of judicial decision making, albeit one that cannot be conclusively proved?

The right answer thesis is problematic. Because the constructive model of legal and moral reasoning may produce more than one "best" legal and moral theory, no single right answer will exist for some questions of the normative order. Furthermore, appeals to the common legal and moral frameworks that these theories presuppose cannot resolve all difficult questions. Finally, it is dubious whether any finite set of assumptions can generate a correct outcome to every conceivable legal and moral issue.

Dworkin is correct in his observation that the existence of practical controversy does not imply the absence of a right answer to a legal or moral question. But this does not ameliorate the theoretical uncertainty that may arise when incommensurable best theories both explain and justify the law; commensurable and conflicting theories are equally explanatory and neither is clearly morally preferable; a single best theory of law produces equally cogent arguments for both plaintiff and defendant, and background morality provides equally ambivalent guidance; or internal paradox occurs within a single best theory of law.[23] Such examples undermine the plausibility of the right answer thesis. A critic cannot prove conclusively that such theoretical uncertainty must occur, but given the fragility of our language and logic the prospects seem high.

Moreover, the right answer thesis does not rule out the possibility that a "tie" judgment may be the right answer to particular cases. Despite Dworkin's denial that the presence of the theoretical uncertainty grounding the possibility of ties undercuts the right answer thesis,[24] it can be argued that ties must be broken, and to break them judges must exert discretion of the sort Dworkin claims is unnecessary. Thus, the right answer thesis may preserve an area for (strong) judicial discretion after all.

The thesis is designed to support Dworkin's view that judges discover rather than create the law. But a judge who adopts in good faith a controversial version of the best theory of law cannot go back and decide differently those cases adjudicated in accordance with what she takes to be incorrect theories. The original choice of theory has an immediate impact on the instant case, future cases, and on the law itself.[25] Although a sophisticated theory of mistakes might allow judges to ignore decisions ultimately proved incorrect, Dworkin adumbrates only the beginnings of a simple theory of mistakes. Furthermore, Dworkin precludes a judge's chosen theory of law from stigmatizing a relatively large body of common law decisions as mistakes. To pass the threshold requirement of "fit," as few past decisions as possible can be labeled errors. Given that legal principles develop in reference to each other, it seems that any allegedly mistaken decisions, even after a judge's legal theory has uncovered them, already have had an effect of some sort on legal doctrine and on the best explanatory theory of law itself. It may be charged that because of the self-regulatory aspects of judicial decision making, "mistakes" are even more persistent than original sin. If this charge is accurate, it further corrodes the support for a right answer thesis that is built in part on the possibilities of purifying past judicial errors.

All these criticisms are symptomatic of a more general malady: if different judges acting in good faith may legitimately construct different best theories of law that generate conflicting answers to a particular case, and if it cannot be demonstrated that one of these is the uniquely correct solution, what purpose does Dworkin's persistent claim that there is a single objective right answer to such cases serve? If it is beyond the powers of even Dworkin's jurisprudential giant "Hercules" to demonstrate without begging the question which of these "right" answers is preferable to the other, then it may be argued that Dworkin is merely rehearsing a hope or methodological assumption that springs solely from faith. Belief in such an assumption seems every bit as mysterious as belief in other unprovable entities such as gods, hobgoblins, and extraterrestrials.

Moreover, we do not always assume a right answer in confronting questions of value. Is there a correct "right answer" to the question of whether Tony Bennett was a better singer than Frank Sinatra? Or Cardozo a better judge than Brandeis? Or whether abortion is morally permissible?

Dworkin may retort here that his methodological assumption is necessary in order to give sense to the questions judges ask when deciding legal cases. If there is not a "right answer" to the question at bar, what could account for the way judges proceed and the rational constraints they experience? Underlying appeals to fairness, the Rule of Law, and separation of governmental powers might also be invoked to support Dworkin here.

It must be made clear, however, that even if there is power to this retort, the resulting implication is that judges must act as if there are right answers (the faith in right answers thesis), not that there are right answers (the right answer thesis), to all legal cases. The next question is paramount: Does the methodology of judges acting as if there are uniquely right answers to hard cases result, quite properly, in more fairness, more respect for law, and more societal support for the legal system than would otherwise occur? Or is the right answer thesis an elaborate hoax that artificially truncates political conflict and thereby brazenly serves the often illegitimate interests of the political status quo?

Perhaps the only way to adjudicate whether Dworkin's faith in right answers thesis is acceptable is to examine the moral acceptability of centrist politics. Such an inquiry goes well beyond the scope of this work, but it underscores the connection between jurisprudence and moral and political theory. No pretension of political neutrality is acceptable here: one's stand on philosophy of law is connected in many ways to one's evaluation of the current normative order.

*Politics and Law.* Political criticisms of Dworkin's theory come from both radical leftists and centrist conservatives. The radical left howls that Dworkin's theory is sham, a mere apology for dominant centrist ideology, which accepts docilely the overwhelming majority of status quo theory and practice and shamelessly employs it as a foundation for what ought to be. Animated by the presupposition that moral and political conditions are more or less as they should be, Dworkin permits only incremental changes and marginal adjustments to the current normative order. From the perspective of the political left, Dworkin is a sycophantic idolator of the false consciousness gestated by centrist politics.[26]

It is apparent to leftists that Dworkin is content with the fundamental structure of the centrist political regime. Spurred by the desire to prevent the wholesale destabilization of that structure, he must ensure that legal disputes remain untouched by conflicts involving full visions of social life. He must therefore halt discussion before it evolves to the level that would undermine the possibility of secure centrist doctrine. By disguising law as a compendium of principles, policies, and purposes, and by arbitrarily immobilizing certain relations as beyond dispute, he is able to conceal the inherently malleable nature of legal doctrine.

Centrist conservatives, on the other hand, claim that under Dworkin's notions the law will become less certain and less determinate than it is under Legal Positivist jurisprudence.[27] Because Dworkin's judges must develop hypotheses about the existence and implications of rules and abstract principles of justice and make coherent the entire body of law, the desired predictability and consistency of law may thereby be sacrificed. Conservatives doubt whether Dworkin's exclusive reliance on judicial arguments of principle will produce fewer defeats of litigants' reasonable expectations than would a Legal Positivist's partial exercise of arguments of policy in hard cases.

Dworkin can reply that it is Legal Positivism that makes hard cases indeterminate because that version of jurisprudence concedes in such cases that the law has run out and that judges must legislate an answer using policy and morality; it is Dworkin who insists that virtually every legal question has a preexisting answer and who denies the necessity for (strong) judicial discretion.

But a host of new questions emerge here: Is Dworkin's view of the determinacy of law in hard cases a myth? Does his view shift the boundary of settled and unsettled law, making more legal situations seem like hard cases? Would abstract and seemingly indeterminate general principles of law bear on each instant case? Would Dworkin's view encourage and legitimate judges' reliance on their normative preferences? Is there too much tension between conflicting rules, principles, maxims, and precedents to warrant a belief in the coherence of law? Are logic and language themselves too indeterminate to support the right answer thesis? How can controversial preexisting rights—rights that often no one can demonstrate or establish exist or are correct—ensure fairness and guide judges to a single correct answer? Would judges who exercise such a methodology be engaged in a self-deception, clandestinely or unconsciously applying their normative preferences when deciding legal questions, while piously invoking the authority of principles they "discovered" in preexisting materials? In controversial cases, is it ever true that a judge will decide against her own normative preferences because the best theory of law, which she has constructed, so decrees?

The purpose of all these questions is to challenge the cornerstones of Dworkin's jurisprudence: the determinacy and coherence of law, the alleged absence of (strong) judicial discretion, the presence of right answers that are often controversial, and the resultant rationality of judicial decision making.

*A Brief Rejoinder.* Dworkin can make, and has made, a number of responses to the criticisms outlined above. He tells us:

> I hope to persuade lawyers to lay the entire picture of existing law aside in favor of a theory of law that takes questions about legal rights as special questions about political rights, so that one may think a plaintiff has a certain legal right without supposing that any rule or principle that already "exists" provides that right. In place of the misleading question, whether judges find rules in the "existing law" or make up rules not to be found there, we must ask whether judges try to enforce the rights they think parties have, or whether they create what they take to be new rights to serve social goals.[28]

Dworkin means to deny that the law of a society is a discrete collection of specific rules, principles, and policies such that it makes sense to ask whether a particular rule, principle, or policy is or is not a member of the collection. His appeal is more closely tied, not to physical or behavioral facts, but to the facts of consistency and coherence. He adds that

> in "Hard Cases," I offered an account of what it means to say that a principle is "embedded in" or "implicit in" or may be "inferred by analogy" from a set of earlier decisions. I said that a principle bears that relationship to earlier decisions, or other legal material, if the principle figures in what I called the best justification of that material.[29]

Thus, he intends to elude charges that assume the outdated model of "existing law" complemented by normative extralegal material and, instead, talk about the enforcement of political rights in legal contexts. In that same vein, the mere fact that reasonable people disagree does not entail the absence of a right answer to such questions. The import of legal questions centers around fairness: not merely on the narrow focus of providing notice to litigants, but on the wider equitable concerns of the nature of the litigants' prior entitlements. To defeat a litigant's right to a political decision is, other things being equal, unfair.

Here we may well suspect that Dworkin is slicing the bologna too thin. What theoretical gain is made by replacing the model of existing law complemented by extralegal material, law that must be applied by a judge to the case at bar, with the model of applying the preexisting political rights of litigants, rights that are discernible from the best justificatory theory of law? Is the Dworkinian model any more tractable than the former model? Is the constructive method of "discovering" the best justificatory theory of law clearly morally preferable to the stigmatized model of applying "existing law"? Are Dworkin's methods more efficient and practical? While Dworkin decries the weaknesses of conceiving law as a preexisting set of discrete materials, it is certainly unclear that conceiving legal questions as inquiries about preexisting political rights uncovered by the constructive model of reasoning is a demonstrable improvement.

Moreover, Dworkin subtly nudges the controversy from the question of whether there are right answers to hard legal cases to the question of whether judges "think they are enforcing the rights the parties have" as opposed to "creating what they take to be new rights." The power (and implausibility) of the right answer thesis stems from its assertion that there are preexisting right answers to all or virtually all legal questions. When Dworkin is assaulted by the fuselage of critical commentary, however, he is inclined to retreat to milder versions such as the faith in right answers thesis (judges should act as if there are preexisting right answers) or the judicial belief in right answers thesis (judges think they are discovering and applying the right answers, not creating new answers). While these three theses are not necessarily incompatible, they surely bear numerous different implications. For example, arguably there may be sound reasons to act as if there are right answers to all legal questions even though we cannot demonstrate the existence of right answers in at least some cases. Likewise, although the mere fact that judges think there are right answers does not imply that right answers exist, if right answers do exist that would certainly be a good reason for judges to believe that they exist and act accordingly.

The point is this: when confronted by critics, Dworkin has a tendency to slip too easily among the protective shields of various layers of distinctions. Too facilely employing the language and distinction of convenience, he advances considerations supporting the faith in right answers thesis or the judicial belief in right answers thesis when the issue at stake is the right answer thesis itself. Gleefully brandishing the truism that the mere fact of disagreement does not imply the absence of right answers, he ignores the equally effective truism that the mere fact of agreement does not imply the presence of right answers. He brushes off what is paramount: in an area where neither existence nor nonexistence may be demonstrable, which is more plausible, the right answer thesis or competing jurisprudential models? When positing initially surprising entities, such as objective right answers in hard cases, hobgoblins, or trolls, who has the burden of persuasion?

*Law as Integrity.* In his later works, *A Matter of Principle* and *Law's Empire,* Dworkin deepens and to some extent alters the thesis of *Taking Rights Seriously.*[30] In *A Matter of Principle,* he labels his position "naturalism" and contrasts it with conventionalism and pragmatism.

*Conventionalism.* A strict conventionalist, as depicted by Dworkin, "restricts the law of a community to the explicit extension of its legal conventions like legislation and precedent."[31] Relying on general societal understandings about which institutions have the authority to govern, and motivated by the central ideal of protecting settled expectations, conventionalists discover litigants' rights in the plain meaning of legal materials, the past intentions, and other political actions of legal officials. When such conventions are absent—when there is no convention that adjudicates a case at bar—judges have (strong) discretion and must rely on extralegal material to create what they take to be the best future policy pertinent to the case. Thus, judges will often be cast in the role of legislators as the conventionalist's positivist impulse often succumbs to instrumentalism in hard cases.[32]

Dworkin believes that strict conventionalism can explain a certain amount of judicial practice, but not the judicial obsession with the past even in those cases where no obvious convention decides the matter at hand. Judges in such cases still look to the past for a right answer based on the policies and principles underlying the applicable statutes.[33] As a descriptive account of judicial practice, strict conventionalism fails, because in hard cases "judges actually pay more attention to so-called conventional sources of law like statutes and precedents than conventionalism allows them to do."[34] Moreover, a judge embracing strict conventionalism views an instant case as governed by existing legal materials if and only if that case is part of the explicit extension of those materials. Dworkin portrays such an extension as "the set of propositions which (almost) everyone said to be a party to the convention accepts as part of its extension."[35] Given that it is clear that judges acting in good faith often disagree about the identification and application of legal material in specific cases, there are significant gaps in the law under a strict conventionalist explanation. Thus, as a theoretical account of the judicial role, strict conventionalism fails because it concedes to judges an excessive degree of discretion that is inamicable to the aspirations of the Rule of Law.

In view of such objections, one might be tempted to soften conventionalism a bit and concede that "the law of a community includes everything within the implicit extension of these conventions."[36] But this concedes too much, says Dworkin, and undermines the distinction between law and politics that is the avowed foundation of conventionalism. In fact, Dworkin takes soft conventionalism to be a "very abstract undeveloped form of law as integrity."[37]

Some critics, such as Stanley Fish, have taken Dworkin to task for attacking a straw person.[38] Given the fact that language is not self-executing, the words of statutes, judicial precedents, and constitutional provisions could not possibly emit explicit imperatives that could fully bind the actions of legal officials. By positing a theory, conventionalism, that from the outset is logically impossible because of the nature of language, Dworkin has created an easily defeatable patsy to contrast with law as integrity. But the bully of the block gains no glory from a successful assault on the feeble.

Although I am sympathetic to assertions of the manipulability of language and the necessity for interpretation when confronting a text, the suggestion that Dworkin assails a straw person seems too strong. There are still a group of "card carrying" originalists who insist that only loyalty to the "plain meaning" of the Constitution or the "actual intentions" of the framers can ensure a faithful and justifiable observation of the judicial role.[39] Thus, there are thinkers who maintain a perception of language that is directly contradictory to Fish's favored version. Such people think that originalism is not only a possible but the only acceptable mode of judicial decision making. Accordingly, the impossibility of conventionalism may not be as clear as Fish suspects, and it is a bit unfair to take Dworkin to task on this basis. Fish's point is better fashioned as calling into question whether Dworkin has constructed a conventionalism that captures the subtleties and nuances of refined Legal Postivism, which is truly the opponent Dworkin wishes to savage here. Construed in this manner, Fish's remarks have considerable force.

*Pragmatism.* Dworkin conceives pragmatism, sometimes called "instrumentalism," as completely abrogating reliance on the past when deciding a case at bar.[40] A judge should effect the best solution given his world vision and should not feel constrained to extract his decision from preexisting legal materials. A pragmatist has a conception of the human and societal good and stands "ready to revise his practice"[41] and his view of litigants' rights in accord with what his vision implies will best facilitate the good in the context of the instant case. His holdings constitute "a set of discrete decisions"[42] that are logically disconnected but for the structure imposed by the judge's strategic use of his vision for the future good. He has "no underlying commitment to any fundamental public conception of justice,"[43] and he cares about the past only prudentially: he must claim that his vision is truly compatible with or a flourishing of the past. If he cannot do this plausibly he must insist that the past is too chaotic to discern. In sum, pragmatists conduct themselves as act-consequentialists and say, "Judges do and should make whatever decisions seem to them best for the community's future,"[44] regardless of "any form of consistency with the past as valuable for its own sake."[45]

Dworkin, predictably, excoriates pragmatism as a false and deceptive observation of the judicial role. For reasons of prudence, judges would explain their decisions on the basis of past doctrine, and they would act as if the litigants had rights that were now being enforced; but at the same time these judges would know that their vision of the good, not past doctrine, was the true source of their decisions. This deception, much like Plato's "noble lie,"[46] would no doubt be rationalized as being itself justified on consequentialist grounds: because of the appeal of Rule of Law rhetoric most citizens do not want the judiciary acting as act-consequentialists. However, the best long-range good for society is effected by pragmatists acting in that fashion; therefore, on consequentialist grounds judges should act pragmatically but simultaneously hold themselves out as protectors of the Rule of Law.[47] For Dworkin, such a posture is ersatz practice because pragmatists act as legislators while donning the garb and rhetoric of the judiciary. Their repudiation of the intrinsic value of the past, their refusal to acknowledge the constraint of discovering litigants' rights by constructing the best justification of law, and their self-conscious use of their particular societal visions in an act-consequentialist manner strike Dworkin as undermining the integrity of law.

Stanley Fish protests that Dworkin has created an impotent opponent for purposes of easy thrashing. Regardless of what pragmatic judges may think and say they are doing, says Fish, all their decisions must be affected greatly by the past.[48] Their vision of social good and their determinations of the community's future must be generated, at least in part, from their socialization, which is inevitably connected with the past. Thus, Fish concludes that judicial decisions cannot be "discrete," and that any judge who so reports his actions is making

> the mistake of assuming a direct and causal relationship between one's account of one's practice and the actual shape of that practice. The mere fact that a lawyer or a judge says that he is doing something impossible (acting freely and in disregard of the past) doesn't make him capable of doing it.[49]

Because pragmatism is "not [a position] one could put into practice,"[50] Dworkin's diatribe against it strikes Fish as irrelevant and moot.

I do not think that a pragmatist judge truly claims to be severing all connection to the past. To do so would be to strip oneself of important constitutive attributes such as past learning, societal context, and ideology, attributes necessary for personhood. Rather, a pragmatist judge demands that past legal material is not of itself dispositive in deciding the case at bar; that is, the judiciary should act instrumentally and secure the solution best able to effect future societal good. Of course, in making this determination judges must consult the past if for no other reason than to view the consequences of past decisions and policies. Moreover, no act-consequentialist, whether in the moral or legal sphere, enters the decision process with a "blank slate."

The distinguishing characteristics of a pragmatic judge, for Dworkin, is not her literal divorce from the effects of the past but her refusal to bow down antecedently to the authority of precedent when formulating for the instant case a holding compatible with her ideological vision for future societal good. Dworkin conceives a pragmatic judge as, at least sometimes, saying to herself, "My ideological vision for future societal good suggests a decision for D; therefore, I will decide in favor of D and 'justify' that decision by claiming either that a decision for D is compatible with past doctrine or that past doctrine is incoherent and incapable of generating an answer on this question."

A pragmatist does not revel in a complete disassociation from the past but denies the absolute authority of the past in determining the case at bar. Such a judge's decisions will themselves have a structure and at least a loose consistency based on their common genesis: the judge's ideological vision for future societal good. Her decisions will not be "discrete" in the strong sense of "unconnected from the past" but in the weaker sense of "not dictated by the past." Therefore, Fish's assertions are effective only against a pragmatic position much more uncompromising than the one portrayed by Dworkin.

Dworkin's portrayal of pragmatic judges, however, could be a bit more subtle. The power of pragmatism is anticipated in Fish's denunciation of the possibility of conventionalism. Because language is not self-executing—all reading requires interpretation and is subject to ideological bias—and past legal doctrine itself is incoherent, pragmatists charge that neither conventionalism nor Dworkin's "law as integrity" is a possible mode of judicial decision making. The pragmatic assault on the two other modes of jurisprudence is not necessarily based on its belief that its ideological vision of future societal good is superior. Rather, pragmatists announce with stentorian bravado that it is the other modes that are engaged in a grand deception: deluding themselves that language, logic, and doctrine are determinate enough to provide firm rational constraints on the judiciary and to allow compliance with the aspirations of the Rule of Law. If pragmatists are correct, then conventionalists and Dworkinians are the ones who are trying naively to do the impossible.

In sum, Dworkin champions law as integrity as demonstrably superior to other theories in that it justifies the law as manifesting a paramount political value: integrity. He criticizes conventionalism because it looks exclusively to explicit conventions, thus giving an unsatisfactory description of what judges in fact do and ceding too many gaps in law that can be filled only by judicial use of (strong) discretion. On the other hand, Dworkin charges that pragmatists perpetrate the grand deception of acting as if litigants have rights while in fact deciding cases on act-consequentialist grounds. For their part, pragmatists allege that conventionalists and Dworkinians delude themselves about the nature of language, logic, and doctrine and end up trying to do the impossible: apply past doctrines that are presumably determinate enough to decide instant cases. As for conventionalists, they vow that pragmatists are judicial renegades who arrogate to themselves powers far exceeding the legitimate bounds of the judicial role and that Dworkinians are merely pragmatists who disguise their judicial activism in disingenuous invocations of "implicit and embedded principles" and in pompous pronouncements of the aspirations of the Rule of Law.

In *Law's Empire*, Dworkin clarifies and deepens the themes of his earlier works.[51]

*Stages of Interpretation.* For Dworkin, the interpretive enterprise as applied to law has two parts. First, legal practice has a purpose, a value that can be articulated independently of describing the constitutive rules of legal practice. Second, the general behavior and specific judgments required by legal practice acknowledge that purpose and value.[52] Construed in such a fashion, the interpretation of any social practice consists of three stages: preinterpretative, interpretive, and postinterpretive.

During the *preinterpretive stage* the subject gathers the rules, standards, conventions, and descriptions of participants' defining roles and of normal behavior and activities that are generally agreed among insiders to constitute the practice. Such elements provide the data that, although not uninterpreted in the sense that they are self-executing, are "raw" relative to the practice. Here the subject "needs assumptions or convictions about what counts as part of the practice in order to define the raw data of his interpretation."[53]

During the *interpretive stage* the subject "proposes a value for the practice by describing a scheme of interests or goals or principles that the practice can be taken to serve or express or exemplify."[54] This is the familiar attempt to formulate the best coherent theory that both fits past doctrine and provides a normatively sound justification for law.

What is different in *Law's Empire* from Dworkin's earlier works is the fuller explanation of the relationship between coherent fit and normative soundness when constructing a best theory of law. Recall that in his earlier works, the suggestion, which Dworkin himself admitted was "crude,"[55] was that the criterion of coherent fit was the threshold requirement after which the criterion of normative soundness adjudicated between conflicting theories that equally fit past doctrine. In *Law's Empire* Dworkin makes clear that both coherent fit and normative soundness are implicated at each point in the interpretive process.

The first requirement for the "best" legal theory remains a minimum level of coherent fit with past doctrine and practice ("the preinterpretative data"). A few possible theories will flunk here because of their inability to provide even this minimum level of fit. Accordingly, their normative soundness cannot even be considered. However, several conflicting interpretations of "best" legal theories will survive this threshold requirement.[56]

The second requirement involves definitional aspects of normative soundness. This filter demands a minimum level of compliance with certain formal elements of justification: standards of sufficient generality, reliance on distinctions connected plausibly to wider justificatory schemes; and expression of purposes and values appropriate to legal practice, such as principles of justice, fairness, and individual rights.[57] A few more possible theories will flunk here because of their inability to comply with these formal requirements.

The third requirement is a more complex adjudication of the remaining competitors for the honorific title "best theory of law." Here the interpreter must reflect legal practice in its "best light."[58] The interpreter must judge competing legal theories from her background view about how various moral–political principles should be weighed relative to each other. For example, what is more important—due process for each litigant or correctness of substantive result? In other words, she must determine which of the remaining legal theories constitutes the best normative justification of law.

Moreover, the interpreter must again consider the coherence of the remaining legal theories' fit with the preinterpretative data; that is, which of the theories requires the least amount of that data to be stigmatized as "mistakes"? Here considerations of fit and considerations of normative soundness are judged together. This is possible, says Dworkin, because fit and normative justification are intimately linked: "the constraint fit imposes on substance, in any working theory, is . . . the constraint of one type of political conviction on another in the overall judgment which interpretation makes a political record the best it can be overall."[59] The pertinent political conviction embodied by the requirement of coherent fit is integrity. Thus, the requirement of fit emerges not merely or mainly from the demands of logic but rather originates in the prescriptions of political morality.

In this vein, Dworkin admits unsqueamishly that "interpretive claims are . . . dependent on aesthetic or political morality all the way down."[60] At this level of interpretation, integrity, as embodied in the requirement of coherent fit with preinterpretative data, may find itself in conflict with other substantive moral convictions, as embodied in the interpreter's background vision of justification, in order that a single best legal theory emerge. Accordingly, the subject's view of the complex relations between the requirement of coherent fit and the prescriptions of background morality within competing interpretations of law will suggest her choice of the "best theory of law." In making that decision, however, she must heed one further restriction: her resolution of those complex relations must acknowledge the distinction between "interpreting" and "inventing." She is free to interpret, and in fact she must interpret, the data and adjudicate the interpretive conflicts she encounters, but she cannot create new facts or mold the data to suit her purposes.[61]

It must be made clear that Dworkin does not assume that propositions that partially constitute an interpretive enterprise must be capable of validity. Rather, he advises that we approach the matter empirically: "We should first study a variety of activities in which people assume that they have good reasons for what they say, which they assume hold generally and not just from one or another individual point of view. We can then judge what standards people accept in practice for thinking that they have reasons of that kind."[62]

During the *postinterpretive stage* the subject may marginally adjust her view of the demands of the practice to reflect better her theory's normative justification of law. The interpreter "adjusts his sense of what the practice 'really' requires so as better to serve the justification he accepts at the interpretive stage."[63] This is not an attempt to rewrite the history of law but rather an acknowledgment that a formal feature of constructive interpretation is that the interpreter must strive to depict the object of interpretation in its best light: "Constructive interpretation is a matter of imposing purpose on an object or practice in order to make it the best possible example of the form or genre to which it is taken to belong."[64] The point here is that the proper description of legal practice is revealed by the best interpretation of law as constituted by one's best coherent theory explaining and justifying law. When different subjects advance conflicting best coherent theories of law, they are to be taken as offering conflicting views about what past legal materials and practices truly are and require of participants; such conflict should not be construed, says Dworkin, as different proposals for legal change.[65]

Dworkin's claim for the coherence generated by Law as Integrity is connected to his views on political legitimacy. Genuine communities truly obligate, says Dworkin, only if their members perceive their communal obligations as deriving from a general duty of concern they have for other members of that community, and the community's practices must manifest equal concern for all members.[66]

*The Chain Novel.* Dworkin employs the metaphor of a chain novel when describing the maturation of law. Imagine a novel written by a host of different authors. The first author writes a chapter of the novel and passes the text on to a second author, who writes another chapter, and so forth. Each succeeding author is presumably constrained by what was written previously: she is obligated to discover an interpretation of the text that best fits the material supplied to her by the previous authors. While it is true that each new author is not constrained completely by the intentions and product of preceding authors, neither is she completely free. She is limited by the need to acknowledge and develop what is handed down to her, as characters have been nurtured and a plot formed by the preceding authors.[67]

While it will not be possible to arrive at an interpretation that explains every structural aspect of the text, the chain novelist must arrive at an interpretation that coherently fits the greater part of the work. In the event that more than one interpretation meets that test, she must "judge which of these eligible readings makes the work in progress best, all things considered."[68] Some competing interpretations will fit more of the previously written material, while other interpretations may make the novel more artistically valuable. Here, as in legal interpretation, the interpreter must make subtle judgments among competing values, one of which is integrity.

*The Political Aspects of Law.* Dworkin reiterates the acknowledgment made in *A Matter of Principle* that legal decisions are a species of political decisions. Rather than conceiving of judicial decision making in an antiseptic, formalist fashion, Dworkin admits straightaway that legal decisions are inevitably motivated by political theory. Because he conceives political theory as ultimately based on morality, and because moral theory is so important in developing and sustaining the best theory explaining and justifying law, it follows that legal decision making inevitably incorporates normative elements.[69]

Dworkin is staking out a middle position between those who advocate the separation of law and politics and the concomitant view that a judge's political convictions must play no role in her decision making, and those who claim to have unmasked the underlying identity of law and politics and who conclude that judges decide on the basis of their personal political convictions and thus act merely as unelected legislators.

In contrast, Dworkin avers that judges may appeal only to those political principles (the political rights of individual citizens, as opposed to policies that contend that a particular decision will nurture the general welfare and public interest) that they sincerely believe constitute the best coherent justification of law.[70] It must be clear, however, that Dworkin's admission that law inevitably implicates politics is not so striking as one might first think. He distinguishes carefully between partisan politics and political theory, in effect stigmatizing the former and citing the necessity for the latter. Moreover, his background view of political and moral theory has always contained the assumption that the constructive model of reasoning redeems normative theory from mere arbitrary assertion of will. Dworkin thus does not consider the slogan "law implicates politics" as an admission of the impossibility of achieving the aspirations of the Rule of Law or as a surrender to the realist forces who highlight the nonrational aspects of legal decision making.[71]

*Rule of Law.* Dworkin charges that the "rule book"[72] conception of the Rule of Law is inadequate. This conception portrays the Rule of Law as a requirement of formal justice: treating like cases alike; providing prior and clear notice of the requirements of law; formulating general, impersonal laws; renouncing the use of ex post facto application of law; and generally aspiring to the goals of notice, objectivity, and consistency in the making and applying of law. Under such a view the actions of state officials are deficient if these actions are contrary to the specifications of the rule book. The rule book conception, however, does not address the issue of the substance or content of law. This version of the Rule of Law reflects a minimalist objective of compliance with certain logical requirements of justice. Therefore, it self-consciously advances necessary but not sufficient conditions for justice.

Dworkin instead champions the more ambitious "rights" conception of the Rule of Law. This conception "assumes" that citizens have moral rights and duties with respect to one another, and political rights against the state as a whole.[73] The rights conception holds state officials accountable if the specifications in the rule book do not "capture and enforce moral rights."[74] It requires that officials comply, not only with the formal, but also with the substantive requirements of justice. Whereas the rule book conception outlines only one area where state officials might fall short, the rights conception delineates at least three types of deficiencies.

> A state might fail in the scope of the individual rights it purports to enforce. It might decline to enforce rights against itself, for example, though it concedes citizens have such rights. It might fail in the accuracy of the rights it recognizes: it might provide for rights against the state, but through official mistake fail to recognize important rights. Or it might fail in the fairness of its enforcement of rights: it might adopt rules that put the poor or some disfavored race at a disadvantage in securing the rights the state acknowledges they have.[75]

Dworkin insists that the two conceptions of the Rule of Law have important jurisprudential implications: "The character of judges is a consequence of the theory of adjudication in force."[76] The rule book conception, which Dworkin connects to Legal Positivism, instructs judges to decide hard cases by referring to what is truly in the rule book and not by reference to their own political judgments. Under the rule book conception, to do otherwise is to substitute judges' prescriptive visions for the formal demands of justice. The rights conception, on the other hand, comports with Law as Integrity: it will demand that "at least one kind of political question is precisely the question that judges faced with hard cases must ask. For the ultimate question it asks in a hard case is the question of whether the plaintiff has the moral right to receive, in court, what he or she demands."[77]

*Skepticism.* Dworkin confronts squarely those who are skeptical about the interpretive enterprise. He distinguishes two kinds of skepticism: external and internal. The external skeptic contends that propositions regarding the point or value of a social practice "are not descriptions that can be proved or tested like physics."[78] Rather than discover the value of a social practice in preexisting material, we project our value judgments on social practices, says the external skeptic. Relying heavily on the fact of wide cross-cultural and intracultural disagreements about values, the external skeptic questions whether normative judgments, given their nonverifiability, make any sense.

Dworkin insists that external skepticism is incoherent. He maintains that all interpretive projects are launched from within some web of evaluative assumptions, while the external skeptic challenges the entire notion of correctness.[79] From within the practices of normative argument, the charges of the external skeptic—denials that normative claims correspond to transcendental reality or bear foundational justification—are without force so long as such charges themselves are not legal or moral arguments. If such a skeptic maintains truculently her position, she disables herself from making any comment on the relative merits of conventionalism, pragmatism, and law as integrity. She in effect remains outside the enterprise entirely and marginalizes herself to the point of irrelevance. On the other hand, if she contends that she can still make value judgments because valuing is distinct from one's attitude about what we are doing when we value, she is engaged in the normative enterprise and becomes an internal skeptic.[80]

The internal skeptic concedes that some social practices are better than others but believes that no interpretation that implicates normative reasoning can be right or wrong because value judgments are merely personal preferences. This position, says Dworkin, is more easily stated than lived. Anyone who believes that, for example, racial discrimination is wrong is thereby committed to there being a right answer to the question of the moral value of racial discrimination.[81] Internal skepticism, however, has the virtue of at least being a coherent position asserted from within an interpretive practice.[82]

*Rational Constraint and Objectivity.* It should by now be clear that Dworkin subscribes to the existence of rational constraint in law.

Interpretation is not merely the projection of the subject's partisan preferences, nor is it an attempt "to report ontologically independent meanings scattered among the furniture of the universe."[83] Regarding objectivity, Dworkin tells us:

> I see no point in trying to find some general argument that moral or political or legal or aesthetic or interpretive judgments are objective. Those who ask for an argument of that sort want something different from the kind of arguments I and they would make for particular examples or instances of such judgments. But I do not see how there could be any such different arguments. I have no arguments for the objectivity of moral judgments except moral arguments, no arguments for the objectivity of interpretive judgments except interpretive arguments, and so forth.[84]

> I do think that slavery is unjust, that this is not "just my opinion," that everyone ought to think so, that everyone has a reason to oppose slavery, and so forth. Is this what it means to think that the injustice of slavery is part of the furniture of the universe? If so, then I do think this, but then I cannot see the difference between the proposition that slavery is unjust and the proposition that the injustice of slavery is part of the furniture of the universe.[85]

Moreover, Dworkin denies that we can make a legitimate distinction between substantive arguments within a social practice and skeptical arguments about that social practice. He tells us that "the words 'objectively' and 'really' cannot change the sense of moral or interpretive judgments. If moral or aesthetic or interpretive judgments have the sense and force they do just because they figure in a collective human enterprise, then such judgments cannot have a 'real' sense and a 'real' truth value which transcend that enterprise and somehow take hold of the 'real' world."[86]

Thus, the law's rational constraint is not connected to claims of "objectivity."[87] Rather, Dworkin conceives interpretation as an enterprise where facts both depend on and constrain the theories that explain them. Here Dworkin reiterates the coherentist themes described earlier, that legal materials possess the structure necessary to produce a significant degree of internal constraint.

Dworkin reiterates that the requirement that a judge's theory of law must fit past legal practice constrains judges in two main ways. First, the judge's theory must respond and be sensitive to legal precedents. Second, the judge's theory must also fit past practices about the doctrines of precedent and judicial review. Dworkin believes that these constraints rule out many possible judicial interpretations.[88]

Dworkin aspires to give meaning to both agreement and disagreement about interpretation and to underscore that theoretical
disagreement in law is indicative of the ongoing vitality of legal
practice. The presence of rational controversy within legal practice is
in fact a necessary condition for Dworkin's theory of judicial interpretation. Moreover, such controversy is not merely empirical but
theoretical—disagreement about which criteria to employ in interpreting social practices and traditions. He contends that "members
of particular communities who share practices and traditions"[89] can
engage in authentic disputes about the demands and implications of
those practices and traditions in "concrete circumstances . . . even
though [these] people use different criteria in forming or framing
[their] interpretations; [such disputes are] genuine because the competing interpretations are directed toward the same objects or events
of interpretation."[90] For Dworkin, law, as an interpretive concept,
will always be subject to controversy and disagreements. But such
conflict is valuable because it provides the structure that rescues law
from the chaos of totally arbitrary and situational decision making,
while it also offers a vigor that ransoms law from the dogmatic slum-
bers of mechanical jurisprudence.

*Refinements and Changes.* Dworkin's most recent work, *Law's Empire,* expands and refines the earlier themes found in *Taking Rights
Seriously.* First, he extends his model of coherent interpretation beyond judicial decision making to legislative decision making; that is,
"legislative integrity" requires that legislatures craft statutes that are
internally coherent and that cohere externally with the existing body
of legal materials. Thus, legislators, as well as judges, must construct a best theory of law.[91] Second, Dworkin softens his earlier
claim that one of the main weaknesses of Legal Positivism is its acceptance of "retroactive" application of law. His earlier objection
charged that by advising judges to decide hard cases on policy
grounds positivists were inviting the judiciary to act as legislators in
precisely those cases where the vindication of litigants' rights are
most important. Dworkin is now less eager to brandish allegations
of retroactivity and more concerned with waving the banner of integrity. His argument from integrity, which plays a similar role to
the earlier argument from retroactivity and which is extended to legislators, stresses that political decisions must cohere with the best
theory of law—the best set of political and moral principles that explain and justify past political decisions.[92] Third, Dworkin now highlights the role of interpretation and reveals his own theory regarding
the nature and requirements of the interpretive enterprise. Fourth,

Dworkin seems now to be a bit more reluctant to invoke the right answer thesis. This has led at least one critic to conclude that "Dworkin has abandoned one of the principal claims [the right answer thesis] that catapulted him to the forefront of the contemporary jurisprudential scene,"[93] and another critic to observe that "right answers remain but everything has become a lot more complicated."[94] The second critic is closer to the truth: in *Law's Empire*, Dworkin talks less frequently about right answers; continues to oscillate among the right answer thesis, the faith in right answers thesis, and the judicial belief in right answers thesis; and envelopes his belief in right answers with a thick interpretive context. But he never abrogates the right answer thesis that he expressed in *Taking Rights Seriously*.

Finally, Dworkin for the first time confronts Critical Legal Studies (CLS). He observes that certain themes of CLS replicate the external skepticism of extreme Legal Realists: the denials of objectivism and Metaphysical Realism, for example. But he concedes the freshness of CLS' contradiction thesis, which insists that legal doctrine can only be understood properly through the grid of fundamental contradiction that pervades the human condition. Although acknowledging that such an attack is a legitimate and even instructive form of internal skepticism, Dworkin contends that CLS either "announces rather than defends"[95] such claims or relies on "historical" rather than interpretive arguments to support them. By this he means that CLS aspires to demonstrate that the historical forces and powers that created law do not exhibit coherence or manifest a single overriding vision of the function of law. But this demonstration, even if empirically accurate, misses the mark; for Law as Integrity does not claim that a historical examination of the past will uncover an underlying coherence of legislative and judicial wills or an immanent and uniform functionalist design. Rather, Law as Integrity "tries to impose order over doctrine"[96] through an interpretation that transforms "the varied links in the chain of law into a vision of government now speaking with one voice, even if this is very different from the voices of leaders past."[97]

Dworkin, however, finds a more interesting claim in CLS: the philosophical charge that "any competent contemporary justification [of the different areas of law] would necessarily display fundamental contradictions of principle."[98] But Dworkin objects that CLS, rather than first searching for a less skeptical interpretation of law, begins by trying to show that its skeptical account fits the law.

Nothing is easier or more pointless than demonstrating that a flawed and contradictory account fits as well as a smoother and more attractive one. The internal skeptic must show that the flawed and contradictory account is the only one available.[99]

To the extent that CLS has tried to support its claim, Dworkin adds, such support has consisted of allegations that "Western democracies can be justified only as an elaboration of a fundamentally liberal view of personality and community"[100] and that liberalism's metaphysical and normative assumptions are inherently contradictory and contaminate any attempt to find coherence in law. Dworkin finds this approach flawed because CLS' arguments "begin and end in a defective account of what liberalism is, an account supported by no plausible reading of the philosophers they count as liberals";[101] moreover, CLS ignores the "distinction between competition and contradiction in principles"[102] and, finally, CLS "may want to show law in its worst rather than its best light, to show avenues closed that are in fact open, to move toward a new mystification in service of undisclosed political goals."[103]

*Critic's Corner.* Critics of philosophical texts, like tax collectors and destitute relatives, are always easy to find. Dworkin has been taken to task for his conception of the interpretive enterprise. First, it has been alleged that Dworkin's theory of interpretation is "insufficiently practical, insufficiently intersubjective, and thus . . . insufficiently political."[104] The theory is insufficiently practical because "it assumes that the point or purpose of a practice can be stated independently of the rules and activities that make up the practice."[105] The theory is insufficiently intersubjective because Dworkin's brooding Hercules seems to be engaged in a dialogue with himself as he tries to impose order on preexisting legal material, while in fact understanding that a social practice may require "a conversation with other participants."[106] The theory is insufficiently political because it marginalizes judicial interaction and thereby threatens "to reduce participants in a common practice to windowless social monads."[107]

Second, critics have charged that Dworkin has not offered a true alternative to conventionalism and pragmatism but, instead, invokes both models where it suits his purposes.[108] In other words, Hercules must first, as a descriptive matter, determine the meaning that legal material already bears; then he must, as a prescriptive matter, "wrestle it into another shape according to some prior sense of what it would be best for it to mean."[109] In the first step Dworkin may play the role of a conventionalist who "posits an identity for the object apart from any interpretation,"[110] while in the second step he may play the role of a pragmatist who has "the power of imposing purpose."[111] Dworkin is further accused of oscillating between the view that preexisting materials constrain legal interpretation, a view that is redolent of the excesses of conventionalism, and the position that judges must reshape law and put it in its best light, a position that resembles pragmatism. Thus, Stanley Fish writes: "Either the object or practice is already the best it can be and doesn't need the interpreter's help . . . or by making it the best it can be, the interpreter rides roughshod over the object and refashions it."[112]

Third, Dworkin confidently objects that CLS and other internal skeptics must show that the "flawed and contradictory account [of law] is the only one available,"[113] yet this is impossible under Dworkin's own conception of interpretation, which includes the concession that interpretation will and must involve controversy. By demanding that internal skeptics perform an impossible task, Dworkin seems much like the smitten gods who condemned Sisyphus. Moreover, Dworkin assumes that it is the internal skeptic, rather than Dworkin, who bears the burden of persuasion. We may question why it is the skeptic and not Dworkin who must prove that her account is the only one available. Here we see the fundamental issue pervading the Dworkin and CLS debate: Dworkin takes the current normative order to be basically just and sound and hence in need only of marginal tinkering, while CLS perceives the current normative order as basically unjust and oppressive and hence in need of radical destabilization. Starting from such different political horizons, there is no wonder that Dworkin, who has a stake in reaffirming most of the fundamental social order, assumes that CLS has the burden of persuasion concerning the proper interpretation of law, while CLS, which aspires to reimagine and remake the social order, assumes that a view such as Dworkin's is wildly implausible and involves self-deception.

Fourth, critics have attacked Dworkin's "chain novel" metaphor. As Dworkin portrays the chain novel enterprise, it seems to be a "grand deception,"[114] as each succeeding author tries to obscure the fact that different writers are collaborating. He tells us that the principle of integrity requires judges "to identify legal rights and duties . . . on the assumption that they were created by a single author."[115] Yet this imperative rests uneasily with the historical fact that numerous wills animated by conflicting purposes all helped to mold law.[116] While Dworkin distances himself from relying on historical analysis and embraces instead the position that a judge imposes order in accordance with an interpretation of law in its best light, still there seems an element of disingenousness in the chain novel metaphor. Moreover, Dworkin assumes that consistency and coherence form the only acceptable genre for such a literary work. Yet "the modernist conception of writing could be seen to make it not only acceptable, put positively desirable, to have a novel that is full of fractures, discontinuities, and shifts of genre."[117] Again, we see the truly fundamental issue in the Dworkin and CLS debate: if one, like Dworkin, is convinced that the basic social order is just and sound then one has a stake in invoking a metaphor that includes a writing style that privileges coherence with the past; yet if a group, like CLS, is equally convinced that the basic social order is thoroughly unjust and flawed then it has a stake in conjuring a metaphor that includes "the modernist conception" of discontinuity with the past. With this having been said, it must be observed that Dworkin's theory of interpretation does not rest on the chain novel metaphor; that is, even if that metaphor is dubious, that of itself does not destroy the validity of Dworkin's claims about the interpretive enterprise. The fragility of the metaphor only suggests that by invoking it Dworkin might be ill served.

*Return to the Right Answer Thesis.* Dworkin is quite willing to concede that in some legal cases no conclusion can be demonstrated to be true from the hard facts, the physical facts and facts about the behavior of legal insiders and the litigants themselves. But he still rejects what he terms the "demonstrability thesis": "If a proposition cannot be demonstrated to be true, after all the hard facts that might be relevant to its truth are either known or stipulated, then the proposition cannot be true."[118] A legal proposition can also be true, says Dworkin, if it is required by the combination of the existing hard facts and the propositions's success in narrative consistency with the hard facts. Accordingly, the demonstrability thesis fails in Dworkin's vision because it restricts judicial right answers to those cases where such answers are produced by hard facts alone and precludes attention to the equally important facts of narrative consistency.

But we must now ask Dworkin what he means by his right answer thesis. Consider the following possibilities:

R1 the one and only answer which the court could properly reach

R2 the answer such that any different answer would be wrong

R3  the one and only answer which states what is true

R4  the most reasonable answer available given the hard facts and facts of narrative consistency with existing legal material

A. D. Woozley has charged that Dworkin conflates R3 and R4.[119] Legal issues may well be settled in accord with R4, but that does not imply the antecedent existence of law relevant to that issue that admits of R3. A judge may have reasonable grounds, based partially on facts of narrative consistency, for asserting decision D, but it does not follow that D reflects antecedently existing truth. Woozley observes:

> In some disputes there will be, in advance of the final judgment, no right answer waiting for us in what will be the final chapter. The answer depends on what is written in the final chapter—which has not been written yet. . . . In a decently sophisticated legal system there should be a right answer to the question how to settle a disputed question of law . . . but that does not mean that there was a right answer to the question of law waiting to be found. . . . If a judge's answer survives attempts to modify or reverse it, and if it gets absorbed into the body of law, then there is an answer to the question, "What is the law on this matter?" which is the right answer [in sense R3], because that is how the book has been written—but it was not in the book until it was written.[120]

Clearly, Dworkin aspires to identify his right answer thesis with R2 and R3. Because he admits readily that right answers can be controversial and that equally capable judges acting in good faith can arrive at different answers in certain hard cases, he probably does not subscribe to R1. Finally, it appears that he would endorse R4 while (perhaps) contesting whether it is truly weaker than R3.

Dworkin responds by claiming in effect that Woozley has begged the question against him. Woozley, according to Dworkin, insists on a certain set of rules for defining truth within the interpretive enterprise (what the author of a narrative actually said) instead of the set of rules Dworkin embraces (what the author said combined with narrative consistency with what the author said).[121] Dworkin thinks Woozley is led astray because he has ignored the fact that all our concepts "take the only meaning they have from the function they play in our reasoning, argument, and conviction."[122] Describing philosophers such as Woozley, Dworkin insists:

> They believe in a mysterious and highly blurred idea of "real" truth, which they express only in metaphors, and which I doubt can be expressed in any other way. They can say that a proposition is "really" true only if it accurately describes facts that are "out there," or part of

"the fabric of the universe," or "locked into" an "independent reality" or something of that sort. Then they announce that since moral claims, for example, or claims about what the law is in hard cases, describe nothing that is "out there," such claims cannot be "really" true.[123]

Dworkin continues by reaffirming that he does not think it is possible to entirely separate "talk about what is true" from "talk about what is reasonable to assert."

Will [Woozley] allow me to say that in hard cases at law one answer might be the most reasonable of all, even though competent lawyers will disagree about which answer is the most reasonable? If so I can say everything I want to say, or have said, about this issue.[124]

Dworkin's view of the interpretive enterprise, his response to Woozley, and his criticism of Legal Positivism must be juxtaposed with his continued endorsement of the right answer thesis. There seem to be at least two strands coexisting uneasily in Dworkin's jurisprudence: his notion of the interpretive enterprise and his criticism of Legal Positivism harbor a critical impulse with potentially powerful destabilizing effects, while his continued endorsement of the right answer thesis betrays an apologetic inclination with potentially forceful legitimating effects.

Dworkin points out the compatibility of an answer's being correct and contestable. Yet he makes no appeal to the presence of an actual consensus on substantive matters, nor does he invoke an ideal vantage point from which all ideological distortions would appear to vanish and from which all informed people would reach agreement. Thus, Dworkin recognizes that contestability is an important part of rationality and essential to the interpretive enterprise. With this said, it is still unclear what the single best interpretation of law amounts to. Clearly, it does not mean "the only possible reasonable view" or "closest to the ideal view." Dworkin recognizes all this. Yet if the single best interpretation means "the best that a judge now has reason to accept," that seems too weak to generate a strong version of the right answer thesis. Certainly a judge will claim that her interpretation is better than other competing interpretations, for otherwise there is little reason for her to expound judicial conclusions; but from this it does not follow that the judge must believe that her reasoning is the only proper form or that preexisting legal material can be placed only in one particular version of its best light. Accordingly, the notion of a single best interpretation of law remains problematic.

Compounding this problem is Dworkin's explicit admission that assessments of fit and normative soundness are prevalent in a number of stages of judicial interpretation. John Finnis alleges that this admission "strips away the last veil hiding the problem of the incommensurability of the criteria proposed for identifying a best or uniquely right interpretation, theory or answer."[125] In assessing the criteria of fit and soundness we are left with the usual legal metaphor of "balancing" or "weighing" competing considerations. But absent commensurable considerations "the instruction to 'balance' . . . can legitimately mean no more than bear in mind, conscientiously, all the relevant factors, and choose."[126] Finnis contends that an understanding of the mechanisms of "choice" eviscerates the plausibility of the right answer thesis.

> It is a feature of the phenomenology of choice that after one has chosen, the factors favouring the chosen alternative will usually seem to outweigh or overbalance those favouring the rejected alternative(s). The chosen alternative will seem to have a supremacy, a unique rightness. But the truth is that the choice was not guided by "the right answer," but rather established it in the sentiments, the dispositions, of the chooser.[127]

Moreover, it remains unclear what currency the slogan "uniquely correct answer" possesses "where there is identifiable a set of two or more options/answers which do not violate any rule binding on the judge or other chooser or interpreter."[128] Finnis concludes that the grave conceptual difficulties besetting the right answer thesis also prevent Dworkin from developing a principled distinction between judicial application and judicial creation of law, and between easy and hard cases.

> [Dworkin] has no valid argument against the common sense of lawyers and others who think that in some cases there is only one answer which is not wrong, while in other (not infrequent) cases there is more than one such answer, and reason itself (whether legal or even moral) lacks the resources to identify one as best.[129]

It appears, then, that the meaning of the right answer thesis must be stronger than the theses expressed by the judicial belief in right answers and faith in right answers views but somewhat weaker than "the only solution permitted by reason." Dworkin cannot trade on the alluring intellectual coinage and shocking rhetoric of "right answers" and simultaneously champion the more mundane and realistic themes of contestability and perspectivism.

There is yet another twist to examine regarding Dworkin's prescription that judges must place law in its best light. The content of what this endeavor requires is (understandably) unfixed. Thus, it remains open for a CLS advocate to pretend to adopt Dworkin's methodology, declare that settled hierarchy and division is inherently wrong, and proclaim the disharmonies and discontinuities of legal materials. Such fractures in the neat coherence of the social order, CLS might argue, provide the opportunity for the law as seen in its best light to remedy the wrongness of vested power held disproportionately by certain privileged groups. Accordingly, Dworkin's prescription to view law in its best light might well boomerang and result in judicial interpretations that would repulse Dworkin.

Dworkin's work is the culmination of the formalist vision. By refining the remnants of crude formalism and by adding a subtle view of the interpretive enterprise, he resurrects the case against legal skeptics and leftist critics. Dworkin abrogates several of formalism's listless precepts: its appeal to Metaphysical Realism, its simplistic notions of the power of abstract legal reasoning and antecedently existing doctrine, and its adoration of straightforward application of deductive logic. Yet he retains the crux of formalism's sanctification of law: its faith in the existence of right answers to virtually all legal questions, its denial of (strong) judicial discretion, and its confidence in Rule of Law virtues. Still, for all his analytic skill and unsurpassed philosophical legerdemain, nagging doubts remain about the possibility of the right answer thesis and Dworkin's portrayal of law's justification.

# CHAPTER 4

## Quantitative Analysis and Circular Apologetics
### *Law and Economics*

$T$HE SEMINAL WORK in the Law and Economics approach to jurisprudence is often credited to Gary Becker, Guido Calabresi, and Ronald Coase,[1] although the movement has been identified most clearly with Richard Posner.

*Coase's Theorem.* Coase examined the effect of the allocation of legal rights, especially property rights, on the production of "external costs" (costs resulting from the acts of one economic entity that must be borne by another economic entity).[2] The difficulty here is to account for incentives for self-interested economic entities to pay heed to externalities when planning their acts. If such entities do not internalize their external costs, then they will not always act to maximize the value derived from productive resources. The traditional way to influence economic entities to internalize their external costs has been through governmental intervention: taxation or tort liability.

Coase argued that the manner in which legal rights are assigned has no effect on methods of production: where "transaction costs" are low, all rules of liability will lead to the same allocation of resources. Transaction costs are those costs that may cause the market to arrive at an inefficient result. They include information costs, bargaining costs, and third-party effects. Thus, tort law is superfluous when transaction costs are low: "The same amount of smoke would be released from the factory's chimney whether the factory owner or the householder was legally responsible for the smoke damages."[3]

Coase argued that in circumstances of zero transaction costs the parties will bargain to achieve the efficient solution regardless of how the law designates rights and liabilities. Moreover, marketplace bargaining has the additional advantage of decreasing the administrative costs of litigation. Accordingly, in a competitive market with no transaction costs and full information, efficient allocation of resources is not dependent on the distribution of initial legal rights.

The Chicago School of conservative economists, and particularly Richard Posner, have used Coase's work to argue that the law should aim and act to achieve the ends parties would have produced but for the obstacles presented by transaction costs. This model tends to champion free choice, to protect and sanctify the integrity of private property, and to privilege the realm of contract as that which most efficiently defines legal relations.

## RICHARD POSNER:
## THE CHICAGO SCHOOL

Posner applies the theories and empirical methods of economics to many aspects of the legal system. He tells us that there are four major conclusions of Law and Economics research: participants in the legal process behave as if they were rational maximizers of their satisfactions; many aspects of the legal system have been influenced strongly by the goal of promoting economic efficiency; economic analysis is helpful in developing legal reforms; and quantitative analysis adds much to our knowledge of the legal system.[4] Presumably, participants in the legal process, like ordinary consumers, subscribe to basic economic principles. They buy less of a commodity when the price rises and more when the price falls.

The foundations of Posner's approach are his definitions of *efficiency* and *value*: "Efficiency . . . means exploiting economic resources in such a way that human satisfactions as measured by aggregate consumer willingness to pay for goods and services is maximized. When resources are being used where their value is greatest, we may say that they are being employed efficiently. Value too is defined by willingness to pay. Willingness to pay is in turn a function of the existing distribution of income and wealth in a society."[5] Posner is working from a market paradigm that assumes that in a voluntary trade both transactors gain: value is increased with each party better off in the sense that each has shown by her behavior that she thinks her situation has improved because of the transaction. When we reach the point that no further trades of this sort are possible, optimum efficiency has been realized.

The Chicago School embraces four theses: a behavioral claim that contends that "economic theory can provide a good theory for predicting how people will behave under rules of law";[6] a normative claim that asserts that the "law ought to be efficient";[7] a positive claim that states that the "law is in fact efficient";[8] and a genetic claim that argues that the "common law tends to select efficient rules, although not every rule will, at any given time, be efficient."[9] Accepting the behavioral and normative claims allegedly permits an official to adjudicate legal conflicts in a principled fashion: "The normative claim identifies efficient behavior as the criterion for choosing among rules; the behavioral claim permits one to identify which rules induce efficient behavior. Together, they allow one to resolve all legal disputes."[10]

*Wealth Maximization Principle (WMP).* According to Posner, the dominant goal of the legal system should be economic, by which he means the maximization of wealth: "wealth is the value in dollars or dollar equivalents . . . of everything in society. It is measured by what people are willing to pay for something or, if they already own it, what they demand in money to give it up."[11] Posner summarizes the implications of WMP in this way.

> [WMP] implies, first, an initial distribution of individual rights (to life, liberty, and labor) to their natural owners; second, free markets to enable those rights to be reassigned from time to time to other uses; third, legal rules that simulate the operations of the market when the costs of market transactions are prohibitive; fourth, a system of legal remedies for deterring and redressing invasions of rights; and fifth, a system of personal morality (the "Protestant virtues") that serves to reduce the costs of market transactions.[12]

Reiterating his allegiance to the normative claim, one of Posner's recurrent themes is that legal rules and social institutions should be judged by their ability to promote WMP. His notion of wealth includes the aggregate of the market values of all property held as well as consumer and producer surplus.[13] Such surplus values result when commercial entities and individuals hold certain properties because they affix higher values to those properties than the current market does. It is clear that WMP prizes only utility and preferences that are supported by buyers' willingness to pay and sellers' willingness to relinquish. WMP is supported by the argument that value itself is a human creation, different people have different values and preferences, and aggregate value is increased if products are under the control of those who value them most. Thus, WMP's goal is an allocation in which products are under the ownership of their highest valuing user.[14]

*Criteria of Efficiency.* The term "efficiency" is used by Posner not merely as a technical but also as a normative standard. The normative usage hinges on the extent aggregate human satisfactions are maximized in certain ways by increasing economic efficiency. At least three different criteria of economic efficiency must be distinguished.[15]

1. Pareto Superiority: an allocation of resources (A1) is Pareto superior to another (A2) if and only if at least one person is better off under A1 than under A2, while no one else is worse off. The relevant test for better and worse off is each individual's conception of her or his own interests. Thus, it is permissible, as judged by the criterion of Pareto Superiority, to move from A2 to A1 if no one prefers A2 to A1 and at least one person prefers A1 to A2.

2. Pareto Optimality: an allocation of resources (A1) is Pareto optimal if and only if there are no other competing allocations of resources that are Pareto superior to A1; that is, any move from A1 to another allocation will result in at least one person being worse off as judged by her conception of her own welfare, regardless of how many, if any, are made better off.

3. Kaldor–Hicks Superiority: an allocation of resources (A1) is Kaldor–Hicks superior to another (A2) if and only if some people (P) are so much better off under A1 than under A2 that P could compensate fully those who are worse off under A1 than under A2, and P would still be better off. Under this criterion, P do not actually have to forward the compensation in question, but this criterion requires only that such compensation could be made in principle with P still being better off under A1 than under A2.

Posner argues that judges should take special notice of WMP for the same reasons that Pareto efficiency has allure: moves sanctioned by the criterion do not force people to do what they prefer not to do; as the criterion is based on the principle of consent, the criterion results in a net increase in utility because no one's position is worsened and at least one person's situation is improved. In fact, Posner tells us that calculations of Pareto efficiency must implicate appeals to consensual transactions: "Because of the impossibility of measuring utility directly, the only way to demonstrate that a change in the allocation of resources is Pareto superior is to show that everyone affected by the change consented to it."[16] Thus, if two people engage voluntarily in a transaction, the assumption is that, as rational maximizers of their interests, they both achieve a utility gain.

However, Pareto efficiency has limited use in the real world because transactions often have effects beyond their constitutive parties and often impose costs on outside parties: "Because the crucial assumption, . . . the absence of third-party effects, is not satisfied with regard to classes of transactions, the Pareto-superiority criterion is useless for most policy questions."[17]

This leads Posner to the adoption of Kaldor–Hicks. Because adoption of this criterion produces winners and losers, Posner must morally justify the losses. He advances two basic arguments as moral justification of Kaldor–Hicks. The first is that some losses suffered by those in transactions that maximize aggregate wealth can be treated as if they were consented to antecedently. Ex ante consent is evidenced, in part, by the willingness to pay a price that discounts the risk of loss ("the consent argument").[18] The second maintains that it is in the interests of most persons that law affix losses to some in order to maximize aggregate wealth so far as this is done impersonally and without prejudice ("the interest argument"). Posner illustrates these claims in a variety of ways. As applied to the negligence system of motor vehicle accident liability, Posner asks:

> In what sense may the driver injured by another driver in an accident in which neither was at fault be said to have consented to the injury, so as not to be entitled, under a negligence system, to compensation? . . . We must consider the effect on the costs of driving of insisting on ex post compensation, as under a system of strict liability. By hypothesis they would be higher. . . . Would drivers be willing to incur higher costs of driving in order to preserve the principle of ex post compensation? They would not. . . . Negligence is the more efficient system, the sum of the liability and accident insurance premiums will be lower under negligence, and everyone will prefer this.[19]

This illustration is designed to highlight the interest argument, which, in turn, provides support for the consent argument: if X can be demonstrated to be in the interests of almost everyone, then it is fair to infer that almost everyone would have consented to X had they been afforded the opportunity.[20] Accordingly, Posner claims that in the general area of law, individuals can be imputed to have given ex ante consent to legal rules that maximize wealth. Thus, WMP and specific legal doctrines that incorporate it are grounded ultimately on a version of social contract theory.

The justifications for Kaldor–Hicks and WMP, however, are highly suspect. The connection between consent and self-interest is not so neat. Policy X may be in my interest, but I may not actually consent to X if afforded the opportunity. Likewise, I may consent to

Y even though Y is not in my interests. This is so for a variety of reasons: I may not know my best interests, I may know them but subjugate them to other values, I may aspire to a policy that favors my interests even more than X, and so on. Moreover, the normative force of counterfactual consent is problematic: "A counterfactual consent provides no reason in itself for enforcing against me that to which I would have (but did not) consent. . . . Counterfactual consent . . . can provide no further argument beyond whatever argument the self-interest itself provides. . . . Counterfactual consent is in itself irrelevant to political justification."[21]

It is also not so clear that in most actual cases people consent in advance to losses they incur as a result of WMP. Willingness to pay a price that discounts the risk of loss is not equivalent to consenting to accept the loss; and the price paid may not from the outset always accurately discount all the risks of loss.[22] Furthermore, appeals to antecedent interests are dubious because it is never clear how and when a person's antecedent interests should be recognized, and what weight, if any, antecedent interests have now. If WMP is alleged to be in almost everyone's interest prior to its application in a particular case, it still does not follow that those who lose that case have reason to regard the application as morally sound.[23]

*WMP and Utilitarianism.* Although at first blush WMP may appear to be a straightforward instance of consequentialist thinking, Posner takes pains to distance himself from the utilitarian standard that holds that the moral worth of an action is assessed by the aggregate surplus of pleasure over pain the act produces.

Posner addresses three of the main problems he finds with utilitarianism. The first is the "boundary problem": Which entities are to count when we make our calculations of pleasure and pain? All humans? Those humans close to us? All current and potential humans? All sentient beings? If we take the maximizing of utility seriously, Posner says, then animals, foreigners, and the unborn should be included in our calculus. But, "there is something amiss in a philosophical system that cannot distinguish between people and sheep."[24] Those utilitarians who recognize this try to exclude entities such as animals by "dividing up preferences into 'higher' and 'lower' on inevitably shifting and subjective grounds."[25] Moreover, the boundary problem with respect to foreigners and the unborn cannot be resolved on utilitarian grounds themselves.[26]

The second problem is "the lack of a method for calculating the effect of a decision or policy on the total happiness of the relevant population."[27] Utilitarians must rely too often on hunches and guesswork because their calculus lacks "a psychological metric that [would] enable happiness to be measured and compared across persons (and animals?)."[28] As a result, utilitarians end up "[basing] rights of great importance on no firmer ground than an empirical hunch that they promote 'happiness.' "[29]

The third problem is "moral monstrousness."[30] This takes two forms: the inability to distinguish types of pleasure and the willingness "to sacrifice the innocent individual on the altar of social need."[31] Because of the first form, a "utility monster" who has a great capacity for deriving pleasure from acts generally considered to be noxious might add significantly to the aggregate surplus of pleasure and thus be judged a better person than another, who has a lesser capacity for deriving pleasure from acts generally considered to be permissible. Because of the second form, utilitarians must permit the murder of an innocent person if that act somehow increases aggregate pleasure.

*WMP and Kantianism.* In Posner's view, Kantianism fares no better. It embodies the "fanaticism"[32] of categorical duties that do not allow trade-offs or exceptions. Thus, true Kantians can never tell a lie or do any evil regardless of the overall positive consequences that such acts may have in certain circumstances. Moreover, flexible Kantians, who try to delineate exceptions, collapse back into utilitarianism: "[Such Kantians] will say that torture is wrong even if it could be shown to be . . . on balance happiness maximizing but then admit that if torturing one person were necessary to save the human race it would not be wrong to torture him. Once this much is conceded, however, there is no logical stopping point."[33] Thus, Kantianism is seen by Posner as impaled fatally on the horns of a dilemma, either fanaticism or self-destruction.

Accordingly, Posner contends that WMP and Kaldor–Hicks efficiency, as applied to resource allocation, stake out an appealing middle position between uncompromising Kantianism and unbridled utilitarianism. Unlike Kantianism, WMP substitutes a kind of hypothetical consent for express consent. This substitution presumably produces fewer constraints than Kantianism on the maximal satisfactions of preferences: goods and services are reallocated on the basis of what parties would have agreed to had their transactions been easier to undertake and conclude.[34] Moreover, unlike utilitarianism, under WMP individuals' preferences count only if they are supported by a willingness to pay. Thus, unlike utilitarianism, under WMP goods cannot be reallocated from X to Y without X's consent merely because Y has a greater desire for the goods.[35] Posner sharpens this point by noting that a theft of property can sometimes increase the aggregate surplus of pleasure over pain and is thereby justified under utilitarianism, but would not be justified under WMP.[36]

Furthermore, Posner claims that WMP embodies more determinacy than utilitarianism: because willingness to pay includes both the desire and the ability to secure ownership, it is easily observable in the market. Finally, Posner makes the bold claim that WMP grounds other commonly accepted moral values more soundly than either utilitarianism or Kantianism.

> Other ethical values can also be grounded more firmly. Economic liberty is an obvious example. . . . Free markets . . . maximize a society's wealth. . . . Less obviously, most of the conventional pieties—keeping promises, telling the truth, and the like—can also be derived from [WMP]. Adherence to these virtues facilitates transactions (and so promotes trade and hence wealth) by reducing the costs of policing markets through self-protection, detailed contracts, litigation, etc. Even altruism (benevolence) can be interpreted as an economizing principle.[37]

*WMP and Moral Intuitions.* Posner presses the case for the normative soundness of WMP by addressing and deflecting potential conflicts between WMP and our common moral intuitions. He does this to underscore the differences between WMP and utilitarianism and to highlight the moral superiority of WMP. First, WMP eludes the problem of the utility monster: "[Potential utility monsters] would have to buy [their] victims' consent, and these purchases would soon deplete the wealth of all but the wealthiest. . . . [Their] victims are protected by a rights system which forces the monster to pay his victims the level of compensation that they themselves determine."[38] Second, WMP can distinguish between the moral worth of various human preferences. It ascribes value only to wealth-creating activity, which has the effect of transcending mere self-interest. Third, WMP appears indifferent to egalitarian values in resource allocation. But Posner points out that "the specific distribution of wealth is a mere by-product of a distribution of rights that is itself derived from [WMP]. A just distribution of wealth need not be posited."[39] Also, the reward-by-economic-contribution principle is not compromised by indolent inheritors of wealth: "Nor is the justice of this reward system undermined when some people live off inherited wealth and make no personal contribution to augmenting the wealth of society. The expenditure of inherited wealth represents simply the deferral of part of the accumulator's consumption beyond his lifetime."[40]

*Troubling Cases.* There are other sorts of cases, however, that Posner finds troubling. For example, he recognizes the possibility that the presence of a few members of an unpopular racial or religious group in a neighborhood might be so disconcerting to their neighbors "as to depress land values by an amount greater than the members of the minority would be willing to pay to remain in the neighborhood."[41] Unhappily, under such circumstances segregation based on race or religion would seem to be wealth maximizing. Posner can only add that "it is however rare that the ostracism, expulsion, or segregation of a productive group will maximize the wealth of a society."[42]

Moreover, Posner acknowledges the possibility that WMP might advise externally limiting birthrates when taxing births to limit population growth is insufficient.[43] Also, WMP's unyielding reliance on negative freedom as morally self-validating may conflict with common moral intuitions. Absent explicit force, fraud, duress, and incapacity, WMP embraces voluntary transactions as dispositive of value and thus as enhancing wealth. But this can lead to morally odd results: "If A . . . sells himself into slavery to B, or if C borrows money from D with a penalty clause that provides that in the event of default D can break C's knees, there is no economic basis for refusing to enforce either contract unless some element of fraud or duress is present."[44]

Furthermore, Posner accepts unsqueamishly the possibility that under WMP a motor-vehicle driver confronted with the inescapable dilemma of running over a hundred thousand sheep or running over one human child may sacrifice the child if the aggregate worth of the sheep is greater.[45]

Finally, he admits that WMP may well seem harsh because it excludes from consideration all preferences not backed by willingness to pay: the preferences of both those unwilling and those unable to produce for the community. Such people "count only if they are part of the utility function of someone who has wealth. . . . There is . . . no public duty to support the indigent."[46] He tries to soften the effect of this admission by adding that "this result grates on modern sensibilities yet I see no escape from it that is consistent with any of the major ethical systems."[47] Thus, although "some nonproductive people might therefore starve in a system guided by [WMP],"[48] people are more likely to be destitute in poor nations than in wealthy nations, and nations that reject WMP are more likely to be poor.

But Posner is incorrect in thinking that WMP is morally superior to the crude version of utilitarianism that he criticizes. WMP does provide a more definite solution to the boundary problem than that provided by utilitarianism. Under WMP, nonhumans count but only insofar as they maximize human wealth. Animals, then, have no inherent moral significance despite their sentient capacities. But while utilitarians were ridiculed for seemingly permitting animals to count as much as humans, Posner may be questioned for refusing to allow them inherently to count at all. Moreover, this refusal has a Janus-faced character. Recall the case of the sheep and motorist: if an aggregate number of sheep, although lacking any inherent moral value, has greater wealth maximizing value than does a particular human, then in a conflict situation WMP advises us to save the sheep and sacrifice the human.

This illustrates that under WMP not only do sheep not have inherent moral significance, neither do humans. Thus, those humans who lack productive capacities have no inherent moral claim on those who are productive. Accordingly, Posner admits that "if [an individual] happens to be born feeble-minded and his net social product is negative, he would have no right to the means of support even though there was nothing blameworthy in his inability to support himself."[49]

As applied to the boundaries to be maximized—does WMP apply only to one's nation or to the entire world?—Posner has little to say other than "most trade restrictions hurt both parties to them."[50] Presumably, he is counseling the fewest possible trade restrictions as a way of allowing nations to maximize their wealth through trades undertaken from enlightened self-interest. But more needs to be said to make Posner's claim persuasive because "there are many cases of monopoly power where [Posner's claim] is simply untrue. And what about all the conflicts that arise when there is colonialism, or when the ownership of mineral rights on the sea floor is considered?"[51]

In sum, Posner is able to address the boundary problem in a way that crude utilitarianism could not, but his solution comes with a high price: the discounting of the inherent (non–wealth maximizing) moral significance of sentient beings and the invoking of unrefined principles of laissez-faire trade. Because of the radically counterintuitive implications of this solution, it is highly questionable whether it represents an advance over the difficulties besetting crude utilitarianism.

Also, Posner may be more sanguine than is warranted about the advantages WMP has over utilitarianism in regard to the determinacy of its applicability.

> It is one thing for a court to determine, say, that A agreed to pay B three dollars in exchange for a book, and failed to do so upon tender of the book. It is quite another to determine all of the secondary and tertiary economic effects of all of the possible outcomes of the dispute presented. Economic analyses even of very simple legal problems often involve identifying—and, more importantly, estimating the magnitude of—externalities (costs and benefits accruing to persons other than the parties), transactions costs, information costs, risk preferences, etc.[52]

Economic analysis tends "to identify competing concerns, but to provide no clear way of evaluating their magnitude."[53] Posner announces determinate results in particular cases; he adjudicates between apparent stalemates. But "he does so . . . by making judgments about what the facts as to the magnitudes of competing concerns are likely to be. . . . His judgments are not, however, empirically demonstrable."[54]

Furthermore, we have already encountered several radically counterintuitive implications of WMP: potentially wealth maximizing cases of racial and religious segregation, possible government limitation on birthrates, the general advantages flowing to the wealthy on the basis of their riches alone, the possible sacrifice of a human life in deference to the lives of an aggregate of wealth maximizing sheep, and the enforcement of morally odd contractual arrangements by a principle that takes "voluntary" transactions to be self-ratifying. Posner (courageously) offers other instances. For example:

> suppose that pituitary extract is . . . very expensive. A poor family has a child who will be a dwarf if he does not get some of the extract, but the family cannot afford the price. . . . A rich family has a child who will grow to normal height, but the extract will add a few inches more, and his parents decide to buy it for him. In the sense of value [employed by WMP], the pituitary extract is more valuable to the rich than to the poor family, because value is measured by willingness to pay.[55]

Posner tries to deflect the force of such examples by labeling them "very rare."[56] But their power is not so easily neutralized. There are at least four major problems here: first, Posner does not consider deeply the source of wealth. It is not enough to know that one family is wealthier than another and has a stronger willingness and ability to pay for a scarce good; we also must look at the genesis of that wealth. It is true that Posner would consider theft and fraud to be wrong (non–wealth maximizing and productive of market distortions). But once an individual gets away with such a crime, she possesses wealth that apparently can be used for further wealth maximizing transfers. If there is any truth to the slogan "behind every great fortune lies a crime," then it would seem that the source of a person's wealth is at least morally relevant when determining who should receive a scarce commodity.

Second, WMP not only advises that the rich family is permitted to obtain the extract because of their willingness and ability to pay more for it, WMP also tells us that it would be morally wrong (non–wealth maximizing) if the poor family obtained the extract. The relative vulnerabilities and projected utilities of the two families are irrelevant for WMP.

Third, it is not so clear that such cases are rare. Perhaps cases exactly like the pituitary gland illustration are, but given the vast number of needy people in this country and the world, conflicts over scarce resources between the relatively poor and the relatively wealthy are not at all uncommon. The pituitary gland case underscores WMP's bias in favor of the rich and blindness to a host of morally relevant considerations other than willingness to pay.

Fourth, counterintuitive implications cannot be brushed aside by assurances that the cases that embody them are rare. This maneuver would not be thought to be adequate if advanced by a utilitarian to elude charges of moral monstrosities; so, too, it is inadequate when used by advocates of WMP. Often so-called extraordinary cases expose deeper theoretical difficulties for a moral theory. Regarding WMP, such cases illustrate its fanaticism, reductionism, and disregard of many commonly accepted moral considerations.

Accordingly, it can be argued persuasively that WMP displays most of the maladies Posner found present in crude utilitarianism and Kantianism: radically counterintuitive implications, reductionism, and fanaticism. WMP is distinct from the other two normative theories, and, as Posner reported, it can address certain problems better than its competitors; but it often counsels us less adequately on other problems. Thus, the case for the moral superiority of WMP has not been established.

## THE CASE AGAINST WMP

Ironically, part of WMP's objectivist impulse may incorporate the relativization of moral values. All values are reduced to preferences that count only so far as they are backed by willingness and ability to pay. Thus, WMP assumes that no "value" is antecedently superior to another. Only market forces can determine which of two competing values should be satisfied. It may well seem that moral assessment and normative justification have been replaced by strength of conviction. Worse, even strength of conviction is constricted to a certain kind of belief, the kind backed by currency. As such, many sorts of values will be marginalized and the voices of the less wealthy will often be suffocated. WMP minimizes such values and voices, not because they are inherently less worthy from a wider moral perspective, but only because they are not antecedently dominant in the market. Thus, it can be charged that the quest for objectivity in this context facilitates the further disenfranchisement of the already disadvantaged and eviscerates the power of moral reasoning—all in the interests of a thinly veiled, impoverished libertarian descriptive and prescriptive world vision.

WMP claims to explicitly ignore questions of economic distribution. Wealth may be maximized in a particular situation regardless of how it is distributed. Posner considers a situation that might seem ripe for redistribution, but rejects it: if all income groups had similar utility functions, then overall utility might well increase if some wealth were redistributed from the rich to the poor: the redistribution might increase the pleasure of the poor more than it decreases the pleasure of the rich because the redistributed money would have a greater effect on the well-being of the poor. But Posner reiterates that WMP is concerned with wealth maximization, not necessarily with increasing aggregate utility. Thus, he rejects redistribution because redistribution does not of itself increase wealth, it at best only reshuffles it; and because redistribution almost always involves costs, redistributional strategies almost always reduce aggregate wealth even when they may increase aggregate utility.[57] Mediating the harshness of his attack, Posner concedes the desirability of wealth redistribution under certain circumstances: when poverty has other deleterious social effects, such as increasing crime, WMP may well justify "governmental efforts to reduce the gross inequality (in a wealthy society) that we call poverty."[58]

The normative implications of Posner's position are alarming. Notice that under his rationale poverty is not bad in itself (or if it is bad in itself it is not worthy of redistributional efforts), it is bad (or it is worthy of redistribution efforts) only insofar as it more widely impairs the economy. Thus, "poverty is bad because it hurts the rich."[59] The oddness of this view is that, absent wider social costs such as increased crime, the existence of extreme poverty has no inherent moral significance, and that the poor are now given an incentive to effect wider social costs such as increased crime, especially crime against the wealthy. Indeed, under WMP, poor people seeking redistribution would be foolish if they did not increase the social costs, for only by doing so will they merit attention.

In that vein, Edwin Baker has argued that WMP favors wealthy claimants of rights: "[WMP] favors the claimant of the right whose use is productive over one whose use is consumptive [and] favors the rich claimant whose use is consumptive over the poor claimant whose use is consumptive."[60] Moreover, the initial advantages bestowed on the wealthy because of their wealth, and thus because of their greater ability to support their preferences with money, make it more likely that they will be favored in future situations.

Baker reconsiders an example advanced by Posner: between two dying men in a desert, which has the right to the one available barrel of water? WMP would answer, "The party who, given the existing distribution of water, is willing (and able) to pay the most for the right."[61] Baker calls this the "situation ante" approach because it uses "willingness to pay before the assignment" of the right in question.[62] But absent Posner's stipulated definition of "value," there are other available criteria to determine which party values the right more. Baker advances three alternative sets of criteria.

(1) The party who, if he had the right, would require the highest price from the purchaser ( . . . situation post approach . . . ); (2) the party who, if he had the right, would not sell it to the other party who wanted the right; or (3) the party who, if he did not have the right, would buy it from the other party.[63]

Baker claims that only if Posner is correct that, assuming the absence of transaction costs, "the initial assignment of legal rights does not affect which use ultimately prevails . . . [would] Posner's answer [to the desert case] and the three alternatives . . . all be equivalent."[64] Here, of course, Posner is relying on Coase's theorem. But Baker points out an important qualification that he believes exposes WMP's bias in favor of the wealthy: "The initial assignment of a right can affect the wealth of the parties which in turn can affect the parties' 'valuation' of the right, and thus affects the ultimate use of the resource."[65] In the desert case, Posner's stipulated definition of "value," looking at the situation ante, would favor the wealthy claimant because he would be willing and able to pay the most. Alternatives (2) and (3) are unhelpful: "Neither party would buy because neither party would sell."[66] Applying the situation post approach seems indeterminate because it is likely that neither party, once possessing the right to the water, would sell the right for any price. Alternately, if one of the parties would sell at a higher price than another, it is not clear from these facts alone which of the two that would be.

This suggests, says Baker, that Posner's definition of "value" is biased in a way that the three alternatives are not: "The initial assignment normally affects the relative wealth of the parties . . . [by increasing] the wealth of the party assigned the right. . . . Since a person's wealth affects how much that person is willing and able to pay for a specific desired right, the effect on a person's wealth of the initial assignment . . . will influence how much the person 'values' the right."[67] Accordingly, in many situations the three alternative definitions of "value" would yield answers different from those emerging from Posner's definition.[68]

Furthermore, we must underscore the self-perpetuating nature of the relationship between initial assignment of a right and future entitlement claims: "There will be situations . . . where a right will be valued most highly by whomever is assigned that right, since that party has—by the very fact of that right's assignment—the wealth to outbid the other. Assignment of a right confers wealth, wealth influences willingness to pay, and willingness to pay is for Coase and Posner the proper determinant of whom the right should be assigned to."[69]

The point here is that Posner's definition of "value" favors wealthy claimants in ways that other coherent conceptions of "value" do not, and Posner has supplied no persuasive (and independent) reasons for embracing his definition of "value" rather than the definitions of the alternatives.

Another criticism, of which Posner seems aware, is that wealth maximization depends on the existing specification of entitlements and then serves to legitimate the very entitlements on which it depends. The problem is that there is no wealth maximization without a particular set of entitlements in place—there is no wealth maximization in the abstract. We can only identify wealth maximizing results in relation to the existing distribution of wealth that itself is held together by specific legal entitlements. Different sets of legal entitlements would support different distributions of wealth and thus different patterns of wealth maximization. WMP, depending as it does for its content on specific legal entitlements, cannot then properly be used to explain and justify those same entitlements.[70]

The moral of the story is that it is inappropriate for Posner to make his positive claim that the common law is efficient: "To say . . . that the common law produces efficient or wealth maximizing outcomes is circular: whatever rights structure is produced by law will produce an efficient outcome. . . . Any determination by the common law will lead to a new set of possible results, and no set of outcomes will be necessarily superior (if even comparable) to another."[71]

At times, Posner seems aware of the alleged circularity and tries to turn it into a theoretical advantage when he discusses WMP's apparent indifference to egalitarian values: "The specific distribution of wealth is a mere by-product of a distribution of rights that is itself derived from [WMP]. A just distribution of wealth need not be posited."[72] The good news for Posner is that WMP does not have to conjure an antecedently just distribution of wealth, but the bad news is that his positive claim about law's efficiency becomes trivial.

Furthermore, WMP loses much of its alleged normative bite: "[WMP] cannot uniquely determine which interests the law should promote as rights and which it should inhibit. The law's decision-making processes can work only with selective normative premises as to whose interests are to count as rights, and these premises necessarily have distributive consequences. To argue that [WMP] can determine rights serves only to mask a choice of which interests to protect as rights."[73]

The mutually legitimating relationship between WMP and existing legal entitlements constitutes a process at which Marxists and feminists will immediately snarl "false consciousness" and "circular apologetics." But even those of other political perspectives will be led by all this to seriously question Posner's positive and normative claims about WMP.

Accordingly, WMP embodies a suspicious circularity: economic efficiency is dependent on a particular set of entitlements that themselves are presumably derived from notions of economic efficiency. While this has the alleged advantage of making no explicit appeal to controversial normative assumptions, it has the disadvantage of masking WMP's own implicit normative assumptions. The techniques of economic analysis pose as value-neutral methods of dispute resolution, while in fact they depend on particular descriptive and prescriptive world visions. The pretense to neutrality depends on dubious metaphysical and epistemological assumptions: the divorce of language from the world of experience, the presence of depersonalized intellectual processes allowing a separation of subject from object, and an ahistorical account of the evolution of scientific knowledge.[74] Clinging to the myths of Metaphysical Realism and desperately clutching to an objectivist impulse, economic analysts aspire to distance themselves from fundamental political disputes. The pretense is misplaced and unnecessary; moreover, its veneer is too thin for durability.

The wealth maximizers' objectivist impulse carries over to their use of language designed to avoid the contestability and value-ladenness of moral language and to highlight dispassionate, more "scientific" discourse. But critics have charged that such language does violence to "moral reality" and "anesthetizes moral feeling."[75]

Furthermore, WMP is often charged with embodying a pernicious conservative bias: "Efficiency has been used in the economic analysis as if it were an independent concept, not entirely relative to whatever distribution of wealth existed. And once it has been realized that efficiency is, by definition, a function of a particular distribution (invariably the status quo), the inherently conservative bias of the definition of efficiency becomes clear."[76]

Another kind of conservative bias is present as well. WMP seeks to maximize wealth based on a given set of preferences whose independent value goes unexamined: "Preferences as they once were or might be, as opposed to preferences as they now are, are not a concern [of WMP]."[77] Issues of preference formation and revision seem purposefully marginalized. Thus, WMP ignores the role that preference formation plays in maintaining self-identity through time.

There is yet another, somewhat less tangible, reproach to WMP. WMP's value reductionism, its embrace of "voluntary" agreements as morally self-ratifying, and its infatuation with market transactions leads to a commodification obsession: virtually anything can be traded in a wealth maximizing fashion. But this mindset may be criticized for demeaning important attributes constitutive of self. Bodily integrity and personal dignity, for example, are not generally thought to be properly subject to market forces. The presumption of honoring voluntary trades is rebuttable as evidenced by public policy prohibitions against prostitution, slavery, baby selling, and so on. Moreover, the mere existence of a "noncoerced" contract never settles the question of its underlying moral status. Given pervasive distortions in contracts, such as vastly unequal bargaining power, and radically different vulnerabilities and needs, further questions remain: Is the contract grossly unfair? Does it embody terms that commodify what should not be commodified?

Moreover, treating constitutive attributes as if they are simply other forms of property distances the self from its content: it transforms concrete persons with unique attributes into abstract, disembodied traders. It permits a sort of self-alienation in which what is integral to personhood and self-development is subject to the same market forces as land, basketballs, and Twinkies. Human flourishing may well be impaired as persons internalize the message that self and constitutive attributes can be separated when economically expedient.[78] As we increase wealth and value as defined by WMP, we may literally lose our souls.

## WMP AND THE LAW

An economic approach to law advises paying special attention to WMP. Thus, all areas of law could expand the influence of WMP. Nuisance law could confer rights to the party to whom the rights are most valuable. Negligence doctrine could confer rights and duties so as to ensure that parties will use the cheapest methods of avoiding economic costs. Property doctrine could define rights so that reallocations to the highest-valued user are cheaper. Contract doctrine could aim at facilitating the process of market exchange and reducing exchange costs.[79]

The discourse of the Law and Economics movement rehabilitates legal analysis as a quasi science. Its reductionist tendencies translate complex human interactions and relations into relatively straightforward economic principles. It locates the rationality of law in general propositions derived inductively from actual and hypothetical motivations of parties presumed to act as rational maximizers of their economic interests. Legal arguments and conclusions can then be properly evaluated by whether they support the predictions and aspirations of WMP. Thus, judges can invoke an antecedent, neutral standard of rational behavior in an allegedly objective, universal analysis and comprehensive understanding of law. Basking in the restoration of scientific rigor and championing a methodology that purports to add consistency and harmony to legal decision making, law as economics privileges the roles of enlightened self-interest and voluntary transactions under conditions of resource scarcity. Challenging the outdated dogma that law is autonomous, the movement gazes beyond the law to discover law's legitimacy. At the same time, Law and Economics scorns abstract deduction from presumed moral rights and duties, and, instead, operates from allegedly rational models of economic behavior.

It is questionable whether the economic analysis of the Chicago School captures important elements of the phenomenology of judicial decision making. Judges do not generally take themselves to be "instruments of efficiency, but rather as engaged in a process of trying to understand and protect the values embodied in the law."[80] Rather than perfecting or replicating market activity, the law generally aims at legislating and adjudicating distributional issues.

Of course, the Chicago School never says that judges are necessarily self-conscious of the role economic efficiency plays in law. Moreover, if WMP were in fact the main value embodied in law, then judges who see themselves as protecting embodied values may well be advancing WMP even though they are unaware of it. Still, the earlier criticisms of WMP severely undercut the positive and normative claims of the Chicago School. Thus, the fact that the economic analysis of law is at variance with the phenomenology of judicial decision making carries significant weight.

Posner's analysis of criminal punishment provides another illustration of the discrepancy between economic analysis and what judges take themselves to be doing. Posner tells us that "economic analysis suggests that a combination of low probabilities [of punishment] with very severe penalties frequently is optimal."[81] Thus, erratically applied (highly uncertain) punishments are permissible if the punishments that are meted out are sufficiently severe that the expected value of punishment (the severity of the punishment discounted by the improbability of its application) is equivalent to the cost of the crimes. Under such a regime, there would also be a social gain in a lowering of the enforcement and administrative costs associated with more frequent punishments. Accordingly, a punishment that is much more severe than current practice but that is actually assessed less frequently is acceptable and perhaps even commendable, for example, a punishment five times as severe as current practice but that is assessed against only one out of every five criminal offenders.

The problem here is obvious. Economic analysis undermines at least two fundamental normative principles: like cases should be treated alike, and punishments should fit the crimes. A strictly economic analysis of punishment, one based on the exigencies and expediencies of the market, is in conflict with the sense of justice that partly constitutes judicial practice. Posner might identify this as an area where economic analysis is not yet, but should be, part of law. But my suspicion is that judges and laypersons are not likely to embrace such a claim warmly. Our faith in the two principles of justice would trump the allure of economic analysis.

Moreover, criminals are not merely economically inefficient, they are morally deficient. It is odd to weigh the benefits attending criminal acts as if they were just another neutral factor to be considered. Why should the pleasure of a sadistic murderer count at all given the manner in which it is achieved? Surely, in virtually all cases the pleasures criminals obtain from their acts are irrelevant to the permissibility of those acts.

Finally, economic analysis transgresses the phenomenology of judicial decision making in other ways as well. Because of its preoccupation with legal results, economic behavior, and the general instrumentalism of law, the Chicago School ignores the social and directive functions of law: "Law is not simply an instrument for achieving a certain distribution of items in the world, but a way of creating and sustaining a political and ethical community."[82]

*Brief Rejoinder.* An advocate of the Chicago School could rejoin in a number of ways. First, it has been claimed that the sorts of criticisms raised here, even if devastating, pertain only to the descriptive and normative claims, and possibly the genetic claim, of economic analysis. But the behavioral claim (that economic analysis provides a good framework to predict how people will behave under law) remains intact: "Despite its vulnerability . . . the normative claim is not central to the enterprise of law and economics. . . . A successful attack on law and economics requires a frontal assault on the behavioral claim."[83] Because it is highly questionable whether any successful assault on the behavioral claim has been made, it is arguable that much remains vital in the economic analysis of law: "The behavioral claim is secure in large part because the dominant strain in American jurisprudence requires some theory of behavior under law, and the economic theory of legal behavior is the only systematic theory available."[84]

Posner takes a more direct route to salvage WMP. He takes the charges of reductionism and fanaticism levied against WMP to be cheap shots based on a misreading of his view: "I have argued that [WMP] provides the best theory, both positive and normative, of common law rights and remedies. . . . I have never argued, and do not believe, that [WMP] is or should be the only principle of justice in our society."[85] Critics may be misled by their failure to understand the way Posner allocates responsibilities among government offices: "My argument is not that [WMP] is the only social value that government ought to pay attention to, but that it is the only such value . . . that courts can do much to promote."[86] Furthermore, Posner has reiterated that WMP is not to be taken as the single guide to public policy: "Almost everyone . . . thinks slavery improper even if the slave became such through a voluntary transaction. . . . Torture and lynching . . . [violate] essential personhood even if [they] could be shown to maximize wealth. . . . All of the examples I have discussed are sufficiently troublesome to make me regard wealth maximization as an incomplete guide to social decisionmaking."[87] Elsewhere he has said that "what the economist might be able to say, by way of normative analysis, is that a policy such as mutilation of felons increases efficiency and should therefore be adopted unless its adoption would impair some more important social value."[88]

Regarding the more general relationship between efficiency and justice, Posner tells us that the "most common" meaning of "justice" is "efficiency": "When we describe as 'unjust' convicting a person without a trial . . . we can be interpreted as meaning simply that the conduct or practice in question wastes resources."[89] Acknowledging that this may not capture entirely what we mean by "justice," Posner adds that even when efficiency and justice seem to conflict, "[views of what is just] are [not] completely impervious to what an economic study might show. . . . Would the objection to medical experimentation on convicts remain unshaken if it were shown persuasively that the social benefits of such experiments greatly exceed the costs? Would the objections to capital punishment survive a convincing demonstration that capital punishment had a significantly greater deterrent effect than life imprisonment?"[90]

Regarding the charge that WMP embodies a pernicious conservative bias, Posner retorts that "I am not an advocate of the status quo. Many features of our current social arrangements are not wealth maximizing, and, since they are not supported by any other principle of justice either, should be changed. Although I am not hostile to patriotism or religion, nothing in the theory of wealth maximization lends support to either practice."[91]

Posner is also unimpressed by criticisms of WMP that are based on the limitations and incompleteness of the explanatory powers of economic analysis. To those who contend that rational maximizing of interests provides only a partial explanation of legal behavior, Posner responds that "an economic theory of law is certain not to capture the full complexity, richness, and confusion of the phenomena . . . that it seeks to illuminate. That lack of realism does not invalidate the theory; it is, indeed, the essential precondition of a theory."[92] Moreover, "a theory cannot be overturned by pointing out its defects or limitations but only by proposing a more inclusive, more powerful, and above all more useful theory. . . . The economic theory of law seems . . . the best positive theory of law extant."[93]

*WMP Revisited.* A sample of Posner's rejoinders to critics is enough to show that his work has, indeed, often been misinterpreted. It is clear that at least some of the most common attacks on WMP are too harsh and stem from misreading. Still, WMP is problematic. Posner's rejoinders sharpen a conflict that underlies much of his work. He has a strongly libertarian conception of personhood, the value of (negative) freedom, and the primacy of the individual that often coalesces uneasily with his quasi-utilitarian conception of social policy. As we have seen, placing paramount value on uncoerced transactions and the maximization of aggregate wealth is not always congruent with other commonly recognized values of human dignity and personhood. Posner is willing to acknowledge these other values, but he does not give us a clear idea of their relative weight with respect to WMP. We are told that at times WMP must yield to other values but are given no guidance beyond a few examples in which the implications of WMP would differ widely from our considered (non-WMP) moral judgments. When responding to his critics, Posner underscores the claim that WMP is always a value to be considered among others, but that claim is hardly striking. With the possible exception of a few truculent Kantians, most of us agree that economic efficiency is a value that must be weighed when making moral calculations. What we disagree on is the amount of weight we must accord that value in concrete situations. Much of the apparent panache of WMP is parasitic on the impression that Posner sometimes gives that it is the paramount value in normative theory; but that impression also elicits the strongest rebukes from critics. When Posner softens (or makes explicit) his deeper view that the conclusions of WMP must often defer to other values, he is able to elude some of the critical attack against him, but his position loses a bit of its luster and its determinacy. Thus, the normative claim of economic analysis seems to degenerate into merely noting that efficiency is just another factor to weigh in moral balancing.

In the same vein, Posner is correct in pointing out that WMP does not embody a conservative (in the sense of status quo preserving) bias with respect to all social issues. But what normative theory does or could embody that strong a bias? No extant theory of which I am aware agrees irrevocably and completely with every social policy currently in place. Posner's critics are surely not charging him with doing the impossible—explaining and justifying all current policies and decisions as internally coherent and beyond future revision. As noted earlier, the critics charge that his analysis takes the basic distributional structures, aggregate social preferences, and bulk of extant entitlements as givens. The analysis then shows how these givens are generally wealth maximizing, which in turn legitimates the status quo further. Posner's analysis in fact claims to demonstrate that existing legal doctrines and relations are for the most part economically efficient. Only minor tinkering is required to sharpen the law. Accordingly, it seems that although Posner's response is correct, it does not fully meet his critics' point.

Moreover, Posner makes clear that he embraces WMP as the only value that courts can effectively promote. Given that much of the critical attack against him concerns the dangers of the relentless use of WMP by the judiciary, Posner's response should provide little consolation for his supporters. Unless WMP is the only value embodied in extant legal doctrine or the only value permissibly employed because of special constraints on the judicial role, it is doubtful that Posner is correct. Surely the phenomenology of judicial decision making, the myriad purposes of judicial opinions, and the variety of specific rationales judges use to support their conclusions suggest that Posner overstates his case.[94]

This chapter examined thoroughly the work of the Chicago School as exemplified by Richard Posner. The economic analysis of the Chicago School has been influential in inspiring new waves of quantitative understandings of law. A few of the new approaches include: (1) the development of the basic Chicago School approach to forming nonmarket analyses to explain bureaucratic and institutional behavior; (2) the analysis of legislative and institutional behavior from the perspective of game theory or interest-group theory; (3) the examination of bargaining relations from the theoretical perspective of relational contract (in which future contingencies are uncommonly complex or uncertain) and strategic behavior (used by parties trying to anticipate the moves of the other and act accordingly), which "seeks to provide an understanding of market transactions in the context of long-term relations where bargains are never discrete and where strategic advantage may influence behavior";[95] and (4) the development of a politically liberal form of Law and Economics that rejects the normative claim of the Chicago School, denies that efficiency is the only important value in common law dispute resolution, and advocates law as a sort of public morality. Many new-wave economists are more concerned with analyzing public law and the proper role of the state than with puzzling over the proper resolution of judicial decision making in the common law.[96]

All economic analysts are united in their belief that the law is or can be a rational enterprise based on assessments of interests and understandings of behavior. Law and Economics discourse continues to embrace a quasi-scientific method with its underlying objectivist aspirations. As such the political Left will continue to view the movement with considerable suspicion as slyly masking the ways the oppression of the disadvantaged is justified and legitimated by the mindset of the dominant, as disingenuously favoring the dominant on no deeper reason than their antecedent advantages, as a theoretically bankrupt enterprise in circular apologetics, and as a pernicious exercise of power thinly disguised by quantitative rigor.

As we will see, there is much to be said in favor of the leftist critique. But as long as we assert that economic efficiency is an important value, law and economics analyses will play an important part in our normative and legal debates. Although the more sweeping descriptive and normative claims of the Chicago School at times seem so overblown as to constitute unintended self-parody, we should not allow that to obscure the role that law and economics analyses can rightfully assume as they inform our awareness of the consequences of law and contribute to sharpening our understanding of normative reasoning.

# CHAPTER 5

# Reconceiving Rational Constraints
*The Interpretivist Turn*

UNDOUBTEDLY INFLUENCED by trends in contemporary literary theory and in the resurrection of classical hermeneutics, jurisprudential thought has partaken in the "interpretivist turn": all reading is presumed to involve an active interpretation by which readers come to understand the meaning and values embodied in various texts.

In legal contexts, this seemingly innocuous proposition engenders intense intramural debate: Is legal interpretation subjective, nonrational, and free? Or is it primarily a rational and objective endeavor? Do meaning and value reside stably and undisturbed in texts? Or is the power to interpret the privilege to reimagine and remake? Does the interpretivist turn entail, or at least suggest, that classical metaphysical and epistemological questions are irrelevant to jurisprudential discourse? These questions have persisted: Is the world independent of our concepts and language? What is a justified belief that a proposition is true? Is justified belief different from knowledge? Must we accept certain tenets of classical logic such as the principles of bivalence and stability? Is the meaning of a sentence the set of conditions under which the sentence is true? Are there natural kinds whose essences cause us to refer to them by a common name? Or are such names merely the conventional practices of a linguistic community?

## BOUNDED OBJECTIVITY

Owen Fiss advances a notion of interpretation that at once distances him both from deterministic theories, which champion the authority of the presumably stable intentions of the framers of statutes or the fixed meaning of words,[1] and from nihilis-

tic positions, which portray judicial decision making as the unbounded choosing or creating of meaning from radically indeterminate texts.

*Obedience to Textual Meaning.* Fiss assumes that legal texts such as
constitutions, judicial precedents, and statutes embody meaning
and value. He acknowledges the creative role of the reader in this
process and recognizes that "the meaning of a text does not reside in
the text, as an object might reside in physical space . . . ready to be
extracted if only one knows the correct process."[2] What Fiss affirms,
and what he takes to be the core of the duty of judicial obedience, is
that an interpreter "is not free to assign any meaning he wishes to
the text."[3] Fiss tells us that "the idea of adjudication requires that
there exist constitutional values to interpret, just as much as it requires that there be constraints on the interpretive process. Lacking
such a belief, adjudication is not possible, only power."[4]

*Constraints on Interpretation.* Fiss suggests a difference between
the noninterpretive knowledge gained in the natural sciences and
interpretive knowledge generated by attention to legal texts. The
special data of texts other than those of the natural sciences embody
meaning and self-understanding absent in the natural objects examined by the natural sciences. Thus, for Fiss, it becomes paramount in
an enterprise such as law to explore possible constraints that might
allow us to rescue interpretation from the charge that it is merely a
mask for unbridled force as judges "find" whatever meaning they
desire in the radically indeterminate or conflicting language before
them.

Fiss states that disciplining rules, which are derived from the
specific institutional setting of the interpretive activity and may differ from one type of material to another, constrain readers and provide the criteria by which the community might evaluate the soundness of interpretations. Readers are "disciplined by a set of rules that
specify the relevance and weight to be assigned to the material (e.g.,
words, history, intention, consequence), as well as by those that define concepts and that established the procedural circumstances under which the interpretation must occur."[5] Such rules are a kind of
professional grammar and function much like "the rules of language, which constrain the users of the language, furnish the standards for judging the uses of language, and constitute the language."[6]

Judicial interpretation is also constrained by the community's
conventional morality. For Fiss, "the judge is trying to give meaning
and expression to public values (those that are embodied in a legal
text) and his understanding of such values—equality, liberty, prop-

erty, due process, cruel and unusual punishment—is necessarily shaped by the prevailing morality. The moral text is a prism through which he understands the legal text."[7]

Here Fiss is careful to point out that "interpretation does not require agreement or consensus, nor does the objective character of legal interpretations arise from agreement. What is being interpreted is a text, and the morality embodied in that text, not what individual people believe to be the good or right."[8] Under this view, the Constitution is the foundational authority for judicial decisions because it both "embodies public values and establishes the institutions through which those values are to be understood and expressed."[9]

Accordingly, the test of correctness of judicial decisions is independent of judicial or popular consensus; rather, the "test is whether that decision is in accord with the authoritative disciplining rules. Short of a disagreement that denies the authority of the interpretive community and the force of the disciplining rules, agreement is irrelevant in determining whether a judge's decision is a proper interpretation of the law."[10]

Fiss advances disciplinary rules and community morality as the devices that redeem legal interpretation and allow it to evade the opposite horrors posed by the Charybdis of mechanical jurisprudence and the Scylla of nihilism. Thus, these devices aspire to constrain readers from merely supplying a text with whatever meaning these interpreters antecedently desire, while simultaneously ameliorating the apparent indeterminacy of legal language.

These goals inspire questions about the nature of the devices themselves, however. If they, themselves, are subject to interpretation, then a critic might contend that Fiss merely reproduces the problem of reading texts at the level of the devices: What is the true content of the disciplinary rules and of community morality? What do they require? How must they be applied in legal context? If the devices themselves must be interpreted, it appears that, rather than achieving the middle course he seeks by identifying constraints on legal interpretation, Fiss has merely recast the unappealing problem of mechanism versus nihilism in a different place. On the other hand, if the devices are presumed to stabilize the meaning of texts because their own meaning is determinate and transparent, then it seems that Fiss has fetishized them to a status he hitherto reserved (and even there somewhat reluctantly) for the objects of natural science.[11]

An even more fundamental question is posed by Robin West as she puzzles over the relationship between law and conventional morality: "Is public, conventional morality read into the constitution, or does it emanate from it? Is it a separate 'social text' which the judge is morally but not legally bound to abide by, or is it an addendum incorporated by reference into a contract?"[12] Fiss, it would seem, adopts the view that conventional morality and the Constitution are mutually sustaining. We must assume at the outset that the Constitution is antecedently rich with value, yet we interpret the Constitution through the framework of conventional morality.

Whether this relationship between the Constitution and conventional morality is coherent is further complicated by the conflicts and tensions apparent in American values themselves. Thus far I have conceded for the sake of argument that there is a consistent system of values that we can accurately fix as conventional morality. Given the class fragmentation and diversity in the United States, talk of conventional morality itself may be viewed as a way of glossing over class conflict, of silencing potentially obstreperous minorities, and as a seemingly pious way of further privileging the preferences of the powerful. Rather than conceiving the Constitution as a repository of meaning or as informed by the community's morality, it is at least as plausible to view the Constitution as a battleground of meaning, where competing ideologies wage strategic dialectical wars among a citizenry (and perhaps even a judiciary) that falls far short of constituting a united interpretive community.[13]

Although advancing a claim of objectivity in legal interpretation, Fiss does not also claim the truth of either Metaphysical Realism or Epistemological Foundationalism; rather, his is a more modest version of objectivity.

> Objectivity in the law connotes standards. It implies that an interpretation can be measured against a set of norms that transcend the particular vantage point of the person offering the interpretation. Objectivity implies that the interpretation can be judged by something other than one's own notions of correctness. It imparts a notion of impersonality. The idea of an objective interpretation does not require that the interpretation be wholly determined by some source external to the judge, but only that it be constrained.[14]

While Fiss suggests that the physical world may be "more transcendent, less relativistic"[15] than the objectivity constituting judicial interpretation, he denies that "bounded objectivity is a secondary or parasitic kind of objectivity."[16]

Fiss thus portrays judicial decision making as interpretation constrained by disciplining rules and societal morality, both of which derive their authority from an interpretive community that is bound together by its antecedent commitment to Rule of Law virtues.

Fiss's reliance on disciplinary rule and communal morality will seem to some as an effort, conscious or not, to mask the way both devices emanate from power and to obscure the criteria by which the devices themselves should be measured. Although Fiss adopts the slogan of "bounded objectivity," his descriptive analysis of legal decision making is captured better by the term *conventionalism*. Although he at times attempts to salvage his objectivism by distinguishing between what individual people think is right from the morality that is truly embedded in a legal text, his disciplinary rules are conventionalist in that they constitute the dominant professional grammar and legal rules in place at a particular time. His reliance on community morality is even more obviously an invocation of a conventionalist standard.

Only those as sanguine about conventional wisdom as Fiss can take solace in the way he allegedly circumvents the supposed horrors of mechanical jurisprudence and nihilism. Those who perceive no necessary connection between a community's current legal and moral pronouncements and legal and moral truth, and those who see conventionalism as a mask for power and privilege, will take small consolation in Fiss's middle path. The former will disparage Fiss as just another moral relativist who has purloined and transformed the title "objectivism," while the latter will decry what they take to be the pernicious conservative bias Fiss accepts in law, a bias that threatens to further disenfranchise already disadvantaged groups. By embracing so warmly the constraining force of communal meanings, Fiss is vulnerable to the charge that he disables law from transcending conventional wisdom and from facilitating a society that is better than current constructions.

## ATHEORETICAL PRAGMATISM

To get a clear idea of Stanley Fish's Atheoretical Pragmatism, we need first to examine his criticisms of other writers.

*Critique of Theorizing.* Fish takes to task those theorists who are preoccupied with the underlying metaphysical and epistemological questions noted above. Such issues may make interesting fodder for the minions of critical analysis, but they serve no function when a reader is actually interpreting a legal text: "You don't use your account of knowing in order to 'do' knowing."[17] Fish's point here is that no practical consequences turn on which theoretical account of the underlying metaphysical and epistemological framework of legal interpretation one accepts.

Fish mocks leftist thinkers, such as critical legal scholars, for their "'anti-foundationalist theory hope,' the hope that because we now know that our foundations are interpretive rather than natural (given by God or nature), we will regard them with suspicion, and shake ourselves loose from, their influence."[18] Here Fish reiterates his view that it is a mistake to assume that "insight into the source of our convictions . . . will render them less compelling."[19] Furthermore, he reproaches certain leftist thinkers for their "capitulation to essentialist ideology"[20] as they resort to bogus metaphysical devices such as "real needs" or make reference to our "real nature."[21]

Moreover, he scolds those thinkers who tacitly desire foundationally secure knowledge and who are thus disappointed by the contingency of the knowledge we do possess: "The irony is that the state which is for [closet foundationalists] the precondition of true knowledge—the state of being above all situations and therefore of being in none at all—is the state in which the very idea of knowledge is incoherent."[22]

Finally, Fish criticizes Fiss: disciplining rules cannot constrain interpretation because their content depends on an interpretation. Moreover, Fiss's fear of nihilism is itself another manifestation of the pernicious preoccupation with metaphysical and epistemological questions: "Nihilism is impossible; one simply cannot 'exalt the . . . subjective dimension of an interpretation' or drain texts of meanings, and it is unnecessary to combat something that is not possible."[23]

In sum, Fish castigates those of whatever political persuasion who cling to the myths of presence: that there could be an independent vantage point from which we might purify and externally adjudicate normative debate; the essentialist trap: that there is a core of real human needs from which we might derive a perspective that transcends our present context; the philosopher's illusion: that one's position on or account of underlying metaphysical and epistemological issues has an important effect on legal practice; and the objectivist dilemma: that the only alternative to an objectivist account of interpretation is rabid nihilism.

*Against Metaphysics and Epistemology.* Fish assails the preoccupation with philosophical questions in law because he insists that judicial decision making, and practice generally, is done through tacit knowledge rather than through theorizing or by application of general rules or standards: "[Learning a practice] is not acquired by exclusively verbal means. Rather it comes as one is given words together with concrete examples of how they function in use [nature and words are learned together]. . . . What results from this process is 'tacit knowledge' which is learned by doing science rather than by acquiring rules for doing it."[24]

Thus, judges do not use their theories or accounts of judging, if they have any, to make decisions. Rather, they have tacit knowledge of the practices that form the context of their actions. Accordingly, those who are interested in judicial decision making will find no illumination by studying metaphysical and epistemological issues. Fish's point here is that it is only within an antecedently constrained practice that asking questions about justification and legitimacy is coherent: there is no external perspective or Archimedean point from which an opposing conception of justification is possible.

*Pragmatics and Professionalism.* Fish's description of judicial decision making begins with his insistence that judges may make use of theory "as a component of [judicial] practice,"[25] but theory does not generate either the form or content of judging. We are antecedently situated in a sociohistorical context, and thus we cannot choose the conventions that form our knowledge. We cannot choose them because we are already embedded in them. As Fish puts it: "already-in-place interpretive constructs are a condition of consciousness."[26] However, readers create the meaning, they do not discover preexisting content in the text: "Interpretation is not the art of construing but the art of constructing. Interpreters do not decode poems; they make them."[27] We cannot, according to Fish, compare any given interpretation and evaluate it by the actual text.

Interpretation so conceived is an act of power, not an act of cognition or discovery. There are no final and fixed interpretations to which we must, under pain of charges of irrationality, pledge undying allegiance. At the same time, Fish's concept does not degenerate into the view that he must believe that any interpretation is as sound as any other. While firmly believing that the interpretation he advances is the correct one, he admits that his conviction need not be shared by others, and there is no higher ground from which to adjudicate objectively the dispute.

Fish's subjectivism is, however, constrained by his acknowledgments of professionalism, institutionalism, and contingent power. These are the sources that "give us the values with which we can turn to criticize the whole. . . . There are, at best, alternative 'imaginings.'"[28] Because judges are already situated in and socialized by legal practice, even those who deny the possibility of principled de-cision making in their accounts of judicial interpretation must still engage consistently in the interpretive act. Legal nihilism and un-constrained subjectivism are practical impossibilities because of these antecedent constraints on judges.[29]

Thus, judges must decide legal questions on the basis of their own (often unself-consciously held) biases and assumptions as con-strained by their interpretive communities. Because of the impos-sibility of an internally coherent theory able to generate law in an objective fashion, the contingency and lack of metaphysical founda-tions of the available methods of decision making should not be alarming; they are all we can have. Accordingly, although the Con-stitution is not a repository of preexisting meaning, neither is it a blank slate awaiting and accepting any conceivable interpretation.[30]

Although Fish addresses the potential problem of self-reference, there remains at least one further question in that regard: If we can-not transcend or elude our interpretive constructions, how can we know that they exist and function as Fish supposes?[31] The force of the arguments that Fish uses against Epistemological Foundational-ism and Metaphysical Realism may still also devour his own pre-sumed constraints, or at least our knowledge of them.

Moreover, Fish does not examine the nature or the prescriptive force of our extant institutions and professional contexts. It would seem that their existence cannot by itself render them morally self-validating. This opens Fish to the charge that at bottom he, like Fiss, ends with the crudest sort of conventionalism: mere description masquerading as justification. Fish would, of course, rejoin that this criticism rests on the very belief he repudiates: the possibility of a justification that emerges from a point external to our practices. But there are at least two available responses to Fish. First, he seems to be left with nothing more than rhetorical battles cabined by preex-isting practices—trying to persuade others while knowing that they have no deeper reason to accept his view beyond their immediate attraction to his rhetoric. Fish would not be disturbed by this—he would reiterate that this, in concert with existing legal practice, is all that is available to us, and it is disturbing only if we continue to yearn for the impossible.

Second, there is a stronger response one can make to Fish. Even under his own interpretation of our current situation, we are mem-bers in a variety of interpretive communities and practices, at least some of which allow us to examine and criticize current legal prac-tice and institutions. Thus, it is consistent with his interpretation of our situation that we critically analyze legal practice from the internal vantage point of other (currently existing) interpretive communities and practices. Yet Fish does not do this. He seems satisfied to give the impression (although it is not clear that this is his considered view) that he endorses the prescriptive content of current practice and finds its justification, even in his own limited sense of the term, unnecessary or of secondary importance. Thus the charge of arid conventionalism.

The political fear accompanying the charge of arid conventionalism is that appeals to current practice may further tilt the playing field in favor of the advantaged and against the already disenfranchised. Fish's boundless faith in legal professionalism may well serve to justify further the continued exclusion of various underclasses from full participation in setting the terms of their own existence. Unlike the literary critic or the reader who merely interprets texts, judges wield an authority that has a direct influence on people's lives. If judges are too single-minded in reflecting the practice of their profession, they may be severed from the practices of their wider community.

In a related vein, it is useful to explore the traditional distinction between the context of discovery and the context of justification. Traditionally, scientists and legal theorists contended that there is a difference between the procedures, motivations, and ways by which we discover various truths, and the justifications and explanations by which we demonstrate these discoveries to be truths.[32] Our rational beliefs that a proposition is true, it is often argued, are not necessarily linked with the ways that the proposition was discovered. Under this traditional distinction, a critic can levy a charge against Fish that was often hurled at Legal Realists: even if Fish's description of the way judges make decisions is accurate, that does nothing to address the ways we might justify those decisions. Once again, we return to the question of whether Fish has said anything prescriptively interesting.

Fish, of course, would advance his usual rejoinder: there is no justification of truth beyond the motivations, ways, and procedures employed within a practice to discover truths. The traditional distinction between discovery and justification is fraudulent because it is grounded on the familiar, and ultimately incomprehensible, belief that there can be an Archimedean point by which to judge the claims emerging from our constrained interpretations. But, once again, Fish's rejoinder is troubling. Given that he acknowledges that he cannot make his nonfoundationalism a foundation, Fish may be reduced to the role of rhetorician. He describes his interpretive claims as "a pragmatic strategy by means of which decisions are successfully inserted into a field of practice that requires of its decisions that they be filled with certain forms of talk, in this case with theory talk."[33] But this may well suggest that "Fish is thus not giving us a justification for abandoning metaphysics, only presentational strategies to be used to get others to abandon metaphysics if that is what we want."[34]

There is yet another way in which a subtle appeal to the problem of self-reference haunts Fish. Formulating theory can itself be construed as a practice and should thus be immune from metatheorizing about how such a practice should be done. But Fish seems to engage in precisely this kind of metatheorizing when he informs us that we never apply rules and theories when actually engaging in practice.[35] Moreover, Fish is also a bit too glib in minimizing the impact of theory on practice. As a descriptive matter, judges experience rational constraints in ways that Fish seems to deny.[36]

Furthermore, Fish seems to divorce the writing of judicial opinions from the reaching of the decision itself when he tells us that judicial opinion writing "is not a mechanism by which decisions are generated, but the complex of rhetorical gestures to which one has recourse when a decision, already made, must be put into presentable form."[37] But Fish's use of "presentable form" obscures at least part of what judges are doing: they are using their theories of interpretation to justify their conclusions as the correct interpretation of the extant body of legal materials relevant to the case at bar.[38]

Participants in the interpretivist turn recognize explicitly the need to transcend the objectivist–relativist dilemma; that is, they aspire to reconceive the rational constraints on judicial decision making in ways that neither depend on accepting strong versions of Metaphysical Realism nor embrace Normative Relativism. As such, these thinkers bridge some of the gap between certain versions of analytic jurisprudence and the leftist critique of law. Unfortunately, it is not clear that these thinkers have yet captured the richness of the phenomenology of judicial decision making, understood correctly the respective roles of theory and practice, and distanced themselves adequately from arid conventionalism.

# PART TWO

What's Left of Law?
*Challenging Law's Pretensions*

# CHAPTER 6

## Historical Necessity and Radical Contingency
*Marxist Jurisprudence*

$R$ATHER THAN advancing a refined theory of judicial decision making or puzzling over the nature of law, Marxist jurisprudence offers a critique of liberal–capitalist conceptions of law. As part of its general undermining of bourgeois consciousness, Marxism aspires to manifest the legitimating functions of law as a contributor to ideological distortion and as a solidifier of the political status quo. Accordingly, there is not so much a Marxist theory of law as there is a Marxist unmasking of law's alleged unsavory participation in domination and oppression.

### GENERAL MARXISM

To understand the Marxist critique of law, we must first attend to a few general themes in Marxist thought. I do not intend to advance an innovative or especially controversial interpretation of these general themes; rather, I will adumbrate a standard description of those themes in order to set the stage for the critique of law.

*Alienation.* According to Marxists, alienation results from market forces and the capitalist production process, especially capitalist relations of production, which disenfranchise workers from decision making. Lacking a voice in the production process, workers toil merely to satisfy survival and sustenance needs. As the insipid routinization of capitalist production and its suffocating division of labor overwhelm workers' creative and imaginative capacities, workers are reduced to semihuman extensions of productive machinery. They are thereby estranged from their labor, their employers, their fellow workers, the product, and ultimately from themselves.[1]

Although Marx was not a proponent of a fixed, universal human nature, he viewed alienation as estrangement from historically created human possibilities. His minimalist view of species-being included the conviction that human fulfillment is intimately connected with imaginative, unshackled use of productive capacities. Labor is a distinctively human activity and possesses central normative significance. Humans presumably shape their social world and forge their personal identities through interaction with their material world and its dominant productive process. It is only through free and creative activity that a person realizes unalienated being.[2]

Capitalist social and economic institutions prevent the actualization of workers' potential and thereby disconnect workers from their species-being because they stifle workers' voice, creativity, and imagination; transform labor power itself into a commodity; influence workers to seek the false consolations offered by ideological superstructure; fail to mediate the social aspect of labor by cooperation and solidarity; and produce the ironic and pernicious consequence that the more diligently and more intensely the proletariat class works, the more surplus value is produced, and the greater becomes the power disparity between workers and capitalists.

*Exploitation.* In its most general Kantian–Marxist sense, exploitation occurs when someone uses another person as merely an object for her own benefit without regard for the humanity of that person. In its more particular Marxist sense, exploitation occurs when one class, the proletariat, produces a surplus whose use is controlled by another class, the capitalists.[3] Moreover, the capitalist economic mode differs from other economic modes in that this kind of exploitation occurs absent the use of explicit duress, physical threat, or other noneconomic force. It is through the capitalists' vastly superior economic bargaining power over workers, their ownership of the means of production, and the lack of real alternatives for workers that exploitation flourishes in a capitalist regime. Finally, capitalism, shrouded by its pretensions to neutral, economic processes, is especially pernicious in that it is thereby able to mask the nature and effects of the exploitation of workers.[4]

Capitalists exploit workers by siphoning the surplus value that workers produce by their labor. Capitalists purchase workers' labor power at its value, which is equivalent to a subsistence wage, and sell products at their value. Because the value workers create is greater than the value of labor power itself, surplus value results.

The exploitive nature of the relationship is reflected in the fact that workers do not receive the labor equivalent of what they produce.[5] Moreover, workers' labor is "forced" in the sense that only limited and equally debilitating alternatives are available for workers seeking to satisfy their subsistence requirements.[6] Although there is considerable dispute about precisely which set of necessary and sufficient conditions captures the meaning of Marxist exploitation, the following elements are relevant: workers benefit capitalists; capitalists economically force, in the relevant Marxist sense of that term, workers to supply that benefit; and capitalists wrongfully fail to supply reciprocal benefits to workers.[7]

*Economic Substructure and Ideological Superstructure.* One of Marx's most intriguing and baffling pronouncements concerns the relationship between a society's economic substructure ("the base") and its ideological superstructure ("the superstructure"). A society's mode of economic production includes its forces of production (natural resources, instruments and means of production, workers and their skills, raw materials) and its relations of production (the formal and informal organization of relations among people, or among people and commodities, in the productive process). The base consists, strictly speaking, of the relations of production. The superstructure consists of our political and legal institutions and our forms of social consciousness (what we think, believe, how we understand and experience the world).[8]

It is clear that for Marx the development of the forces of production results in changes in the relations of production. There will come a time when the existing relations of production no longer effectively and efficiently allow the growth of the productive forces. This internal contradiction divides society and will result in the fall of the obsolete set of productive relations.[9] New relations of production will triumph because they have the capacity to facilitate the continued growth of society's productive forces. Thus, Marx provides an economic explanation for political revolution.

But what is his precise meaning concerning the relationship of the base and the superstructure? There are at least three candidates: economic determinism, economic limitation, and economic practice.[10]

*Economic Determinism.* This interpretation holds that the base causes the superstructure, in the sense that our forms of consciousness and the institutions that embody them are the effects of the economic processes of material production. This view suggests that the base is independent of and logically prior to the superstructure.

There are, however, at least three major difficulties with this interpretation.

First, it marginalizes human freedom to the point of fetishizing impersonal economic processes as the animating forces of history. Second, it is clear that the base is not independent of the superstructure. On the contrary, a superstructure of property rights and legal categories is essential for the coherent functioning and sanctioning of productive processes.[11] Third, Engels rejected the crude reductionism reflected in economic determinism by stressing the "ultimate supremacy" of or "determination in the last instance" by the base, which passages concede that elements of the superstructure can produce effects on the base.[12] Moreover, Marx suggested that the relationship of the base and superstructure was historical and complex and that the superstructure was not merely the passive reflector of productive processes.[13] Accordingly, economic determinism unrealistically marginalizes human freedom and serendipitous possibilities and is untrue to the reciprocal interaction between base and superstructure that Marx and Engels sometimes acknowledged.

*Economic Limitation.* This view asserts that the base sets limits on social consciousness; that is, a society's dominant ideologies are constrained in the sense that numerous possible parts of a society's superstructure will not be actualized because those possibilities are incompatible with the society's base.[14] The productive process thus narrows the range of ideas and practices that can gain currency in a society. This interpretation has the advantage of removing the burden of economic determinism from Marx and Engel—it does not insist that the base is the cause of and logically prior to the superstructure. But this gain is purchased at a stiff price: it weakens the Marxist claim about the relationship of the base and superstructure to a point at which many political centrists could agree with Marx and Engel. Portrayed in this fashion, Marxism loses its political bite and becomes too domesticated. Thus, economic limitation is too weak to facilitate Marx's materialistic purposes.[15]

*Economic Practice.* This interpretation has been defended most recently by Richard Schmitt.[16] Under this view, the base is not conceived as consisting of "impersonal economic processes that unfold independent of human wishes and desires, and independent of human thinking and understanding."[17] Rather, the base must also include "what humans do."

> By [the base], Marx means also what human beings do—that is, he refers to their material activities or "production and reproduction." But

those, like all human activities, are thinking activities, because it is the essence of human beings to think about what they do. The distinction between base and superstructure is not one between matter that does not think and thinking that is not material. The base consists of human activities.[18]

Given this refined understanding of the base, the superstructure is viewed as describing, codifying, and defending extant social practices.

The practices that constitute the base may well be understood—people generally know what they are doing—without having been put into words. At some time in the history of a group, the practices are put into words, described, codified, and defended—and these . . . form the superstructure. The base is what we do; the superstructure is how we talk about it . . . it seems eminently plausible that the base determines the superstructure: Our practices determine how we describe and justify them.[19]

The economic practice view willingly renounces the predictive power of the base–superstructure relationship as the price Marxism must pay to avoid worse problems. It still seems to embody the troubling suggestion that the base is logically prior to the superstructure, but it has demonstrable advantages over its two main competitors, and it need not be committed to the position that the base is always logically prior to correspondent intellectual activity in the superstructure. It is also compatible with the Marxist position that a superstructure is needed to organize and stabilize the very base from which it arose.

But the economic practice interpretation triggers different problems. First, it brings a loss of predictive power that may be anathema to a general theory, such as Marxism, that exalts the scientific inevitability and certitude of numerous future events. Second, it expands the elements of the base to include what many Marxists would regard as superstructural elements because not all our social practices seem at first blush to have the requisite materialist connection. Third, it radically threatens the very distinction between base and superstructure: describing, explaining, and justifying our social practices are themselves social practices; describing, explaining, and justifying our first-order descriptions, explanations, and justifications are also social practices; and so it goes. Because talking about what we do is itself inexorably a doing, we may question whether the economic practice interpretation sanctions any clear or useful distinction between base and superstructure. Rather, it is arguable that this interpretation artificially distances the bulk of our social practices from other, specific social practices: our theoretical, introspective reflections on and examinations of all our social practices.

Put this way, the economic practice interpretation may be true but trivial: our social practices, some of which describe, explain, and justify, determine how we describe, explain, and justify! But how could it be otherwise? Alternatively, the economic practice interpretation can salvage a distinction between base and superstructure by showing some principled way to distance the social practices of describing, explaining, and justifying our various social practices from all other social practices that do not describe, explain, and justify our various social practices. This must be accomplished in a non-question-begging fashion that rescues Marxism's scientific pretensions and materialistic aspirations. My suspicion is that the end product of this mission will be an eviscerated historical materialism that lacks the flair and dramatic appeal of "base determines superstructure."

All this is complicated further when applied to law. Because law seems to function in both the base and superstructure, however they are conceived, Marxists have distanced themselves from relentless use of the base–superstructure model when discussing law.[20] Accordingly, whatever the general persuasiveness of the base–superstructure model, modern Marxists wisely acknowledge that this model has limited specific utility when applied to law.

*False Consciousness.* The term "false consciousness" suggests an inverted representation of reality, a representation that Marxists believe is systematically misleading and socially mystifying in that it misrepresents what are in fact the interests of the ruling class as the natural, common interests of society. This misrepresentation, which flows from the superstructure, justifies, stabilizes, and reinforces the social and political status quo. A person who holds a view that is the result of false consciousness is unaware of the underlying motives and causal processes by which she came to accept that view.[21]

"False consciousness" is used specifically when oppressed classes adopt the dominant ideology and perceptual prism. When these dominant ideas do not truly correspond to the experience of the oppressed classes, ideological distortion occurs.[22] Such distortions have a functional explanation: they legitimate the ruling classes' monopoly on power by depicting current social relations as natural, appropriate, or inevitable. In this fashion, the interests of the ruling class misrepresent themselves as universal human interests. Thus, a particular class's perspective comes to prevail on the members of subordinate classes. There is often a tension, which can intensify into contradiction and eventually revolution, between the ideological prism acquired through socialization and the subordinate class's experiences accumulated in productive activity.

A belief is ideological only if it would perish upon the revelation of its causal origins. Because the relationship between false consciousness and nonideological perception cannot be interpreted validly as a species of the general relationship between illusion and truth, ideological distortion cannot be overcome solely by intellectual criticism. Ideological distortion is not the opposite of truth but is, instead, a narrow or one-sided rendering of truth that functions to preserve the practices of the ruling class. Hence, false consciousness dissolves only when the internal contradictions of an economic system—especially evident when relations of production can no longer efficiently make use of developing technology—are practically resolved.[23]

When philosophical adversaries report conclusions or arguments that deny Marxism's central aspirations, they frequently are accused of promulgating the ideological distortions of false consciousness. In effect, Marxism too quickly charges that liberal–capitalists verify certain Marxist tenets by the very way these liberal–capitalists try to refute Marxism. This is not to say that the notion of false consciousness is without currency. There is much truth to the observation that certain views may be the unconscious, conditioned reflection of economic and social oppression and that subordinate classes often become accomplices in their own torment by internalizing the very dominant ideologies that contribute to their mistreatment.

But if applied relentlessly, the notion of false consciousness loses much of its critical bite. If the notion is advanced as a nonrefutable thesis, if all denials of Marxism are taken to be affirmations of the doctrine of false consciousness, then the notion of false consciousness is trivial. Any subjective report that denies any basic Marxist conclusion seems too easily and automatically to stigmatize itself. Marxists dismiss the content of a view because it allegedly can be explained by its determinants. Moreover, such a posture demeans the experiences, and not merely the ideologies, of Marxism's philosophical rivals. In fact, subjective reports of one's inner condition or of one's ideological commitments are neither incorrigibly true nor self-refuting. The challenge for a Marxist is to delineate without begging the question under what circumstances such reports and commitments do and do not reflect veridical perceptions correlated to wider experience.[24]

*Dialectical Method.* Although I can scarcely begin to do justice to the complexities of Marx's dialectical method in a few sentences, it is important to sketch at least a few characteristics of it. The method stresses the process of conflict, antagonism, and contradiction as necessary for progress. Truth is reached, or approximated, by the conflict of ideas; and social change occurs because of class conflict and contradictions in a society's economic substructure. The conflict of opposite views is necessary because each position, taken by itself, contains a partial or one-sided insight into a larger truth. In the same way a thesis (a starting point) evolves into its antithesis (opposite) and then into a synthesis (a balance), earlier stages of the dialectic prefigure and are transformed by later stages. Each stage provides what was lacking in the preceding stage while developing what was of value.

The dialectic has more dramatic shifts and less stable points of equilibrium than more conventional notions of progress. It underscores the mutual dependence of opposites and the partiality and provisionality of current conceptions. It is purported to apply not merely to intellectual progress but also to how humans evolve social life under specific material conditions. Conceiving of societies as organic wholes, Marx reiterates that social change results from contradictions within society's base. However, a sympathetic reading of Marx allows that he did not intend that the dialectic be viewed as a logic that superseded formal logic.[25]

## CRITIQUE OF LIBERAL–CAPITALIST NOTIONS OF LAW

Marxists refuse to construct elaborate jurisprudential theories because they insist that to do so reduces them to being participants in the liberal–capitalist fetishism of law.

*The Fetishism of Law.* The term *fetishism* connotes an unnecessary and distracting obsession. Fetishism involves conferring specific characteristics on objects or concepts, characteristics that take on the aura of being inherent, while in fact they are present because of prevailing social and economic arrangements. The fetishism of law in liberal–capitalist regimes is alleged to be manifest in at least three ways: (1) the necessity of law, (2) the autonomy of law, and (3) the desirability of the Rule of Law.[26]

*The Necessity of Law.* Encomiums to law flow freely in the rhetoric of liberal–capitalist regimes. Law is seen as the body of rules and principles that preserve what is best about humans and protect us all from what is worst. Apologists portray a refined legal system as that which holds a community together, facilitates the progress of civilization, and redeems us from the anarchy of a Hobbesian state of nature.[27]

Marxists deny the inevitability of law. First, they place greater trust than do liberal–capitalists in the informal, customary prescriptions and prohibitions that hold a culture together. Second, and more important, they view the necessity of law as emanating from presocialist historical and economic situations. Liberal–capitalists may be correct that law is necessary in the kinds of regimes they have known. But Marxists are committed to the rise of a new set of social relations in which claims of legal necessity ring hollow.

The inevitable collapse of capitalism—due to the failure of its relations of production to make effective, efficient use of its forces of production—will pave the way for the elimination of the conditions that nurture class division. The elimination of class division speeds along the end of capitalist alienation and exploitation, which, in turn, will permit socialist relations of production to facilitate economic growth.

The transformation of the relations of production and the elimination (or near elimination) of the conditions of scarcity bring about the context from which societal relations can be reimagined and remade. Human social relations and experience will no longer be tyrannized by the pernicious antinomy of self versus others. The perplexing tension between individuality, our felt need to maintain our specialness and uniqueness when confronted by others, and community, our felt need for intimacy, connection, and bonding, will be radically transformed. Because Marxists believe generally that the state and ideological superstructure function to maintain and legitimate class domination and exploitation, the elimination of class division allows much (perhaps most) of the superstructure to "wither away." Marx's mature positon was that law was fundamentally superstructural—a reflection of the ruling class's needs and interests as developed from the conditions of the base. Accordingly, Marxists view with suspicion liberal–capitalists' claims of the necessity of law.

*The Autonomy of Law.* Liberal–capitalists allegedly herald the independence and uniqueness of law to add to law's mystique. Hugh Collins describes the autonomy of law as consisting of three dimensions.

First, there are regular patterns of institutional arrangements associated with law, such as the division between a legislature and a judiciary. Second, lawyers communicate with each other through a distinctive mode of discourse, though the exact nature of legal reasoning remains controversial. Third, legal systems are distinguished from simple exercises of force by one group over another; for legal rules also function as normative guides to behavior which individuals follow regardless of the presence or absence of officials threatening to impose sanctions or failing to comply with the law. Together these three features of law, its institutional framework, its methodology, and its normativity, are considered to make law a unique phenomenon.[28]

Marxists scoff at liberal–capitalist claims of law's uniqueness. True to the primacy it places on economic substructure, Marxism is reluctant to champion law as a separate aspect of social life. Rather, Marxists are more likely to underscore law's complicity in "the manipulation of power and the consolidation of modes of production of wealth."[29] Law is taken to be another part of the superstructure that tends to mask the reality of the base and that contributes to the illusions of false consciousness. Furthermore, although law is superstructural, it functions in the economic base as the definer of productive and property relations.

*The Rule of Law.* Liberal–capitalist systems consistently extol the allegedly formal and necessary Rule of Law virtues: like cases must be decided alike; there can be no ex post facto law; notice must be given to citizens of the laws' requirements; laws must be crafted generally and impersonally; and the most fundamental aim of a legal system must be the impartial application of law and the principled restraint of the power of legal officials.

Marxists view the Rule of Law as a primary culprit in the liberal–capitalist legitimation of the status quo. The seductions of paeans to due process and to the principled restraint on the power of legal officials function to defend the naturalness of existing social arrangements. Behind the Rule of Law's mask of formal neutrality lies a conglomeration of processes, doctrines, and structures that serve generally to advance certain class interests and to defeat or marginalize other class interests. The formal equality of the Rule of Law places an imprimatur on substantive inequality. Yet the individualistic presuppositions and intoxicating effects of Rule of Law rhetoric impede the development of class consciousness. Thus, Marxists tend, not to praise the Rule of Law, but to interrogate it; not to offer a set of necessary and sufficient conditions for the existence of the

Rule of Law, but to ask what functions the Rule of Law has served and whose interests it has advanced.[30]

*The Critique of Law.* It should now be clear that the Marxist critique of law has two main elements: (1) a functional explanation of the legal system and (2) a firm conviction in the contingency of law.

First, to avoid participating in the fetishism of law, Marxists cannot treat law as if it were unique and independent. Thus, when they examine the functions of law, they take their object to be that which is conventionally perceived as law.[31]

We have already sketched Marxism's reductionist explanation of the function of law: law serves the interests of the ruling class. But Marxists have come to see this reductionist explanation as too crude to portray accurately the machinations of the modern capitalist state. The ruling class, the owners of the means of production, have much less direct control over the workings of government than they did in the days of Marx and Engels. Moreover, there seem to be numerous examples of the intervention of the government and the legal system that have enfranchised workers and the underclasses at the expense of the narrowly conceived interests of the owners. When confronting the myriad changes capitalism has undergone, alterations which have prevented the collapse of capitalism that early Marxists insisted was imminent, modern socialists advance the notion of the relative autonomy of law to refine the reductionism of their predecessors.[32]

Under this view, one of the most important functions of law is ideological. Law plays the fundamental role of preserving the status quo. Not only is there a conservative bias built into law by Rule of Law doctrines such as the observance of precedent and faithfulness to the intentions and policies of the past, but law assumes a paramount educative role. Law interprets and resolves social conflicts and relationships, mediates the potentially disruptive tensions in economic substructure, and issues authoritative proclamations that purport to be the product of an objective, neutral, rational process. As such, the dominant ideology is filtered through a series of legal surrogates, purified of direct contamination by the ruling class, sanctified as the outcome of eminently fair procedures, and solidified as part of society's core common-sense normative beliefs. As citizens further internalize the decrees of law and come to accept these judgments as their own, they are further victimized by the ideological distortions of false consciousness and are thereby less likely to vent the rage necessary for meaningful social transformation. Marxists contend that in this manner the dominant ideology secures the consent of the oppressed in their own oppression. To put a finer point on it: because of the power of its educative function, law is in part the instrument by which the disenfranchised become accomplices in their own subordination.

I must stress, however, that Marxists are not contending that state officials are engaged in a self-conscious, grand conspiracy that seizes law as its bludgeon. The educative role of law is not a linear, relentless indoctrination by the dominant ideology. Because contradictions in the economic base give rise to counterpart tensions in ideological superstructure, legal officials can be viewed as mediators not merely of particular disputes among citizens but also of potentially disruptive economic and ideological disharmony. The dominant ideology itself is not a fully coherent, monolithic whole. Moreover, there are usually competing ideologies, articulated to varying degrees, that confront the dominant ideology.[33]

The legitimating and educative functions of ideology grant Marxists the ability to transcend crude instrumentalism and permit them to underscore the fashion in which certain ideas become entrenched as common sense.[34] The mediating role of ideology allows Marxism to refine crude instrumentalism, but at a price. What passes for a "dominant ideology" in liberal–capitalist regimes is hardly a solidified, fixed body of doctrine from which specific, determinate conclusions must be drawn. Moreover, specific laws and their justifications are not easily linked, clearly and inexorably, to material conditions in the economic base. Because specific laws themselves admit to interpretation and their genesis is rarely unambiguous, Marxism seems to have two choices. One is to downplay the link between the material base and the content of law, highlight the relative autonomy of law and the superstructure, and soften its depiction of dominant ideology. Such concessions to plasticity make Marxism more plausible but attenuate and domesticate the radical panache of historical materialism and scientific socialism.

Alternatively, Marxism can give ad hoc analyses of specific laws, analyses which purport to show how the dominant ideology provides an indirect linkage of the material base to those laws. This approach aspires to preserve the integrity of historical materialism and scientific socialism, but it is highly improbable that its piecemeal explanations would ever constitute a coherent whole. As such, this approach could be seen as circular apologetics: Marxists have a theory that says the material base B is indirectly linked to law by dominant ideology I; here is a given law L; L is linked to B by I in the following way W, but W may be quite different from (and perhaps incompatible with) the other Ws by which other Ls are linked to B. The main difficulty with circular apologetics is that its various explanations are so elastic that they do not admit of possible refutations and thus trivialize themselves.

This unappealing journey between the Charybdis of servility and the Scylla of triviality results from the tensions in Marxism's understanding of the relationship between base and superstructure, its acknowledgment of relative autonomy, its commitment to scientific socialism, its understanding of the role of ideology, and the reality of law. All is not lost: Marxism is left with several general, plausible claims about the structure and form of law, but these lack the explanatory specificity and political acuteness to which Marxism originally aspired.

The second Marxist critique, the denial of the necessity of law, is closely linked with its exposition of the functions of law. Because Marxists deny that those legitimating, educative, and mediating functions will be required in the "final form" of society, law will wither away along with other superstructural elements.

Lenin is credited with being "the first to subscribe explicitly to the thesis that law will wither away in a Communist society."[35] But even he conceded that a communist society would require customary normative rules and principles to guide social life. The emphasis here is on less formal action by fellow citizens—ranging from social disapproval to sanctions administered by "comrades' courts"—and away from highly institutionalized dispute resolution conducted primarily by state officials. This difference in emphasis manifests the conviction that a society lacking class division has no need for and cannot logically sustain institutionalized forms, such as law, that promote primarily the interests of one class. In a society where the antinomy between individual and community is transformed, the entire society will affirm and protect its normative foundation.[36]

There is another reason Marxists deny the necessity of law. Often—perhaps usually—liberal–capitalists argue that law is necessary to constrain humans, who are by nature self-interested, motivated by material incentives, and competitive. It is claimed that law is required to enforce the social contract that itself is required to mediate our baser strivings and selfishness. But Marxists deny any thick and substantial notion of human nature. They insist that liberal–capitalists have such a notion because their economic base encourages, sustains, and rewards the very traits that come to be seen as natural. The familiar processes and products of legitimation and fetishism, not inherent human attributes, give rise to our commonsense belief that law is necessary to save us from ourselves. Once humans are liberated from the productive relations and other material vestiges that nourish this commonsense conviction, they will be empowered to transcend those traits hitherto thought of as inherent and untransformable. Marxists believe generally in the plasticity of human nature and subscribe only to a thin notion of inherent human attributes: our species-being consists of our collective ability to change our traits along with our material circumstances, and our general predisposition to find fulfillment in unalienated labor. Accordingly, the fall of capitalism and the emergence of communism provide the presuppositions for a classless society, unalienated labor, collective human transformation, and the end of law.

Some non-Marxists have argued that the flair of the slogan "law will wither away" is misleading for two reasons. First, Marxists concede that even under communism, the final form of society, "there will be both rules for the administration of a planned economy and elementary rules of social life."[37] But these are not termed "laws" because under communism they would not function as instruments of class oppression: in the final form of society, differentiated classes, and thus class struggle itself, have vanished. Accordingly, it may well appear that "the whole thesis of the withering away of law rests upon the dubious definitional fiat that rules which serve any other purpose than class oppression cannot be law."[38] Second, there seem to be functions of law that go beyond class struggle: "It is hard to connect laws concerning abortion, drugs, homosexuality, and rape with the instrumental pursuit of their interests by the ruling class."[39] There is reason to believe that such laws would not pass from sight even if communism were realized.

There is merit to both points, but neither is totally devastating to Marxism's aims. The first remark raises the question of whether the radicality of claims about the contingency of law rests on a mere tautology: "law" is stipulated as that which serves class oppression; there is at least one society in which class oppression is not necessary, or even possible; therefore, law is not necessary, or even possible, in all societies. While it is true that stipulative definitions generally produce uninteresting conclusions, we should not take this semantic quibble as fatal to Marxism's goals. Indeed, its main purpose here is to undermine liberal–capitalist dogma that law is what necessarily holds any society together, what preserves the best and discourages the worst in us. Seen in this light, the thrust of Marxism is that eliminating class division, effacing the distinction between individual and community, and facilitating opportunities for unalienated labor are the more fundamental ways to bind a society and to actualize our species-being. The prime error of legal fetishism is that by privileging law by proclaiming law's necessity, it deflects attention from the more essential conditions required for human progress. Thus, Marxism perceives the unwavering commitment to the necessity of law as an ideological obstacle to societal transformation.

At first blush, the second remark seems unassailable. In a communist society there would be deviants to whom the structure must respond. Moreover, even within a class or in a classless society, personal relations among members admit to regulation. Furthermore, contemporary socialist doctrine has seemingly acknowledged this: even prior to glasnost and perestroika, we have witnessed an increase in the importance of law in socialist societies.[40]

But, again, Marxism is not defenseless. It would probably try to account for the nature and extent of deviant behavior in our time by pointing to economic scarcity, alienated relations of production, and ideological distortions. A truly communist society would presumably ameliorate such conditions and the concomitant behavior. Moreover, we must also note the "while law has grown into an indispensable principle of social organization in the civilization of the West due to the particular historicity of that civilization, that is not the case with other civilizations wherein law and its concomitant principles, such as equality of humans, are deemed, as in China and Japan, as dehumanizing."[41]

Still, the critics' point seems powerful: not all law is eliminable even in a communist paradise. But, remember that Marxism acknowledges the need for elementary rules governing social life and for community pressure as a response to destructive behavior. It is not as if Marxism is now or ever was blind to the critics' point.

Marxism begins by castigating liberal–capitalist claims of necessity and inherency in the areas of human nature, social relations, and the legal order. Ironically, Marxism itself ends with a series of necessitarian claims: the inevitable fall of capitalism and rise of communism, the apodictic withering away of law, and the incontestable metamorphosis of the human species. Infatuated by a particular, distorted view of the methods of the natural sciences, Marxists peer back at the past and assert confidently the existence of historical and economic laws.

But the evidence that is the past does not come so unambiguously packaged. The data underdetermine any particular theory and admit to numerous interpretations. Those who look back and try to harness these data into a coherent whole usually find what they seek: they begin with an intuition or hypothesis about the future, project this vision onto the indeterminate meanderings of history, and selectively embrace past events that are consistent with their original vision. They put the rabbit in the hat, pull it out, and then proclaim their insights to the world. Unfortunately, their claims of necessity ring at least as hollow as those of their philosophical rivals. Post-Marxian history has not revealed the working class to be the vanguard of the communist revolution, and it has not manifested a pattern of revolutionary activity in advanced capitalist countries; instead, it has witnessed capitalism maintain its basic structure while incorporating numerous marginal adjustments that have permitted it to mediate its alleged internal contradictions.

Marxists appear to have been trapped by their own presupposition that only an objective analysis of the social order, an examination based on their simplistic view of the natural sciences, could claim persuasively to have eluded the mystification of liberal–capitalist false consciousness. While liberal–capitalist ideology may well be hostage, to one degree or another, to social practices and material conditions, so, too, Marxist ideology may well be a pawn to this simplistic view of the natural sciences.

It is not so obvious, although it is probable, that critics are correct in thinking that in a communist society not all of that which is conventionally described as "law" can disappear. Even if taken literally, however, it has not been proved that Marxism's claim that law will wither away is either plainly false or trivially (tautologically) true. Moreover, taken less strictly, the claim serves several Marxist purposes: it highlights the fundamental changes required for human progress, changes allegedly retarded by paeans to law's necessity; it insists that numerous layers of institutionalized legal mechanisms must be viewed as unessential; it reveals the allegedly reactionary implications of our sanctification of law; and it challenges us to reconceive a nonlegal response to the polarity of self and others. All these theses, whether ultimately convincing, retain much vibrancy and provide difficult challenges to conventional wisdom.

Although Marxism's depiction of law seems at times reductionist or simplistic and at other times does not hang coherently with general Marxist theory, much remains about it that resonates in history. Marxist themes about the contingency, relative autonomy, and functions of law are refined in later movements such as Legal Realism, Critical Legal Studies, and feminist jurisprudence. Mark Tushnet captures this sentiment well when he says that in one sense Marxism is the only remaining secular view that is committed to fighting domination wherever it occurs. . . . Law may be taken as a metaphor for all those facets of our social relationships that seem to us necessary for us to get along in the world and that also seem somehow imposed on us. Marxism is then a metaphor for a world of radical contingency, in which we know that social regularities are constructed by our own actions, have no life of their own, and may be challenged and reconstructed whenever and however we want.[42]

This, then, is Marxism's ultimate irony: despite its original pretensions to scientific objectivity and historical necessity, its greatest legacy may be its challenge to those very pretensions and its affirmation of radical contingency. Seen in this light, Marxism's own internal contradictions dialectically generate its most profound contribution.

# CHAPTER 7

## The Fundamental Contradiction and Nihilism
### *Critical Legal Studies*

$\mathbf{C}$RITICAL LEGAL STUDIES (CLS) is the name applied to a movement composed of heterogeneous thinkers whose views are held together, if at all, by three common themes: the radical indeterminacy of law, law's complicity in political legitimation and mystification, and the ideological foundation of law.[1]

## COMMON THEMES

*Radical Indeterminacy.* CLS denies that there is a pure method of analysis that is capable of yielding determinate answers to legal questions. There is no self-evident point where justification of received opinion ends and revision must begin; that is, there is no available metalogic capable of determining the correct relationship between justification and revision. Rejecting the possibility of an immanent moral rationality, CLS also dismisses the possibility that legal doctrine can be articulated by a single coherent theory.[2] CLS takes the radical indeterminacy of law to imply that legal reasoning cannot be validly contrasted with political rhetoric. Hence, law is nothing more than the product of the contingent outcomes of power struggles, historical accidents, and ideological conflict.

*Political Legitimation.* CLS claims that traditional jurisprudential theories mystify and often deny the value choices inevitable in the selection and application of legal rules. Political legitimation, in part, results from law's complicity in proclaiming the political status quo as fundamentally correct, as corresponding to a transcendentally appropriate standard, or as resulting from an inherently fair process of choice. The practical result of this (usually subconscious) legitimation process is to freeze the fundamental terms of social debate, refract social conflict, and thereby constrict the possibilities for widespread political destabilization. In contrast, CLS asserts that no particular scheme of human association has conclusive authority.[3]

*Law as Ideology.* CLS contends that law can be manipulated to "justify" numerous rationalizations for various outcomes. Moreover, a plausible argument can be made that any of these rationalizations and their corresponding outcomes have been predetermined by pre-existing legal doctrine. This is true because legal doctrine is nothing more than an elaborate, highly stylized vocabulary and litany of manipulable techniques for categorizing, describing, and comparing; it is not a method for reaching substantive outcomes.[4]

Instead, competing visions of ideal conceptions of moral good, political right, economic welfare, and social justice animate law. Law provides another arena where ideologies engage each other in battle, where temporary victories are earned, and warring theories advance and retreat during the social and economic flux of history. This ubiquitous ideological conflict is unremitting and unarbitrable—it cannot be mediated by any neutral arbitrator or through appeals to objectively grounded metaethical or metaepistemological principles.[5]

*Distinctive Features.* Three features of CLS are of special interest: its claim that the incoherence of legal doctrine is a result of a more general metaphysical problem, "the fundamental contradiction"; the nature of its allegations about the pervasive indeterminacy of law; and its attempts to confront directly the charge that CLS is self-refuting and thus nihilistic.

The fundamental contradiction, CLS proclaims, is that legal and political conflict are at the heart of human experience: our yearning for intimate connection with others and the recognition that others are necessary for our identity and freedom coalesces uneasily with the fear and anxiety we experience as others approach.[6] We simultaneously long for emotional attachment yet are horrified that our individuality may evaporate once we achieve it. These impulses are thought to be contradictory because our desire for close personal connections and our desire for radical individuality cannot be fulfilled simultaneously.

CLS takes the liberal regime of rights to be a device intended to mediate, or even deny, the presence of the fundamental contradiction and thereby disguise our "painfully contradictory feelings about actual relations between persons in our social world."[7] Such rights delude us into believing that individualism and collectivism each has a natural proper sphere, and that rational analysis of doctrine can determine or discover those spheres. But, according to CLS, pretending through rational analysis to find the separation between, for example, state coercion that violates individual freedom and state coercion that is necessary to facilitate that freedom only reiterates the problem. The unresolvable contradiction will reemerge at each level of generality and at each stage of analysis. Legal doctrine, says CLS, is replete with instances of the fundamental contradiction, such as the battle between the use of bright-line rules and the exercise of ad hoc standards as ways of resolving disputes; the tussle between a devotion to maintaining the fact–value distinction and a commitment to obliterating that distinction; and the scuffle between commitment to the intentionalist discourse of human free will and dedication to the determinist discourse of social conditioning.[8]

Mainstream legal thought, it is argued, privileges one of the impulses of the fundamental contradiction and marginalizes the other. The privileged impulse is treated as the descriptive and prescriptive rule governing the bulk of cases, while the opposing impulse is relegated to governing a small pocket of exceptions.[9] Camouflaging the reality that rational and normative imperatives do not force the choice that was made, the law conspires with the process of political socialization to "beautify" the privileged impulse as natural and morally required. In this manner, the legal process helps to suffocate the possibility of pervasive political debate over the fundamental terms of social life.

In fact, says CLS, subsuming a legal case under one set of rules and principles rather than another demands a choice between the opposing impulses of the contradiction.[10] All attempts to conjure law as coherent and determinate are efforts to mollify our existential dilemma and distract us from the irresistible connection between power and political–legal results. Thus, the fundamental contradiction is at once an insurmountable obstacle to the discovery of firm general resolutions to legal questions and an invitation for society to construct intellectual smoke screens to obscure from our consciousness the inevitability of nonrational choice in legal decision making.

Much of what CLS avers on this issue is alluring. Many, perhaps all, of us do experience the dread of simultaneous attraction and repulsion at the approach of others. Moreover, this disharmony may never be fully reconciled once and forever, and so we find ourselves making uneasy compromises and adjustments during our life's journey. If this fundamental contradiction is indeed so pervasive, it is not implausible to suspect that its effects might resonate in legal and moral reasoning.

But prior to donning our "CLS Does It More Existentially" T-shirts, we should pause and consider a few questions: Do we truly endure these conflicting impulses in the uncompromised way CLS describes? Are they really contradictions? Is the dichotomous analysis that CLS employs the result of the fundamental contradiction? Or is it the creator of that phenomenon?

By explicitly invoking the term "contradiction" CLS makes itself vulnerable to a straightforward interrogation from the minions of propositional logic: few, if any, persons experience the tension between individualism and community as contradictions. Do we truly desire, even for a moment, a total and unqualified individuality that would make us completely immune to external intrusion? Do we truly desire, even for a moment, a total and unqualified immersion into community such that we are indistinguishable from "the one"? To be contradictions, one of these extreme impulses must be true and the other false at any particular moment. It is more likely that these conflicting impulses are contraries: they cannot both be true but both may be false at any particular moment.

It is misleading to announce the discovery of two uncompromising impulses, both of which are necessarily beyond our attainment. In fact it is probably the case that we antecedently desire precisely what we end up with: a mixture of individualism and community, a measure of both the experience of specialness and uniqueness, and the fulfillment of intimate connection with others. On a more mundane level, I may enjoy immensely the gustatory delights of fettucini alfredo but also take pride in my trim figure and low cholesterol level. Am I now beset by a fundamental contradiction by virtue of which I am paralyzed from making principled dietary decisions? I suspect not. My impulse was never to eat all and only fettucini, nor is my conflicting desire a motivation never to indulge in an iota of fat or cholesterol-producing food. Through use of judgment and a minimum of rational reflection I can satisfy both impulses more or less to the degree I antecedently desired. Accordingly, I suspect that the alleged fundamental contradiction besetting humans is more of this sort than the dramatic existential crisis that CLS reports.

Critics can reasonably charge that CLS is, indeed, trapped in the false dichotomy of thinking that, unless a distrinction can be mechanically and uncontroversially delineated, then it is an imposter. The antidote to such thinking is the acceptance of complexity, fallibility, and imprecision as part of human rationality. CLS will retort that it does not claim that normative reason is affected by mere tension, conflict, or disharmony; rather, it claims that the fundamental contradiction permeates rationality. As such, no principled reconciliation is possible, and appeals to the acceptance of the critics' looser standard are irrelevant.

But it is precisely the presence of contradictions that I dispute here. On my view, CLS has inflated the presence of human internal opposition and disharmony into caricatured claims of logical contradiction. My fettucini illustration concerns a rather trivial matter of personal taste, but the point remains: the dichotomous form of analysis favored by many in CLS invites hyperbole.[11] It lures CLS into distorting the content of our competing impulses and endowing them with the potency to disable principled rational reflection. This need not be true in mundane matters or in legal decision making unless we mistakenly accept the very objectivist–relativist duality that incinerated the vigor of the formalist–realist debate.

*Pervasive Indeterminacy.* CLS repeats and then transcends Legal Realism's indeterminacy manifesto. While agreeing with those realists who stress the referential vagueness of legal rules and principles, CLS accents its own metaphysical postulate that the legal system, mirroring the fundamental contradiction experienced by humans, embodies contradictory justificatory schemes that generate opposite results in specific cases. Independent of the indeterminacy of language, there is necessarily present an indeterminacy of normative vision. Assuming that we are all simultaneously enticed to contradictory world images, judges must necessarily make political choices when selecting and applying preexisting legal doctrine. This is true because all such doctrine will contain conflicting elements that echo the fundamental contradictions of their creators.[12]

Moreover, functionalist explanations of law, whether endorsed by the political right or political left, are suspect because studies have shown no consistent link between various societies' social and economic conditions and their legal statutes and decisions. Also, it is unclear that any attempted generalized legal response will receive the same interpretation at its various levels of application.[13]

This is not to say that legal practice within our country is widely unpredictable or arbitrary. CLS recognizes that legal insiders and savvy outsiders, based on their knowledge of current political trends and the views of the officials in charge, can formulate solid expectations of how most legal questions will be decided. But notice that predictability here gestates from factors external to judges' explicit arguments and rationales. In fact, CLS announces with stentorian bravado its belief that centrist–capitalist regimes privilege the classical liberal–individualist values while marginalizing the more socialistic communitarian values. However, CLS alleges that the marginalized principles, those that would radically destabilize current political practice, are always available, for they are already embodied in preexisting legal doctrine.[14]

The force of the indeterminacy thesis is parasitic on the persuasiveness of the fundamental contradiction thesis. Thus, to cast doubt on the latter is to question the former. But there are a few nuances here to add to the previous criticism of CLS.

First, we must interrogate CLS about the meaning of "legal indeterminacy." That term might mean, among other possibilities, "without ability to aid in arriving at legal conclusions" or "unable to compel or dictate specific legal answers."[15] Under the first interpretation legal doctrine is irrelevant to judicial decision making, while under the second, legal doctrine in itself is insufficient to explain legal answers.

The first interpretation implicitly assumes another improbable reductionist dilemma: either the selection and application of legal doctrine is fully determinate or judicial decision making is fully indeterminate. Embracing such an assumption puts CLS in league with extreme formalists–extreme realists. Thus, this first interpretation seems too uncompromising, even for CLS. CLS has trumpeted the importance of legal doctrine as a way of destabilizing the political status quo and unsettling vested power.[16] Moreover, legal doctrine seems important on CLS' terms as a normative embodiment of the fundamental contradiction. Finally, the phenomenology of legal decision making certainly includes the experience of insiders taking preexisting doctrine seriously. Even if they are mistaken in doing so, the fact remains that their thinking and actions will be, at least in a limited way, a self-fulfilling prophecy.

The second interpretation more likely constitutes CLS' favored position. But CLS needs to say more. Most traditional and contemporary legal theories will admit an element of politics and interpretation in judicial decision making but not join in CLS' bolder conclusions.[17] Only an extreme formalist would think that legal doctrine is self-executing and thus sufficient to explain and justify judicial decision making. On one hand, if CLS is merely claiming that legal doctrine underdetermines judicial conclusions, then its position is subdued and is compatible with a host of mainstream theories, because several (non-CLS) contemporary theorists accept that the selection and application of legal material is not strictly required by logic.[18] But they also accept, apparently contrary to CLS, that the selection and application of legal material are not unconnected to rationality and are not merely a matter of choice and passion. Accordingly, CLS must take a more defiant position to distance itself from the competing theories it disdains. On the other hand, any bolder claim comes perilously close to accepting the anachronistic reductionist dilemma that judicial decision making must be either fully determinate or fully indeterminate.

Robert Gordon describes the indeterminacy thesis in this way.

> The same body of law, in the same context, can always lead to contrary results. This is because law is indeterminate at its core, in its inception, not just in its applications: because its rules derive from structures of thought (collective constructs of many minds) that are fundamentally contradictory.[19]

Under Gordon's interpretation, it is not that legal doctrine is irrelevant but that its rules and principles always direct us to contradictory conclusions. Judges must, therefore, make choices concerning classification, selection, and application, choices not compelled by legal doctrine.

But how far is Gordon willing to go? Surely he is not saying that a particular judge cannot make decisions that form (more or less) a coherent whole, for he would accept the significant predictability of law. Moreover, he cannot be saying merely that judicial decision making involves politics, for that is a posture many contemporary opponents of CLS accept. Finally, if he means only that different judges acting in good faith and attending closely to the presumed boundaries of the judicial role can arrive at different conclusions, we must still wonder what is unique here, the allegation that doctrine does not strictly necessitate conclusions? The accusation that there is contradiction, not merely disharmony, in law? The claim that this contradiction bursts forth from human thought patterns afflicted by the fundamental contradiction? The revelation that inherent doctrinal instability leads to inevitable legal change?

The first possibility—that doctrine does not necessitate conclusions—seems merely to mirror a much-acknowledged precept: evidence or doctrine underdetermines conclusions. The second and third possibilities—that contradiction saturates law because of the fundamental contradiction besetting humans—is dubious given what has been said earlier. The fourth possibility—the inevitability of legal change—can be accepted by most CLS opponents, although their attribution of the reasons underlying change will differ greatly.[20]

In sum, CLS equivocates when using the rhetoric of indeterminacy. At its most persuasive, the movement points out forcefully that legal doctrine underdetermines judicial conclusions and that legal decision making implicates politics; however, although CLS's manner of revelation may be distinguishable from other theories, the underdeterminacy thesis has been advanced by others. At its most radical and daring, the movement appears to deny the rational connection between legal doctrine and judicial conclusions, but this at bottom may depend on CLS' acceptance of yet another disreputable instantiation of the objectivist–relativist dichotomy.

*Nihilism.* Much as ethnic slurs enrage those who are proud of their national heritage, no charge more inflames a member of CLS than the accusation that CLS is nihilistic.[21] It is not difficult to figure out why such a charge is levied against CLS. The argument supporting CLS' attack on centrist ideology, adhering as it does to social contingency, jurisprudential indeterminacy, and pervasive conditionality flowing from the fundamental contradiction, seems to preclude CLS from establishing a normative justification for its own vision. CLS' critical attack seems to cut the heart from all efforts to provide non–question-begging adjudication of epistemological and moral truth claims.

This nihilistic paradox, in which CLS' critical attack is so extreme that it prohibits CLS from constructing persuasively its own alternative vision, is occasioned by an equivocation in CLS' main theses: its explicit denial of foundationalism and objectivism and its implicit use of objectivist standards when criticizing other jurisprudential views. On one hand, CLS truculently declares that we lack independent grounding and univocal justification for the conceptual grid that animates our perceptions of the world, for any attempt to articulate such a justification occurs within the boundaries of that world and grid. Spurning the presence of an a priori bridge that might link our conceptual grid to a transcendent metaphysical linchpin,[22] CLS pays homage instead to our unresolvable fundamental contradiction. On the other hand, when criticizing other jurisprudential views, CLS reveals itself as composed of frustrated supraobjectivists who posit a standard of reasoning and argument for normative debate too lofty and inaccessible for human (nontrivial) conceptual endeavors: straightforward deductive argument from unmanipulable, true premises. Once it demonstrates the inability of centrist–capitalist ideology to attain this standard, CLS snickers, smugly proclaims its skepticism, and takes sanctuary within the bosom of the fundamental contradiction.[23] Accordingly, when shrieks of "nihilism" flow freely from the mouths of critics, CLS may well be reaping what it has sown.

Some CLS members directly confront the nihilistic paradox and attempt to eviscerate it by denying that political and legal commitment needs or should seek rational justification. Nihilists, CLS can claim, must hold an antecedent belief that normative decision making must either be justified foundationally or it is arbitrary; then argue that normative decision making cannot plausibly be construed as justified foundationally; and conclude, nihilistically, that normative decision making is arbitrary and mere sham.[24] Some members of CLS repudiate explicitly the antecedent belief that distinguishes nihilism. Accordingly, the first part of CLS' strategy is to deny that its abrogation of foundationalism and objectivism leads us down a slippery slope to chaos and arbitrary normative decisions. In this vein, Joseph Singer writes:

> When I convince someone that her theory did not compel her to reach the normative results she advocated, she does not immediately give up all her moral beliefs or her political positions. She continues to hold certain beliefs deeply despite an inability to derive them logically from principles that are grounded in reason or consensus. And she is right to do so.[25]

And:

> Morality cannot require anything because it is an abstraction, and abstractions are what we make them. Virtue may not be knowledge, but it certainly is not callous indifference. Why? Because I assert it to be so. What we do and believe matters. It does *not* matter that I cannot prove this to be so; what matters is the human assertion of responsibility. (emphasis in original)[26]

Singer states that there is nothing mysterious about moral decision making so conceived. These decisions are no different from mundane choices such as marriage, childbearing, moving to another country, or changing jobs. How do we make such choices? Singer tells us we take a look at what we want in life, imagine what life would be like if we choose one way rather than another, talk with people whose opinions we value, argue with others and self, and decide.[27] Singer speculates that normative decision making, like other areas of practical choice, is not a matter of logically deriving foundational truths, but rather a matter of emotion, experience, and dialogue.[28]

In similar fashion, Mark Tushnet declares:

> Instead of having political positions flow from social theory, the dominant CLS project simply takes political positions. But not just any political positions. *The politics of the dominant position is the politics of decentering, disrupting whatever understandings happen to be settled, criticizing the existing order whatever that order is.* Some CLS proponents are attracted to small-

scale decentralized socialism. But that attraction must be understood as the embodiment of a critique of large-scale centralized capitalism. It cannot set forth a permanent program, the realization of which would be the end of politics. In fact, in a socialist society, the critical legal scholar would criticize socialism as denying the importance of individual achievement, and decentralization as an impediment to material and spiritual achievement. (emphasis added)[29]

The second part of CLS' strategy is to deny that it is composed of closet supraobjectivists. Rather than equivocating on its alleged commitment to objectivism, CLS can argue that its attack on centrist legal ideology is empirical and immanent; that is, CLS assumes high foundational standards when criticizing other theories, not because it is revealing an implicit objectivist impulse, but rather as a form of immanent critique, as a way of holding other theories accountable to the standard to which those theories themselves aspire. It is the centrist who is trapped by dichotomous thinking, CLS may charge, and it is she who cannot formulate a positive program capable of withstanding her own critical assault.

Thus CLS claims neither to subscribe to the animating supposition of nihilism nor equivocate on its own position regarding objectivism. Only if this response is successful is it clear that the charge of nihilism that critics lodge against CLS is misplaced.

Unfortunately, neither part of CLS' strategy is fully compelling. First, Singer's account of normative reasoning is woefully inadequate.[30] Both the phenomenology and impact of moral and legal decision making differ from the phenomenology and impact of the everyday decisions that Singer cites. We believe and act as if our most important normative decisions are more than mere reflections of rough hunches mediated by experience and conversation. Moreover, the discourse, reasons, and arguments viewed as appropriate for normative choice are very different from those of everyday, nonnormative decision making.

Singer's account oscillates between mere avowal of will—"Because I assert it to be so"—and sentimentalization of passion. But if normative choice reduces merely to subjective assertion of power, Singer's claim that CLS is not nihilistic evaporates into lame posturing because that position is precisely to what nihilism is reduced. Moreover, the invocation of passion and emotion hardly illuminates a solution. If moral choices are groundless, then they are no more than random events; and if they are based on reasons, then these reasons are subject to scrutiny from some common standard, or they are mere reiterations, and not explanations, of the choices. If the choices emanate from pure passion, whatever that is, the questions are unavoidable: Why sentimentalize a particular set of passions rather than its competitors? How do we adjudicate among competing visions, choices, passions, and political structures if all are in unremitting, unarbitrable conflict?

Singer tries to mediate this problem through use of currently fashionable slogans such as "conversation," "experience," and "imagining" the consequences of our actions. But we need to know what is and what should be decisive or evidentiary in normative decision making beyond its assimilation to all other areas of personal choice. Surely the discourse, standards, and considerations endemic to matters of mere personal taste—Which flavor spaghetti sauce should I create tonight?—differ radically from those attending to moral and public policy dilemmas such as abortion and euthanasia. By marginalizing reasons, knowledge, and standards for correctness, Singer distorts and reduces the phenomenology of normative choice.

The program of the "dominant CLS project" fares no better. It self-consciously venerates a ceaseless rebellion against whatever is currently in place. Lacking any content other than the salutary effects of insurrection, impoverished by the absence of an underlying vision of a human good, and devoid of any hope that it can transcend interminable critique, this program can do no more than prostrate itself before the false idol of exaggerated provisionality.

Second, CLS' claim that it is practicing immanent critique rather than equivocating on its commitment to objectivism is only partially successful. If CLS intends through its critique to denigrate only those opposing legal thories that consciously affirm foundationalism, then the thrust of its attack languishes, because the only viable candidates to impugn are the few remaining versions of extreme formalism. But extreme formalism is not the current dominant theory of legal practice or the mode indigenous to liberal–capitalist thought. In large measure extreme formalism is a caricature or heuristic device rather than a thriving school of jurisprudential thought. Worse still, those adherents who without shame still label themselves formalist do not subscribe to a simple-minded application of deductive rationality to legal decision making. Moreover, until CLS can advance a positive program that can withstand its own critical assault and avoid reductionist dualities, it is in no position to sling mud at centrist–liberals for their presumed frailties. Accordingly, to the extent CLS makes the claim of immanent critique to elude the nihilistic paradox, the movement exposes itself to the reproach that, at best, it has merely assaulted every contemporary theorist's favorite whipping boy, and, at worst, it has attacked a straw person.

The intuitions of CLS are correct: it does need to transcend the acceptance of the objectivist–relativist dilemma to exonerate itself from the allegation of nihilism. But to recognize and promote that fact is insufficient. The difficult but necessary work involves a new vocabulary, different standards for measuring truth, and a thorough examination of the relationship between persuasion and rational acceptance. My suspicion is that once CLS attends seriously to such matters some of its bolder positions will be domesticated, and members of the movement will assemble with the rest of us and try to persuade others that their descriptive and prescriptive worldview is a sounder account given whatever common framework we share.

## ROBERTO UNGER

The apex of work in the CLS genre is that of Roberto Unger.[31] While retaining the three classic CLS themes—pervasive indeterminacy, political legitimation, and law as ideology—and remaining loyal to the fundamental contradiction thesis, Unger adds elements that rescue him from charges of nihilism. By taking theory seriously, by including a more thorough picture of human nature than his CLS comrades, and by mitigating the contradiction-in-law thesis, Unger is able to evade clearly the charge that he is a closet worshiper of the objectivist–relativist dichotomy, the implication that he courts ceaseless rebellion for its own sake, and the allegation that he conjures logical contradiction from the presence of meager disharmony in law.

### Background Argument: A Theory of Persons

*Existential Dilemma and Human Passions.* Unger tells us that we all experience the "problem of contextuality": ambivalent feelings of being necessarily embedded in a thick cultural and social context that seemingly defines the limits of the possible and impossible and being able to transcent cultural contexts and limits as we experience modes of thought and being that cannot be translated adequately by the logic and language of current norms.[32] The paramount animating drive of human passion is to transcend the cultural contexts that are provided by the established forms of personal relations, intellectual inquiry, and social arrangements.

Unger is concerned with our "existential dilemma," which manifests itself as simultaneous yearning and fear when in the presence of others. The passions are centered around the duality of our undeniable need for others and our felt danger at their approach.[33] To this extent, accepting the fundamental contradiction thesis, Unger demands that to advance self-understanding and mediate our existential dilemma, we must open ourselves to a full life of personal encounter, thereby giving full expression to our need while accepting the accompanying danger.

*Human Plasticity.* Unger tells us that there is only one noncontingent fact of human personality: contingency itself;[34] that is, the capacity of human personality to transcend the limits of the culturally determined possible and impossible is the only noncontingent fact of human nature. For Unger, we are most truly ourselves when engaging in activity in which we deny the false necessities generated by the structures of social life. It is during such activity that we celebrate the possibilities of our infinite personalities.

Unger invokes three rhetorical questions to provide additional support for his plasticity and empowerment theses: Do his conceptions suggest more readily verifiable or falsifiable ideas? Are his theses compatible with a persuasive and potent social theory? Are his theses validated by the qualified introspection of humans?[35]

Implicity acknowledging the contentlessness of the plasticity claim, Unger seeks a normative conception of human personality that fuses description and prescription but does not fall prey to skepticism or abject relativism.

*Images of Personality and Convergence.* According to Unger, the four main images of personality, as reflected in literature and philosophy, are the heroic ethic, fusion with an impersonal absolute, Confucianism, and the Christian–Romantic ideal.[36] Unger instructs us that if we take these four images and cleanse them of aspects that deny the infinite quality of personality, we will discover that the remaining theoretical ideas converge and give us similar answers to our most important normative questions.

The resulting conception of human personality includes the primacy of personal encounter and love, and a commitment to social iconoclasm. Aggrandized mutual vulnerability is a prerequisite for advancing self-understanding, and, according to Unger, we are most empowered and most truly ourselves when we engage in context-transcending activity informed by faith, hope, and love.[37] Unger insists that the concept of infinite personality allows us to avoid relativism, while the phenomenon of convergence offers us a reason to accept a normative conception of human personality that escapes contentlessness.

Unger has been taken to task for allegedly adopting the classical method of logically deriving normative conclusions from a particular view of human nature.[38] Critics have argued that it seems puzzling to derive anything from claims about the plasticity of human nature.[39] Such claims appear to be an admission that we cannot discern who or what humans are. Thus, to begin from conditionality and indeterminacy and then purport to derive substantive conclusions seems preposterous.

It may seem strange to criticize Unger, one of the founding fathers of CLS, from a CLS perspective, but such a criticism is available. Because his efforts can be viewed as just another failed attempt to use classical logical categories to deduce substantive (and ahistorical) moral and political conclusions, CLS advocates can plausibly charge Unger with intellectual treason. By his apparent acceptance of the standards of proof, truth, and argument that, from their perspective, emanate from the false consciousness of the dominant centrist regimes, Unger may be viewed as trying to play the other guy's game while adding only one more rule or assumption—his one unconditional fact of human personality. The charge is that all Unger has done is changed the initial premise of a tired and disreputable centrist political argument and in so doing merely amended that argument by moving from a closed theory of human nature to an open theory. Despite the breadth of his thought and the originality of his political program, he is doomed to failure by his very acceptance of some mainstream philosophical categories and ways of carving up and describing the world. Moreover, by accepting such categories Unger may be revealing an objectivist impulse that would repel most CLS advocates.

In defense of Unger it must be noted that classical thinkers such as Plato and Hobbes derived substantive normative conclusions from fixed theories of human nature. In contrast, Unger contends that fixed theories of human nature are too often merely projections of the current social and political order and not the discoveries of ahistorical truths about human personality. Fixed theories of human nature, therefore, artifically restrain thought and action. Accordingly, Unger is less a prisoner and more a liberator of the classical method.

This defense of Unger, although true, does not meet the critics' point. Critics here do not necessarily dispute the type of theory about human nature that Unger advances but the very method of trying to derive moral conclusions from a theory about human nature. However, a stronger defense of Unger is available. He is not at all deriving moral conclusions from a theory about human nature. Rather than there being an antecedent, determinate theory of human nature that might set the boundaries of normative disputes, it is one of the tasks of moral theory to help form the most acceptable nature for which persons should strive. Unger posits only one non-contingent fact about human personality: its ultimate plasticity. But he recognizes clearly that no substantive conclusions can follow from such a starting point. To avoid the charge of contentlessness he provides a more substantive view of human personality—one informed by the convergence of the four main available images purged of those aspects that deny plasticity. But even here he does not pretend to derive deductively his programmatic vision from his substantive view of human personality.

Unger would agree that we cannot appeal to an antecedent and disembodied theory of persons as an axiomatic starting point in our quest for moral theory. Rather, a theory of persons partly constitutes particular versions of moral theory, and the acceptability of a moral theory helps determine the acceptability of its component theory of persons. The notion of "acceptability" used here is much looser and contestable—appealing to concrete experiences of human personality more than formal categories—and this suggests strongly that Unger is not trying to meet the strict standards of deductive proof. Hence, the critics' charge is misplaced.

His critics here are the "ultra-theorists,"[40] to use his own term. Renouncing attempts to develop general explanations and comprehensive plans for political transformation, they mercilessly thrash the conclusions and justifications of the dominant ideology and often conjure images of a more desirable social life; but they do not formulate deep theoretical justifications for their favored practices. At their most radical, they ridicule all normative discourse and revel explicitly in arbitrariness and nihilism.

For Unger, ultra-theorists, by obliterating the link between normative discourse–theoretical insight–explanatory power–practical action, cripple effective and liberating theory and practice.[41] Lacking an underlying explanation of the respective roles of contexts and context-smashing in human flourishing and empowerment, ultra-theory collapses into a nominalistic form of standard social science or degenerates into the most virulent forms of existential rebellion for its own sake.

It has also been argued that Unger's program merely restates and does not solve the problem of the fundamental contradiction.[42] Although promising to liberate social conflict from its marginalized place in centrist politics, Unger ends by creating yet another structure, his "structure of no structure," that is immune to destabilization. Thus, Unger has merely relocated the point at which social conflict is prohibited.

Unger has a response here that will not seem terribly persuasive to CLS' committed ultra-theorists. Given that he believes that there is one objective nonconditional fact of human personality and driven by the need to mediate the indeterminacy and contradiction theses to avoid the difficulties adumbrated previously, Unger cannot go all the way and claim that everything is always up for grabs. To do so would court a nihilism that he decries. But he does more than merely relocate the point of conflict; he provides a structure that is designed to allow the fullest amount of social conflict consistent with his commitment to honor and facilitate the infinite human personality. It seems that once he denies that everything is contingent he must build from that which is objective. In so doing he avoids some of the starkest problems besetting CLS but invites rebuke from alienated ultra-theorists. This is probably a small price to pay.

However, Unger's notion of progress seems puzzling. He tells us that, despite our inability to transcend all conditionality, progress is possible as we "loosen the limits" of conditionality. But if progress means that some conditional forms are less conditional than others, or that some conditional forms are better than others, Unger may be presupposing a standard by which to evaluate conditional forms that itself is not conditional. Alternatively, if progress acknowledges that all forms are equally conditional—a democracy of conditionality—then it is not clear to what progress amounts. Is it simply the explicit recognition that our modes of discourse are conditional and the appreciation of the freedom we exercise when we continually recombine and reimagine contexts? Or is progress simply the process of recombination and reimagination itself? Finally, it is not clear that the prescription to accelerate revision follows from the assumption that all forms of social life and all modes of discourse are conditional. We might well decide that, given the fact of conditional forms and modes, we should not accept any given structure as ultimate truth; we might well allow a reasoned process of change in our structures and modes, but why choose to accelerate revision? In the absence of evidence indicating that such a change would be an improvement (a higher form of conditionality? a closer approximation to a nonconditional standard? a realization of freedom?), why advocate change for change's sake?

Unger would probably reply that his model is based on a modern view of science. Science progressed from the Euclidean paradigm to another. The best science is viewed as capable of accelerating self-revision and recognizing and absorbing anomalies and incongruous perceptions, but without destroying itself or repressing the facts it has found. Science might be viewed by Unger as transforming the fact of conditionality into an intellectual advantage and theoretical method.[43]

More fundamentally, progress can be defined in terms of Unger's one unconditional fact of human nature: its ultimate plasticity. Unger acknowledges that the act of context-smashing creates a new context; we are never unencumbered and unsituated. However, we progress as we ascend to looser contextual structures that encourage their own destabilization, thereby giving currency to human personality. We are not engaged in self-defeating rebellion for its own sake but transform contexts for a purpose: to liberate human personality so that its one objective aspect can flourish. We never discover the Archimedean point that might arrest all future context-smashing; we never create a nontranscendable context that is indisputably superior to its competition; but neither are we trapped by a democracy of conditionality. There is a nonconditional standard by which to evaluate various conditional contexts, the one objective feature of human personality. Some conditional contexts are superior to others based on their flexibility and acceptance of destabilization. The contrast here is between rigid structures that resist attempts at destabilization and flexible structures that facilitate their own transformation.[44] Moreover, Unger tries to document how plasticity has been paramount in military, economic, and social triumphs throughout history.[45] Accordingly, we should accelerate revision to precipitate an understanding of ourselves and as a requirement of worldly success.

## Programmatic Vision: Beyond Capitalism and Communism

Unger uses the ultimate plasticity of human personality in contending that political and social arrangements, rather than being depicted classically as a set of concrete social institutions defining a fixed and closed structure, should incorporate destabilization mechanisms. Such mechanisms must undermine existing social arrangements and unsettle hierarchical relations before these firmly solidify into entrenched power. Thus, rather than advancing a particular, substantive political situation—such as socialism, liberalism, republicanism—toward which all societies should aim, Unger concentrates more on the process and necessity of social change.[46] Unlike other theories, such as classical liberalism, which purports to deny pervasive conditionality and to highlight processes of social change while remaining neutral on the specific content of the "good life," Unger's goal is to acknowledge the contingency of our institutional and social arrangements and open them to transformation. His project can be viewed as placing a radical framework on the classical method of arriving at normative conclusions from a conception of human nature. His programmatic vision can be captured by the slogan, "Today's political domination was yesterday's liberation."

Deviationist legal doctrine employs a method similar to the "loose form of criticism, justification, and discovery that is possible with ideological controversy itself."[47] For Unger, abstract concepts such as "right," "economic market," and "freedom," have many possible specific institutional embodiments. Although philosophers using the analytic tools of conceptual analysis may purport to discover the dictates of Reason and, miraculously, demonstrate how the present institutional structures of democratic–centrist regimes are more or less morally sound; in fact, this is an exercise in false necessity. For things can well be otherwise.

The proponent of deviationist legal doctrine looks at pockets of doctrine outside the acknowledged core of law and tries to extend the use of that peripheral doctrine.[48] For example, in the law of contracts, the principle that every contract must be entered into with good faith is peripheral to the acknowledged core principle, every contract must involve arm's length bargaining. By extending the use of the peripheral principle and marginalizing the hitherto core principle, the law of contracts changes considerably, and certain balances of social power are altered as a result.

Critics will charge that Unger has subverted the traditional judicial role by advocating deviationist doctrine. It seems that an advocate of deviationist doctrine is intentionally choosing to decide overwhelmingly important political issues on the basis of a pocket of legal doctrine that is not, and is acknowledged by judges not to be, where the weight of precedent lies. At first blush this certainly appears to be an illustration of unelected judges creating rather than interpreting law and imposing their own political preferences on citizens rather than following the precepts of *stare decisis*.

Here Unger would dispute the implicit alternatives embraced by his critics: a nonpoliticized judicial decision making based on strict adherence to the plain meaning of constitutional provisions and legislative enactments ("textualism"), or grounded on the intentions of the framers of those provisions and enactments ("intentionalism"), or derived from the rational or normative order immanent in the law ("formalism"). The CLS attack on formalism is by now clear and will not be repeated. Instead, CLS' assault on textualism and intentionalism (known jointly as "originalism") is worth summarizing.

In constitutional contexts, originalism is support by a variety of rationales. First, it is claimed that judges must act within the Rule of Law. Second, social contract theorists claim that the governed have consented only to participate in, and are thus required to abide by, an association defined by its original political understanding. Third, some advocates of originalism may admit a preference for the substantive values held and espoused by the politically powerful in the late eighteenth century in America.[49]

The CLS repudiation of originalism is in some respects compatible with the tenets of centrist–liberal jurisprudence. It should be clear that textualism and intentionalism are in conflict. The alleged literal reading of a provision may be at odds with the intentions of its framers. What we intend is not always reflected clearly in what we say, much less how others interpret what we intend and say. Thus, there may well exist a conflict between the alleged plain meaning of a provision and the animating intent of its framers.

Moreover, all reading requires interpretation that is subject to ideological biases and the currents of history. Presumed literal readings all too often disingenuously mask political preferences. Even the most fervent idolaters of textualism would be hard pressed when confronted with terms such as "due process," "freedom of contract," "cruel and unusual punishment," and "equal protection." These and most other paramount constitutional clauses have no static meaning and are subject to rival, contestable interpretations.[50] Accordingly, textualism is flawed because every significant constitutional provision lacks a preexisting, determinate meaning.

Intentionalism, on the other hand, may pretend to appeal to either the actual intentions of the authors of a provision at the time of framing ("explicit intentionalism") or the intentions these authors would have expressed had they anticipated the cases and historical events that actually occurred after the framing of the provision ("imputed intentionalism"). Furthermore, proponents must confront an ambiguity between applying what they take to be the true and explicit intentions of the framers and what the framers themselves said and thought their explicit intentions should be interpreted throughout history.

Once intentionalists construct a metatheory to resolve these conflicts and ambiguities, they face additional obstacles: Our Constitution was the product of many people, and it is unclear how the notion of "intention," which is primarily predicated of individuals, can be coherently applied to a group in which many may have no specific intentions about a particular provision but desire merely to ratify the Constitution as a whole. Furthermore, many current social practices did not exist at the time of the framers, and thus the framers developed no explicit intentions about such practices. It is doubtful that any social practice exists with exactly the same social meaning throughout history, and it is also unclear at the outset how our Constitution gains everlasting legal authority simply through self-proclamation.[51]

Finally, and most important, the three underlying rationales for originalism are neither internally consistent nor persuasive.[52] The Rule of Law doctrine seems unassailable until we demystify its undeniable tension with originalism: given that many judges throughout history have not acted as textualists or intentionalists—these are the judges sneered at by originalists for being "judicial activists"—there are many nonoriginalist decisions embedded in law. An originalist judge confronting a politically important case today may well be in a position of either reaffirming a prior nonoriginalist decision to conform to the Rule of Law or overturning that prior decision to be true to her commitment to originalism. If she does the former she betrays originalism, and if she does the latter she destabilizes the very Rule of Law that presumably supports originalism. Accordingly, it is clear that even if the Rule of Law provides a foundation for originalism when we consider the issue abstractly, the relationship becomes much more complex when we ponder the issue in its historical context.

The contractual claim fares no better. The existence and legitimacy of an ongoing social contract based on an agreement made by those no longer alive, an agreement that binds progeny and later immigrants, is a notorious problem. How do we give consent? How are we bound to the social contract? If the answer involves the fact that we came voluntarily to these shores or we remained uncoerced within this political association, a further question arises: How do such facts bind us to the original understanding of the social contract? At most, it seems that we are bound to the current social understanding of our national community, an understanding that includes many nonoriginalist judicial and political decisions. Again we encounter a conflict between the contractualist claim and originalism's animating impulse.

The infatuation with the substantive values of the framers is also misplaced. The framers were simply particular people who lacked omniscient vision and who adhered to several fundamental values contrary to present social understandings. We can reasonably view the framers as predominantly racist, sexist, privileged, elitist white males who projected many of these attributes in their substantive policies. While we should not demean their many accomplishments, it is doubtful whether they embodied once and forever all available moral truths and insights.[53]

In sum, Unger would conceive of judicial interpretation as an encounter between reader and text. He would deny that there is a literal reading in constitutional provisions for textualists to discern. Moreover, the pretensions of intentionalists evaporate when the intramural tensions between explicit and imputed intentions are exposed and the deep conflicts between the abstract rationales for originalism and the concrete historical situation encumbering originalist judges are highlighted. For Unger, those who proclaim the need for originalism in fact yearn to truncate artificially the various levels of "intentionality" in order to "find" the level that most closely comports with their political preferences. Thus, to assert the slogans of originalism is to act in bad faith and to mask political reality.

But still, critics might rejoin, there are degrees of judicial politicization. Our alternatives cannot merely be either originalism–formalism or Unger's deviationist practice. Surely Unger's program transgresses against the sanctity of precedent and trespasses on legislative prerogatives more seriously than current centrist practice does. After all, Unger's call to make judicial use of peripheral legal principles as a mode of political transformation is parasitic on his admission that there are core legal principles that constitute the weight of precedent.

At this point Unger might well plead guilty to the critics' charge and accept unsqueamishly the condemnation of the minions of centrist politics. For at bottom he aspires to efface the distinctions between political official and layperson, political expert and follower, and judge and citizen. Moreover, he would claim that deviationist doctrine abrogates nothing concerning the judicial role that centrist regimes have not already lost.

Internal development is animated by two themes: no one scheme of political association has conclusive and everlasting authority, and the mutual correction of abstract political ideals and their specific institutional embodiments offers the best chance of significant political change.[54] Internal development is the process by which we create new institutional embodiments for our ideals and alter our ideals and the spheres of their domain.[55]

For Unger, political change cannot be achieved by advocating violent revolution, by abrogating law or democracy, by vilifying the policies of the United States, or by fantasizing a new abstract idea of society; rather, it is achieved by the internal development of existing legal doctrine, social relations, and political institutions. The locomotive of social change is fueled by alterations in the relative functionality and transformation of existing formative contexts, not by the unveiling of comprehensive alien ideologies or the inauguration of novitiate utopian visions.

Social power must no longer be viewed, as it is by the disciples of false necessity, as antecedently right or necessary, but is instead seen as laden with contestable political presuppositions. Here the distinction between officials such as judges and lawyers, and laypersons becomes less clear as deviationist doctrine and internal development employ looser and more contestable standards of rationality and produce tentative conclusions.

Some ultra-theorists would claim that Unger's is a romantic and ultimately impotent vision.[56] Fueled by the background assumption that rational argument can raise social consciousness and liberate us from the chains of dominant ideology, Unger renounces violent revolution as the instrument of political change. Yet, some will argue, true and lasting fundamental change is not produced by better rational demonstrations or more comprehensive theories; it springs from widespread alterations in the perceptual grids through which humans view and understand their daily activities. Such sweeping upheavals only dog the footsteps of successful violent revolution.

This criticism hits at the practicality of superliberalism and its prospects for implementation. Unger's predicament here is clear: if he advocates violent revolution, he can be attacked as Utopian because the prospects for successful revolution in the major centrist-capitalist regimes are worse than dim; if he advocates consciousness raising and exalts the role of theory as the engine of social change, he can also be attacked as Utopian, because many believe that theoretical vision plays at best a minor role in the restructuring of fundamental politics. But this predicament merely underscores the present power of dominant centrist ideology in the West.

To escape from the attack that his program is impossible to implement and doomed to be mere theory divorced from practice, Unger could cite the advances made by feminists. It is undeniable that by raising social consciousness without threats of violent revolution feminists have succeeded in effecting significant change. While it may be countered that feminism has in fact been co-opted and assimilated by centrist–capitalist regimes, Unger can still maintain that the necessary link between violence and political conversion is hardly unbreakable. At worst the prospects of success for meaningful political change in the West seem no dimmer for consciousness raising than for violent revolution.

On the other hand, centrist critics will be tempted to inquire whether Unger's program of recurrent conflict and incessant appeals to conditionality will invite the rise of overtly authoritarian regimes. In the absence of objectively true moral and political standards, Unger's program may seem to encourage relentless instability as all moral and political issues appear to be permanently up for grabs. Under such conditions, critics fear that totalitarian regimes will eventually be embraced as a way of providing security and order in the face of political anarchy.

Unger, however, has a plausible retort to such a criticism. He could claim that the rise of totalitarian regimes is not implied by the fact of conditionality or by the presence of recurrent political conflict but is instead generated by the depoliticized character of large segments of unorganized and manipulable citizens. If this is correct, then his program constitutes an antidote to totalitarianism because his central aspiration is to extend the political franchise to more citizens in more areas of their everyday existence. Moreover, Unger's program is not a celebration of permanent, overt revolution. Unger aspires only to efface the distinction between full-blown revolution and total stagnation. Thus, he would strive to disassociate conflict from fundamental, nonnegotiable issues and confine it to concrete proposals capable of being compromised. For Unger, our political choices are not confined to "anarchy or totalitarianism or centrism."

Institutional structures include a system of rights, a central economic principle, and an organization of government. Although Unger leaves their specific embodiments to the collective deliberations of the people, he does provide the following general outline.

He begins by affirming that we must radicalize the available conceptions of rights to avoid solidifying forms of privilege and hierarchy. A scheme of rights should not reify a particular version of social life, because such a sanctification is yet another manifestation of false necessity. The internal development of existing ideals of rights and democracy when combined with respect for our infinite personalities will afford humans a measure of security without concomitant domination. Unger takes an altered scheme of rights as important for its own sake and "also for its encouragement to a systematic shift in the character of direct personal relations and, above all, in the available forms of community."[57]

The central economic principle is the establishment of a rotating capital fund. The central agencies of government would set outer limits to disparities of income and authority within work organizations, and to the distribution of profit as income. Capital would be made available, temporarily and at a low rate of interest, to teams of workers. The fund, which would disaggregate the control of capital into several tiers of capital takers and givers, would aim at maintaining a constant flow of new entrants into the economy and ensuring that no economic enterprise could use legal devices to seclude itself from market instabilities.[58] The long-range aim of the fund might involve more decentralization and economic experimentation.

Critics will be concerned that Unger's program might result in perennial economic insecurity. His heralding of long-range decentralization, a rotating capital fund, and disaggregated property rights will strike many as anathema to traditional entrepreneurial incentives and destructive of citizens' confidence in business enterprise. Moreover, both his specific economic and general programs may seem hopelessly indeterminate and vague.

To meet such criticisms, Unger advises that we constitutionalize some of the procedures and rules of the rotating capital fund, thereby shielding them from radical instability. But given his view of the judicial role, the importance of deviationist doctrine, and general aversion to freezing the terms of social life, it is doubtful whether this maneuver would be desirable or effective. He is more likely to subject the issue of the relative amount of economic security to recurring public conflict. His economic program gambles that constraints on individual and family capital will be outweighed by the greater mobility of and access to capital made possible by the rotating capital fund.

Unger's economic program must be viewed in the light of his other prescriptions concerning the reorganization of work. Abrogating public ownership of the means of production, Unger denies as well the rigid distinction between task definers (employers and managers) and task executors (workers).[59] Rather, he strives to accelerate interaction between the two work sectors and to insulate none of the components of the workplace from politics and the logic of recombination.

Although this program remains indefinite, he feels such problems beset any programmatic vision that tries to avoid transcendental appeals without lapsing into abject skepticism. Viewing his program as a contestable proposal that itself is subject to political conflict, Unger prefers it to what he takes to be the illusions of current democratic–centrist practice that gives large-scale investors explicit monetary incentives and that insulates managers and owners from the possible destabilizing effects of mass democracy. Unger suggests that current centrist practice falsely extrapolates from one possible economic predicament: underconsumption during periods of economic growth. Unger decries present practice, through which a relatively small group of investors has a disproportionate voice in the market. Instead, he places his faith in the greater mobility of and increased access to capital by more groups of entrepreneurs.

At bottom, Unger has no clear retort to the critics' charge. His firm conviction is that current democratic–centrist practice rests on the illustion that our particular form of the market is necessary. But this illusion nourishes economic rigidity that can only end in long-term economic inefficiency. Moreover, centralized–communist attempts to maneuver macroeconomic aggregates by a combination of public ownership and the authority of technical experts has also failed. His alternative is vague and indeterminate, but his vision is unwavering: increased mobility of and access to capital, when combined with restructuring of workplace relations and recurrent political conflict, will result in greater long-term efficiency than current practice and will serve to invigorate and transform our market.

More generally, critics have charged that Unger's preferences for context-smashing and destabilization, while exalted by modernist intellectuals, are not representative of ordinary people.[60] Most humans, it is claimed, yearn for increased security and more firmly settled contexts, and experience upheaval and radical change as unwelcome threats. Thus, Unger's call for "increased human empowerment" through the transcendence of fixed structures is in fact an elitist's self-indulgent fantasy. The masses of people, who are denied the material comforts that upper-class intellectuals take for granted, appreciate the security of a fundamental structure susceptible to alteration no more disruptive than marginal adjustment.

The jurisprudential version of this criticism would highlight Unger's apparent failure to understand the virtues of the stability of the Rule of Law: constraints on rampant discretion, security in forming expectations and predictions over time, protection of civil liberties through general applications of law, and its contribution to economic efficiency.

Unger's retort to such a criticism would undoubtedly point out the stabilizing aspects of his own program: immunity and solidarity rights, constitutionalization, and the right to remove oneself from political conflict or leave the state entirely. Moreover, he might reiterate that the fear of context-smashing is simply another manifestation of the paralyzing effects of the illusion of necessity communicated by centrist ideology. Rather than accepting the alleged longing of the masses for security as a basic independent fact of human nature, Unger would perceive it as damning evidence that dominant ideology has been successful in retarding the flourishing of our infinite personalities. Accordingly, we should take the critics' charge as further proof of the need to liberate the masses from the political status quo and not as a demonstration of any presumed inadequacy in Unger's account.

To adjudicate this dispute we would have to deal more fundamentally with Unger's claim that there is one and only one noncontingent fact of human personality. In other words, is the masses' craving for security a sign of a deeper fact about human nature, or is it merely further evidence of the corrupting influence of dominant politics? Is the Rule of Law a ruse by which citizens are further entrapped by false necessity, or is it a necessary, but not sufficient, condition of justice?

Critical Legal Studies is a vibrant and refreshing addition to jurisprudential debate. Its associates are bound together by a few general themes and a common abhorrence of centrist politics. Although there are numerous ways to classify this movement, which itself resists classification, my favorite consists of three groups: (1) those, such as Unger, who say they are not nihilists and clearly are not ("super-theorists"); (2) those, such as Singer, who say they are not nihilists but who can still be plausibly affixed with that prejorative label ("mezzo-theorists"); and (3) those who seem to accept the label "nihilist" as the ultimate act of political and moral defiance ("ultra-theorists").

Super-theorists will be criticized by one or both of the other groups for accepting and thereby legitimating the foundationalists' political game. Motivated by the good intention of freeing us from the shackles and fantasies of false necessity, Unger's efforts are nonetheless in vain because he buys into and plays the same old disreputable foundationalist hustle: trying to establish a proof that might yield abstract, cognitive support for what are in fact radically contingent political and social arrangements.

Ultra-theorists, the group most likely to make such charges, offer an alternative that will strike most professional academics as hopelessly anarchistic because it denies the abstract philosophical quest for conceptual grounds. Ultra-theorists perceive the absence of conceptual and cognitive grounds as a liberating postulate. Rather than demobilizing us and making all moral and political action problematic and arbitrary, ultra-theory claims to undermine social and cognitive tyranny and to open us to other forms of life and alternate social arrangements. Rather than appealing to abstract categories or intellectual proofs, we should start from our concrete experiences of love, truth, and power: the politics of everyday life in local, specific personal encounters. As an antidote to the maladies of mainstream politics and jurisprudence, ultra-theorists counsel that we should adopt a kind of Ungerism, but stripped of its intellectual baggage.

Such a position will be assaulted immediately by centrist political theorists, whether foundationalists or nonfoundationalist super-theorists such as Unger, as relativistic or nihilistic. Ultra-theorists, however, brush off these charges. In their view, such accusations are telling only from the perspective of those who accept certain of the categories of abstract philosophy. Ultra-theorists could admit that from the perspective of mainstream theorists a radical CLS position is hopelessly inadequate, but, after all, that perspective is precisely what ultra-theory denies. By not playing the mainstream game, ultra-theory from the outset could not hope to satisfy that game's standards and criteria of intellectual success. Unless there is some higher or common ground to adjudicate this dispute—a perspective that begs the question in favor of neither ultra-theory nor the mainstream—it is unclear how to proceed.

While the centrist tradition accuses ultra-theorists of relativism and groundlessness, ultra-theorists criticize the mainstream by citing its numerous historical failures in trying to satisfy its own criteria of intellectual soundness.[61] Mainstream thinkers, foundationalists and nonfoundationalists alike, although purporting to establish their conclusions by means of rational argument, in fact ultimately rely on some unargued for and axiomatic intuition or first principle. It may seem that both mainstream thinkers and ultra-theorists are in the same position: both can offer only circular arguments or unsupported claims in defense of its conclusions. Ultra-theorists might contend that we are inevitably cast back to nonrational commitments, historicism, and decisionism.

The ultra-theorists in CLS and mainstream philosophers, whether foundationalists or nonfoundationalists, speak from radically different horizons. Ultra-theory contends that any modernist reconstruction of moral and political judgments is doomed insofar as it accepts certain foundationalist categories and thereby aspires to privilege cognition at the expense of volition, whereas mainstream thinkers' charge that ultra-theorists are anti-intellectual, nihilistic, and lacking in appreciation for the tangible, practical achievements of analytic philosophy. Each camp does or should understand that its conclusions and reasoning seem hopelessly naive when judged from the perspective of the other. Yet no common and higher ground seems available to ameliorate the war of words and deeds between these two alien factions.[62]

At the same time, nonfoundational but nonnihilistic radicals such as Unger try to pour content into CLS's political and jurisprudential aspirations—and mezzo-theorists talk and act like ultra-theorists while denying that they are nihilists. For their efforts, super-theorists such as Unger are assailed as traitors by the ultra- theorists and vilified as assassins of the Rule of Law by the foundationalists; whereas at least some of the other groups perceive mezzo-theorists as enigmatic, lacking the courage of their convictions, and ultimately acting in bad faith.

# CHAPTER 8

# In Search of Dialogue
## *Feminism Unmodified*

T HE FEMINIST MOVEMENT is so diverse that it is presumptuous and inaccurate to talk about "feminist jurisprudence" as if that were a monolithic school. I will, instead, explain and address what may well be the most interesting strain of feminist jurisprudence: the "feminism unmodified" (FU) of Catharine MacKinnon and Ann Scales.[1]

## FEMINISM UNMODIFIED

*Critique of Abstraction and Objectivism.* FU stigmatizes the quest for universal legal rules that claim to go beyond and control the results of particular cases. Such rules masquerade as neutral and are claimed to emanate from the demands of logic and objective reality, but in fact these rules project the aspirations of those males powerful enough to make the decisions relevant to the recognition and acceptance of the rules. The notions of "value-free" and "aperspectivity" are viewed by FU as political and regressive.

> In order to apply a rule neutrally in future cases, one must discern a priori what the differences and similarities among groups are. . . . One must first abstract the essential and universal similarities among humans; one must have strict assumptions about human nature as such. Without such an abstraction, there is no way to talk about what differences in treatment are arbitrary and which are justified. Underlying this approach is the correspondence theory of truth: The sovereign's judgments are valid only when they reflect objective facts. . . . There must be a list of sex differences that matter and those that do not. Notice, however, that abstract universality by its own terms cannot arrive at such a list. It has no 'bridge to the concrete' by which to ascertain the emerging and cultural qualities which constitute difference.[2]

In this manner, through male ideological assumptions and the disingenuous selection of relevant differences and similarities and through the connivance of the patriarchal myth of objectivity, women are kept in their place by legal means. The holding of power puts males in the position of setting the terms for notions such as "knowledge" and "truth," which allows them to establish a viewpoint and through objectification anoint it as "reality." Although such notions are socially constructed from the situation of male domination and female subjugation, sex differences come to be viewed as the justification for male power rather than the result of it. MacKinnon echoes this observation: "Men *create* the world from their own point of view, which then *becomes* the truth to be described. This is a closed system, not anyone's confusion. *Power to create the world from one's point of view is power in its male form*" (emphasis in original).[3]

Moreover, by measuring rationality in terms of alleged aperspectivity, "what counts as reason will be that which corresponds to the way things are."[4] The failure of women to meet male standards and the relegation of women to carefully circumscribed inferior positions is accounted for and justified by their differences from men. Furthermore, a successful objectification project enlists the aid of the subordinate classes in their own continued subjugation. The method of detached justification and scientific explanation of the social order can secure a powerful stranglehold on the underclasses.

FU views the injustice of sexism as not merely legal error—a few mistakes made at the margins of doctrine—but as an integral part of an entire social system geared for the advantage of one sex at the expense of the other. Regardless of whether the imposition of male legal standards is part of conscious sex discrimination or "merely" an unintended side effect of the shared male point of view, the effects on women are devastating. At best, women must suppress their differences to meet male legal standards and become equally "male"; at worst, women who refuse to submit are tyrannized further by a system that proclaims its objectivity and universality.[5]

*The Centrality of Sexuality.* In feminist thought much is made of a distinction between "sex," conceived as biological, and "gender," portrayed as a social construct. MacKinnon, however, uses sex and gender more loosely and interchangeably. She is more concerned with talking about "sexuality," which she takes to be fundamentally social.

> Sexuality is that social process which creates, organizes, expresses, and directs desire, creating the social beings we know as women and men,

as their relations create society. . . . Sexuality to feminists is socially constructed yet constructing, universal as activity yet historically specific, jointly comprised of matter and mind. . . . The organized expropriation of the sexuality of some for the use of others defines the sex, woman. Heterosexuality is its structure, gender and family its congealed forms, sex roles its qualities generalized to social persona, reproduction a consequence, and control its issue.[6]

She takes "male" to be a social and political, rather than biological, notion. As such, what is male is severed from any claims of necessity or inherency. Moreover, she issues the "standard disclaimer"[7] that the male perspective is not shared by all and only (biological) males, "although most men adhere to it, nonconsciously and without considering it a point of view, as much because it makes sense of their experience (the male experience) as because it is in their interest."[8] Here she underscores the hegemonic function of the male perspective, which takes itself to be nonsituated and universal.

According to MacKinnon, the issues pervading definitions and determinations of rape provide one illustration of the intersection of the centrality of sexuality and the male quest for legal abstraction and objectivity. She tells us that the law places primacy on the issues of consent, on the existence of prior social interaction as an indicator of consent, and on distinguishing rape from normal sexual encounters. But in so doing, the law ignores the general societal condition of male domination and the social meaning of gender, marginalizes the victims' perspective, and presupposes a standard of criminality that reflects the meaning of the act to perpetrators.

MacKinnon views rape from victims' experiences and asserts that sexuality is a "social sphere of male power of which forced sex is paradigmatic."[9] Thus, she does not radically separate normal heterosexuality from rape. Under social conditions of male domination, she believes that it is difficult to distinguish the allegedly normal from the violently aberrational: "where the legal system has seen the intercourse in rape, victims see the rape in intercourse. The uncoerced context for sexual expression becomes as elusive as the physical acts come to feel indistinguishable."[10] She takes special umbrage at the widespread legal exemption of marital rape and the law's use of prior social interaction as an indicator of consent that contraindicates rape: "women experience rape most often by men we know. . . . Women feel as much, if not more, traumatized by being raped by someone we have known or trusted, someone we have shared at least an illusion of mutuality with, than by some stranger."[11]

Beyond the issue of consent, MacKinnon vilifies the way the law distinguishes rape from mere sex by the level of force used: "The law does this by adjudicating the level of acceptable force starting just above the level set by what is seen as normal male sexual behavior, rather than at the victim's, or woman's, point of violation. . . . Rape is a sex crime that is not a crime when it looks like sex. . . . Assault that is consented to is still assault; rape consented to is intercourse."[12] Thus, for MacKinnon, whether consent and an acceptable level of force are present in an encounter are not truly variable factual issues that have objective solutions in specific cases. She questions whether consent and acceptable force are from the outset meaningful concepts given the social meaning of gender and the pervasiveness of male dominance. MacKinnon emphasizes that "forced sex as sexuality is not exceptional in relations between the sexes but constitutes the social meaning of gender. . . . To be rapable, a position which is social not biological, defines what a woman is."[13]

A properly feminist approach, MacKinnon insists, must begin in the meaning of sexual encounters from women's point of view. The wrongness of rape (and given the current situation, virtually all other heterosexual sexual encounters?) stems from the subordination of women to men. Under the present conditions of male dominance, legally contested interactions will be or not be deemed "rape" depending on whether men's or women's meaning wins out. Moreover, the law invokes its usual pretensions to objectivity and to the existence of a single, objective state of affairs, which must and can be unpacked by the available evidence. In resolving such questions, judges systematically employ shared beliefs from the dominant male culture to animate legal norms with determinate meaning and legitimacy.[14]

*Rejecting Another Feminist Approach.* There are three main branches of feminist legal theory: the "differences" approach, which claims that women must be allowed full opportunity to compete in the public arena, that traditional stereotypes of women's attributes must be delegitimized by revealing their source in pernicious social practices, and that unequal treatment can be justified only by articulating real differences; the "different voice" approach, which contends that there is a uniquely female way of managing moral and legal questions, a way that has been marginalized in legal doctrine and moral theory; the "dominance" approach, endorsed by FU, which locates gender inequality not in terms of gender differences but in terms of the historical domination of women by men.

One of the most cherished tenets of the classical liberal version of the Rule of Law is that like cases must be decided alike and that similarly situated litigants must be treated similarly. Accordingly, a state official must justify disparate treatment of two citizens by articulating the relevant difference(s) between them. In several instances this "differences approach" has seemingly allowed women to extend their legal rights by asserting their basic similarity to men.

But MacKinnon and Scales are concerned with the numerous cases in which men and women do not seem to be similarly situated," [cases] involving pregnancy, [cases] involving the supposed overpowering sexual allure which women present to men, and [cases] involving the historical absence of women."[15] In their view, the difficulty of the differences approach is twofold. First, there is the problem of distinguishing relevant from irrelevant differences: "How does one tell what the differences are? Does it matter whether the differences are inherent or the result of upbringing? Is it enough to distinguish between accurate and inaccurate stereotyped differences? Or are there situations where differences are sufficiently 'real' and permanent to demand social accommodation?"[16] Second, there is the problem of feminists being co-opted as they strive to identify a number of real, nonstereotypical differences between men and women that might serve as a basis for special rights for women. Some feminists "have let the [legal] debate become narrowed by accepting as correct those questions which seek to arrive at a definite list of differences. In so doing, [they] have adopted the vocabulary, as well as the epistemology and political theory, of the law as it is."[17]

Thus, although the differences approach is often viewed as having advanced the interests of women in certain cases where women were successfully portrayed as being similarly situated to men, in cases where women are not similarly situated to men, those who accept the assumptions of the differences approach may be unwittingly helping to mask real gender issues. Those who advance a discrete list of differences between men and women "only encourage the law's tendency to act upon a frozen slice of reality. In so doing, [they] participate in the underlying problem—the objectification of women. . . . Our aim must be to affirm differences as emergent and infinite."[18]

MacKinnon identifies two separate but related theories of gender equality. The "single-standard" rule claims to be a neutral application of similar treatment for similarly situated parties; as such, it merely echoes a standard Rule of Law aspiration. The "special protection" rule is self-consciously nonneutral as it acknowledges and makes allowances for the allegedly real differences between men and women. MacKinnon joins Scales in assailing both approaches for unknowingly embracing the maladies of gender inequality that the approaches are designed to remedy.

> Under the [single] standard, women are measured according to our correspondence with man, our equality judged by our proximity to his measure. Under the [special protection] standard, we are measured according to our lack of correspondence with him, our womanhood judged by our distance from his measure.[19]

Thus, for MacKinnon the single standard and the special protection rule are related in that they both inadvertently contribute to the hegemonic process that reinforces gender hierarchy and presupposes men as the measure of all things: "Men are set up as a standard for women by saying either: 'You can be the same as men, and then you will be equal,' or, 'You can be different from men, and then you will be women.'"[20] In MacKinnon's view, the classical liberal notion of equality, as embodied in the Rule of Law, ensures that the only women who are advantaged are those who most closely replicate the male norm and enforces a male standard, which has its own point of view, as an allegedly universal point of view and thus as a formal requirement of justice.

## TOWARD A FEMINIST JURISPRUDENCE

FU calls into question some of the central and cherished elements of the Rule of Law: its use of neutral standards of adjudication, its striving for objectivity through manipulation of legal abstractions, and its aperspective rationality. FU views the Rule of Law as an essential contrivance of the male hegemony that systematically appropriates and defines female sexuality.

Of what characteristics, then, would a truly feminist approach be composed? First, a recognition and an understanding of the critique of objectivism and abstraction. Second, an acknowledgment of the centrality of sexuality and the pervasiveness of gender hierarchy. Third, an awareness of different political perspectives and the role they play in adjudication. Fourth, a relinquishment of the myth that proper adjudication involves sifting carefully the "facts" to reconstruct the one true version of the reality of the case, and an abrogation of the fable that the application of the appropriate legal doctrine to that reality unveils the preexisting right answer to the case. Fifth and finally, a good faith effort by judges to structure and perceive a case from a point of view different from their own, especially when a party's perspective challenges the status quo of male domination. Such an approach champions an end to the evaluation of women and their claims by male standards and prefigures the transformation of legal terms to allow women to be judged by their own standards.[21] Thus, FU begins from the vantage point of taking women's narratives and experiences seriously, especially when those narratives and experiences conflict with the perceptions of women held by the dominant culture. The beginnings of a feminist approach to law depend on at least three general themes: consciousness raising, result orientation, and appreciation and acceptance of paradox.

*Consciousness Raising.* A feminist approach to law begins with the collective reconstruction of the meaning and measure of women's social experience. The basic aspiration is to produce not only a political theory focused on the centrality of sexuality, but also to transform in a concrete sense the way women experience their lives.

MacKinnon does not employ an acknowledged methodology (e.g., the scientific method) and apply it to "a different sphere of society to reveal its preexisting political aspect."[22] Rather, consciousness raising appropriates women's experiences—"life as sex object"[23]—to unmask the political foundations of prevalent social practices.

> Taking situated feelings and common detail . . . as the matter of political analysis, [consciousness raising] explores the terrain that is most damaged, most contaminated, yet therefore most women's own, most intimately known, most open to reclamation. . . . The claim that a sexual politics exists and is socially fundamental is grounded in the claim of feminism to women's perspective, not from it. Its claim to women's perspective is its claim to truth . . . determined by the reality the theory explodes, it thereby claims special access to that reality. Feminism does not see its view as subjective, partial, or undetermined but as a critique of the purported generality, disinterestedness, and universality of prior accounts.[24]

*Result Orientation.* FU argues that because women are systematically oppressed on the basis of their sex, appropriate remedial measures must be constructed by reference to sex. FU insists that equal application of the rules of a legal system that embodies and reinforces gender hierarchy cannot cure or even significantly ameliorate women's disadvantaged status. Current legal abstractions and codifications are taken to be "antithetical to the particularity, specificity and contextualization"[25] of women's experience. Taking objectivism to be the "basis for inequality"[26] and spurning the use of legal abstraction as that which "shields the status quo from critique,"[27] FU extols the virtues of "concrete universality."

Concrete universalism takes differences to be constitutive of the universal itself . . . it sees differences as systematically related to each other, and to other relations, such as exploited and exploiter. . . . It regards differences as emergent, as always changing. . . . When our priority is to understand differences and to value multiplicity, we need only to discern between occasions of respect and occasions of oppression. Those are judgments we know how to make, even without a four-part test to tell us, for every future circumstance, what constitutes domination.[28]

Scales underscores what she takes to be the main purpose of law: "to decide the moral crux of the matter in real human situations."[29] In her view, this enterprise depends on understanding the "relation among things, not their opposition,"[30] and employs imperfect analogies whose scope and limits "must be explored in each case, with social reality as our guide."[31] She takes the process to be explicitly "normative, but not illogical."[32]

The process is result oriented, and the measure of its success is whether the decisions it renders ameliorate the oppression of the underclasses. Scales endorses MacKinnon's test for challenges raised under the Equal Protection Clause and under Title VII of the Civil Rights Act: "the test in any challenge should be 'whether the policy or practice in question integrally contributes to the maintenance of an underclass or a deprived position because of gender status.'"[33]

It should be clear that this approach often demands that different legal standards be used for men and women. No generalization about which particular standard must be used at which particular time can be made. Such determinations can be made only after an examination of the particular circumstances of various legal challenges and an investigation of whether the social practice being called into question exploits gender status. Scales admits, however, that the possibility of a feminist approach to law depends on raising the consciousness of incumbent judges about the nature and scope of gender oppression and may well "ultimately depend upon significant changes in judicial personnel."[34]

Visions such as feminism, which critique the possibility of objectivity and neutrality of law so emphatically and indefatigably and which mock so easily the alleged pretensions of the Rule of Law, inevitably elicit charges of "nihilism" from centrist loyalists.

Scales's response to this charge has four parts. First, she abrogates the common epistemological and normative assumptions that underlie the charge, and she reiterates the role these assumptions play in the continued systematic subordination of women. Second, she suggests that even if objectivity is viewed as desirable by some (males?), it is simply unavailable to us: "The business of living and progressing within our disciplines requires that we give up on 'objective' verification at various critical moments, such as when we rely on gravity, or upon the existence of others, or upon the principle of verification itself. . . . Jurisprudence will forever be stuck in a post-realist battle of subjectivities . . . until we confront the distinction between knowing subject and known object."[35] Third, she maintains that FU does not sever "the observer from the observed."[36] FU is thus a prime example of the required confrontation of the distinction between the knower and the known, and FU's method has natural analogues: "The physics of relativity and quantum mechanics demonstrate that nature is on our side: Nature itself has begun to evince a less hierarchical structure, a multidirectional flow of authority which corroborates our description of perception. We warmly embrace the uncertainty inherent in that perceptual model."[37] Fourth, she denies that the law's justificatory foundations require truculent adherence to the myths of objectivity and neutrality: "There must be something reliable somewhere, there must be indicia of fairness in the [legal] system, but neither depends on objectivity. . . . We need standards to help us make connections among norms, and to help us see 'family resemblances' among instances of domination. Standards, however, are not means without ends: They never have and never can be more than working hypotheses."[38]

It is not clear, however, whether Scales is attacking any real, influential philosopher of law. Those philosophers, such as Dworkin and Hart, who do accept objectivity in law have more subtle accounts of right answers and judicial discretion than the clumsy versions of mechanical jurisprudence that seem to be the focus of FU's attacks. Furthermore, FU's disdain for the formal elements of the Rule of Law seems misplaced. FU contends repeatedly that it does not aim at making the Rule of Law better live up to its own self-image but rather strives to eliminate the basic attraction we find it to possess.

But even if we concede, for the sake of argument, the truth of one of FU's claims—that substantive gender oppression results from the application of the elements of the Rule of Law in our male-dominated society—the question arises whether that is due to an inherent weakness in the Rule of Law or to the dominant political ideology that the Rule of Law sustains and invokes. At worst, the Rule of Law is an unconscious collaborator, compelled to participate in substantive inequality by the set of background moral and political assumptions with which it is saddled by the dominant discourse of the male-dominated state. But we can imagine different states—radically egalitarian, female dominated, or whatever—in which following the aspirations of the Rule of Law would result in significantly different substantive legal results. If FU's claim is that the Rule of Law is an unwitting vassal for the background moral and political ideology of whatever state invokes it and that the Rule of Law cannot be an independent force for guaranteeing substantial equality, then FU is correct. But this concession is not damaging to the minions of centrist politics, because they admit straightaway that the elements of the Rule of Law are merely formal requirements: they are necessary, but hardly sufficient, conditions of justice. My point here is only that the Rule of Law of and by itself is not the reason either substantive justice or injustice results from the judicial decisions of various legal systems.

That is not to say that the elements of the Rule of Law are, in any profound sense, neutral. Stripped of any background set of moral and political assumptions, the elements of the Rule of Law are merely inapplicable abstractions. The Rule of Law is neutral only in this trivial sense. But once the elements of the Rule of Law are made applicable, by being commandeered in the service of a dominant ideology, basic neutrality is abrogated. Any dominant ideology already embodies certain moral and political values that invocation of the Rule of Law will tend to sustain. Thus, FU is correct in thinking that the Rule of Law incorporates a conservative bias—it is used in part to preserve the status quo and thus it will significantly mirror the dominant discourse of a state—but that does not reveal inherent defects of the Rule of Law; it only underscores the need to examine more carefully our underlying prevalent ideologies and values.

There may be nuances to FU that my criticism has overlooked. At first glance, denials of the central elements of the Rule of Law seem to renounce many commonly accepted principles of justice. But FU's point may be that preoccupation with traditional Rule of Law virtues blinds us to the fluidity, contextuality, and pluralistic interpretations of social reality. Required to fit fresh cases into rigid, monolithic, legal categories, judges are systematically prevented from giving credence to alternate interpretations of experience. It is not merely that the Rule of Law has a benign or even useful conservative bias but rather that it dangerously freezes our understanding of social life and our ability to assimilate minority points of view. Thus, an advocate of FU might argue that even in a radically egalitarian or female-dominated state, adherence to Rule of Law adjudication would be misconceived from the outset. FU could contend that the metaphysical and epistemological underpinnings of the Rule of Law—a belief in objectivity, neutrality, strict classification—are fatally flawed, from a theoretical standpoint, and are instruments in ensuring the further marginalization of subordinate classes, from a practical standpoint.

This more nuanced rendering of FU expresses much that is commendable. But we must now try to imagine a method of adjudication that would not incorporate the traditional Rule of Law aspirations but that could maintain a measure of reliability and not succumb to ad hoc, case-by-case decision making. FU offers us some boilerplate rhetoric about reliable standards able to discern the family resemblances among various cases of domination and about the need for indicia of fairness. Moreover, FU adds a specific test for certain equal protection and civil rights challenges ("whether a policy or practice integrally contributes to the maintenance of an underclass on the basis of gender"). Finally, FU takes refuge in a "we know it when we see it" approach when addressing the scope of gender oppression.

FU's counsel on these matters is troubling and disappointing. Virtually all its prescriptions can be assimilated into mainstream jurisprudence. For example, its specific test for equal protection and civil rights challenges could be embraced without any violence to centrist allegiance to Rule of Law virtues. Constitutional law already recognizes special levels of strict scrutiny for challenges based on "suspect" classifications such as race, national origin, and alienage, and in fact already recognizes an intermediate level of scrutiny for challenges based on sensitive classifications such as gender and legitimacy. While it would be an error to think that the law's modest recognition of gender challenges replicates FU's prescribed test, it must be acknowledged that acceptance of Rule of Law adjudication does not disable us from giving currency to claims of societal inequalities based on class, gender, or race. It is theoretically conceivable, although not politically probable, that our constitutional law could incorporate a version of FU's prescribed test for gender challenges. The point here is that acceptance of FU's prescription does not necessitate wholesale renunciation of Rule of Law adjudication.

Moreover, FU's talk about reliable standards, indicia of fairness, and family resemblances is reminiscent of the classic, and somewhat tedious, "rules versus standards" intramural debate that has long raged among centrists. Again, there is nothing in such talk that necessarily jeopardizes Rule of Law adjudication. Finally, there is irony in the "we know it when we see it" approach to cases of gender oppression: such an approach is otherwise ridiculed by feminists when offered in place of a definition or test of pornographic material.[39]

My disappointment is that it appears that proponents of FU are dragons without fire: in their descriptive analysis they herald, in an often exciting and perceptive fashion, the deficiencies of Rule of Law adjudication, but their limited prescriptions end up being compatible with the standard elements of that method of adjudication. They seem to pull back from their radicality and end with a theoretical attack on certain suppositions of mechanical jurisprudence that have already been repudiated long ago by centrist philosophers of law. In fact, FU's more general attacks on the metaphysics of presence, objectivity, the correspondence theory of truth, methodological neutrality, and single slices of reality are prefigured in the work of numerous males in the history of philosophy—the Sophists, Nietzsche, Peirce, James, Dewey, Heidegger, Wittgenstein, Kuhn, Quine, Sellars, Rorty, to name only a few. Given that these philosophers, taken as a group, hardly constitute a vanguard of feminism, it is doubtful that repudiating the presuppositions of Metaphysical Realism is necessarily connected with enlightened views on gender equality. By the same token, it is conceivable that one could embrace the "metaphysics of presence" yet decry the excesses of male-dominated society.

*Appreciation and Acceptance of Paradox.* FU acknowledges candidly that its description of the current subordination of women and its prescription for change generate paradoxes and manifest tensions internal to feminism. One such difficulty concerns FU's own claims to veridical perception and its ability to stigmatize the perceptions of politically centrist women as illusory or as emanating from the noxious socialization of male hegemony. MacKinnon says that

> feminism must grasp that male power produces the world before it distorts it. Women's acceptance of their condition does not contradict its fundamental unacceptability if women have little choice but to become persons who freely choose women's roles. For this reason, the reality of women's oppression is, finally, neither demonstrable nor refutable empirically.[40]

A related puzzle emerges when we ask how FU can castigate the "male totality"[41] with such confidence, while simultaneously denying that it does so from a neutral or aperspectival vantage point. At times, MacKinnon denies that this puzzle is a paradox at all.

> Feminism criticizes this male totality without an account of our capacity to do so or to imagine or realize a more whole truth. Feminism affirms women's point of view by revealing, criticizing, and explaining its im-

possibility. This is not a dialectical paradox. It is a mechodological expression of women's situation, in which the struggle for consciousness
is a struggle for world: for a sexuality, a history, a culture, a community,
a form of power, an experience of the sacred.[42]

At other times, MacKinnon denies that the conclusions of FU are
merely "partial" truths.

Although feminism emerges from women's particular experience, it is
not subjective or partial, for no interior ground and few if any aspects of
life are free of male power. . . . [FU] claims no external ground or un-
sexed sphere of generalization or abstraction beyond male power, nor
transcendence of the specificity of each of its manifestations. How is it
possible to have an engaged truth that does not simply reiterate its determinations? Disengaged truth only reiterates its determinations.
Choice of method is choice of determinants—a choice which, for women
as such, has been unavailable because of the subordination of women.[43]

It seems that FU often flaunts contradictions and paradoxes, self-
consciously and proudly. FU attributes to "women" a keen sensitivity and veridical vision of the way things really are—the conditions of male oppression and domination—while simultaneously
portraying them as possessing "an infinite capacity to be duped."[44]
Moreover, FU often uses what it takes to be social practice and appears to manipulate the facts of that practice to support whatever FU
is momentarily trying to establish. As an example of this language of
convenience, FU uses the alleged prevalence of sexual harassment of
women by men as both the explanation of its recognition by society
(cases are too numerous to discount or ignore) and its nonrecogni-
tion (the frequency of sexual harassment obscures the identification
of abuse because it makes harassment seem commonplace and thus
less offensive).[45] Furthermore, FU is convinced that the liberal notion
of women's consent being a prime factor in the legal analysis of various disputes is a fraud because women have not been allowed to
form themselves in male-dominated society; yet FU demands that
women in such a society have their voices taken more seriously.
Likewise, FU counsels a pluralism that demands that alternate ideologies be heard and that judges empathize with visions other than
their own; yet it is likely that FU would sneer at female judges—
"collaborators"[46]—who empathized with male litigants asserting
anti-FU claims.

FU, however, is unlikely to be unsettled by such remarks. For it
takes these very tensions and contradictions as descriptive of
women's condition: "Integral to women's experience is knowing one

thing on one level, and a different, inconsistent thing on another. . . . Knowledge can occur on different levels and in different parts of ourselves. Is not our ambivalence real? Might this ambivalence even be further evidence of men's fraud against women?"[47]

In sum, FU does not claim to be universal but denies that it reduces to relativism; it shuns efforts to make it a science of sexism or an abstract theory seeking "generalities that subsume its particulars."[48] Rather, it prizes contextualism, refusal of polarity, tolerance of ambiguity, and even contradiction: "[FU] does not begin with the premise that it is unpremised. It does not aspire to persuade an unpremised audience because there is no such audience. Its project is to uncover and claim as valid the experience of women, the major content of which is the devalidation of women's experience."[49]

General criticisms of FU's methodology could focus on the following set of questions: Has FU, despite its avowed commitment to pluralistic interpretations, ignored the socioeconomic divisions among women? Has FU provided only the musings of a special-interest group: privileged, educated, upper-middle-class women? Can these reflections truly constitute "women's perspective"? Or are they, rather, class based and thus unrepresentative of an entire sex? More to the point: Does FU manifest the very urges that it otherwise stigmatizes as pernicious and exemplars of the male (power) mindset—tidy classifications, a single and simple interpretation of reality?[50]

FU arrives at a classic dilemma. On the one hand, it has a powerful point: the preferences of a subordinate class are, at least partly, the result of established social rules and practices. Thus, those rules and practices cannot be justified noncircularly by appeals to those very preferences. On the other hand, FU is guilty of philosophical imperialism if it automatically stigmatizes all who dissent from its prescriptions as unwitting victims of the dominant consciousness. This dilemma is not insurmountable, but FU must advance a more refined analysis of the problem than it has to date.

Does FU, despite its refusal to accept reality as a single slice, posit both men and women as undifferentiated classes? Are these classifications based on question-begging definitions? "To be dominant is to be male and to be subordinate is to be female. Who is male? Anyone who is dominant? What is dominance? Whatever males do."[51]

Beyond the call for more power and the critique of male-dominated society, FU is content to wait until women are no longer oppressed. But it is not clear that women can throw off the yoke of male oppression absent a more complete prescriptive vision. Finally, FU seems to accept too easily the doctrine that we cannot assess the values articulated by women in a male-dominated society because such women are not speaking in their "authentic voices."[52] It is not clear that we cannot, at least to a significant extent, separate one's values from one's "authentic voice" and appraise those values.[53]

By identifying male hegemony as the perpetrator of women's oppression, has FU ignored analysis of the economic structure of society? In other words, does FU lack an account or full explanation of women's oppression? Does it merely charge "male domination" at all occasions of perceived disadvantage without any deeper account of the source of that domination other than males' (innate?) desire for "sexual access to women"?[54]

Would FU's legal prescriptions—its special test for constitutional challenges based on equal protection and civil rights claims—ironically invoke and sustain the very gender stereotypes that FU otherwise is determined to eliminate? By framing legal standards in terms of biology, FU may be accused of sending a message to males that they should not abrogate their traditional gender roles because if they do they will bear all the burdens traditionally borne by women but without the special protection that FU's legal standard affords women.[55]

Independent of this problem, the guidance provided by FU's special test for such constitutional challenges is shaky. Determining the moral crux of the matter and assessing whether a particular policy or practice contributes to the maintenance of an underclass based on gender would be matters hotly disputed within feminist circles, much less without. Even those women who are seeking their own voice are unlikely to arrive at a consensus. Inevitably, it would seem, some clearer standard—built by a series of precedents or sharper definitions of the test itself—would emerge to provide determinate content. Yet as soon as this occurs, FU sinks back into the alleged quagmire of Rule of Law jurisprudence. The dilemma here is not between a rigid foundationalism seeking Cartesian indubitability and arbitrary or random judicial decision making. Rather, it is between a Rule of Law jurisprudence that need not depend on the acceptance of Metaphysical Realism and case-by-case ad hoc, analyses in which even those feminist judges allegedly striving for the same goals could issue radically different edicts. Unless one believes that no legal standards are possible, perhaps because each case is totally or overwhelming dissimilar from all others, it would seem that the dynamic of the historical developmental of decisions will lead even FU's test into what FU takes to be the cesspool of liberal legalism.

One is struck by the question whether much is unique to feminist jurisprudence. FU's general assaults on the indeterminacy and malleability of legal doctrine, its acceptance of result orientation, and its debunking of the alleged pretensions of the Rule of Law are by now old hat. Such claims have been advanced and refined by Legal Realists, Marxists, Critical Legal Studies, and can, in large measure, be accepted even by liberal–centrist philosophers of law. Moreover, FU's metaphilosophical attacks on aperspectivity and Metaphysical Realism have numerous antecedents in philosophical literature; indeed, such a perspective partially constitutes one of the more traditional strains of epistemology: skepticism. Furthermore, FU's emphasis on the role of power and the dominance of the ruling class treads a well-worn path. Likewise, FU's modest legal prescriptions, although not currently reflected in the law, are not (at least in several cases) necessarily anathema to centrist thinkers. It would appear that the only truly distinctive feminist contribution to jurisprudential debute is the primacy it places on patriarchal domination and the centrality of sexuality. Rather than identifying class, economic, or racial oppression, FU designates males as the perpetrators of social inequality. It would seem that FU is merely a form of Marxism that substitutes the oppression of women for the oppression of the working class and that does not necessarily call for the downfall of capitalist economics, or that FU is merely a form of Critical Legal Studies that emphasizes the dominance of the male vision rather than the unremitting war of several ideologies, or that FU is merely a form of Legal Realism that brandishes a political agenda that claims to transcend marginal reform and limited social engineering.

The suggestion that FU is little more than a warmed-over variation of other (male-based) theories of law, however, would infuriate FU's authors and confirm in their minds classic patriarchal strategies. They would be firmly convinced that my remarks are a rather pedestrian attempt to defang FU, assimilate it to male discourse, and thus trivialize it as derived and parasitic.[56]

I have assessed several aspects of FU, but I must add a disclaimer. My criticisms flow from a background of analytic philosophy, which FU would stigmatize as an accomplice in the perpetration of the myths of the Rule of Law, and from the acceptance of several epistemological assumptions, which FU would identify as the very assumptions from which it aspires to divorce itself. As such, propo-

nents of FU will not view my protestations as revealing embarrassing implications of FU but as merely restating its position and
contrasting it with the dominant male discourse.

There is a temptation to throw up one's hands and conclude that
analytic philosophers, given our predilection for coherence and disdain for contradiction, and FU, given its appreciation for paradox
and abhorrence of abstraction, are alien discourses that simply talk
around each other. Lacking enough common ground to engage in
genuine dialogue, each merely recasts the other's central aspirations
as criticisms, while the other, recognizing this, sneers back, "So
what!"

But perhaps things are not so bleak after all. While it is probably
true that "there can be no escape from plurality—a plurality of traditions, perspectives, philosophic orientations,"[57] we—Anglo-Ameri-
can philosophers and feminists—share a larger situated framework
that makes it most unlikely that our "conceptual schemes are so self-
enclosed that there is no possibility of reciprocal translation, understanding, and argumentation."[58] Rather than approaching contrasting views as philosophic opponents to be confronted and reduced
gleefully to absurdity, Richard Bernstein advises us to "begin with
the assumption that the other has something to say to us and to
contribute to our understanding. The initial task is to grasp the
other's position in the strongest possible light . . . understanding
does not entail agreement. On the contrary, it is the way to clarify
our disagreements."[59] If analytic philosophers and feminists have
reached the impasse described above, it is because they have shared
an adversarial style of confrontation that precludes the type of "engaged fallibilistic pluralism" that Bernstein exhorts.

> [Engaged fallibilistic pluralism] means taking our own fallibility seri-
> ously—resolving that however much we are committed to our own
> styles of thinking, we are willing to listen to others without denying or
> suppressing the otherness of the other. It means being vigilant against
> the dual temptations of simply dismissing what others are saying by
> falling back on one of those standard defensive ploys where we con-
> demn it as obscure, woolly, or trivial, or thinking we can always easily
> translate what is alien into our own entrenched vocabularies.[60]

In order to break dialogical impasse, feminists must restrain their
inclinations to portray doctrinal analysis in so cynical and one-sided
a fashion, to dismiss Rule of Law aspirations as nothing more than
sham and pretense, to disdain analytic philosophy as merely the
conceptual henchman of male domination, to ridicule the quest for

consistency and coherence as either psychological error or aggressive male weaponry, and to castigate critics of their views as male oppressors or their collaborators. For if FU deflects and disables all criticism—as flowing necessarily from malevolent despots or their sycophants—than FU trivializes itself. Likewise, we analytic philosophers must curb our tendency to assault with deranged avidity the perceived doctrinal weaknesses of feminism. For such butchery serves to blind us to the undeniable insights constituting feminist perspectives: the law's complicity in the historical disenfranchisement of women, the subtle ways in which women's views are marginalized and trivialized in social life, the dangers of a "blind" justice that further oppresses the already disadvantaged, the blatant prejudices and biases built into our language and reflected in our experience, the mystifying effects of the Rule of Law when it is used by politically reactionary elements to support allegedly value-free interpretations of legal material, the inadequacy of a gender-neutral approach in a society that has historically nurtured so much gender oppression, and the gut-wrenching expressions of rage and entreaties for love that transcend analytical dissection but that find validation in experience.

# PART THREE

Law's Aspirations and
Philosophical Method
*Promises, Impasses, and
New Directions*

# CHAPTER 9

## A Dialogue Between Mainstream Methods and the New Guard
### *Is There Any Hope?*

**W**E HAVE JUST witnessed various difficulties the advocates of Feminism Unmodified and the proponents of analytic philosophy encounter when trying to engage each other in meaningful debate. The impasse they labor under, however, affords us an opportunity for further insights. Their seemingly divergent methods of discovery, presuppositions, and rhetorical strategies exemplify a wider debate. To illustrate this, consider the following dialogue. Let X and Y represent participants in any number of ongoing discussions within various disciplines, a few of which I indicate below. The dialogue does not track precisely any of the specific debates listed, but it does display many of the common features of each.

| X | | Y | Field |
|---|---|---|---|
| Critical Legal Studies | vs. | Doctrinalists | Jurisprudence |
| Radical Feminists | vs. | Centrists | Political theory |
| Neo-Pragmatists | vs. | Analytics | Philosophy |
| Modernists | vs. | Rationalists | Literary criticism |

X: You cannot live up to your own standards. Your view rests on Epistemological Foundationalism or Metaphysical Realism.[1] These are unconvincing because of [indeterminacy of language, fragility of classical two-valued logic, impossibility of an Archimedean point].

Y: We don't claim that reasoning is mechanical or that universal agreement is required to establish rational claims. You attack a strawperson. Moreover, your rule-skepticism is self-referentially

211

false, it degenerates into a nihilism that cannot be lived, and it disables you from constructing a positive program. Yet you are the ones who claim to "fuse theory and practice"! [Less frequently: a defense of foundationalism and realism.]

X: We merely hold you to your own pretensions, standards that are not only theoretically bankrupt, but worse, politically noxious because they mask the fact that the terms of knowledge and moral correctness ultimately stem from power, not disinterested reason.

Y: It is your method of critique, not our conception of reason and morality, that results in disabling skepticism. Also, our formal requirements of reason do not imply substantive political results.

X: We reject the neat separation of process and result. Furthermore, our methods suggest nothing disabling. One does not give up one's beliefs or ability to assert claims just because she recognizes that those beliefs and claims are not founded on Epistemological Foundationalism and Metaphysical Realism. Just because our ideological disputes are not justified by God or Nature does not suggest that they are trivial. Making explicit the contingent source of our beliefs does not contaminate their content. Thus, we are hardly disabled!

Y: Such beliefs and claims reduce to nothing more than expressions of preference and taste.

X: We are all antecedently situated in social practices that form a context for our discussions. Our discussions are not arbitrary or mere bleatings of preferences.

Y: That reflects ironically the crudest (status quo preserving) conventionalism . . . from you, the apostles of radical change!

X: You accept the phony dilemmas that we repudiate: either objectivism or relativism, either foundationalism and realism or nihilism. Abrogate those dualisms and you eliminate your apparitions and fears of nihilism. Nihilism is impossible, and there is no need to combat or fear that which is impossible.

Y: Your romance with paradox is a trendy attempt to gloss over your disabling contradictions. You have no constructive program.

X: Our constructive program will emerge from democratic dialogue once we pierce the mystification of the dominant discourse.

Y: The very "situation" and "context" you previously extolled!

X: You are straitjacketed by the principles of bivalence and stability. This blinds you to the fluidity and dialectical tensions of life and in things.

Y: Your claims are not innovative. There have been skeptics, relativists, and pragmatists around in the minority strains of Western philosophy from the start.

X: That was a transparent rhetorical move! You try to assimilate, domesticate, and co-opt our position to the dominant discourse. This allows you to ameliorate our political threat. An example of this is your tendency to stigmatize any of our radical programs as "Utopian" and thus unrealizable and to ridicule our less radical programs as "assimilable to the dominant discourse" and thus mere reformism that makes our theoretical assertions unnecessary.

Y: We only report the ways things are.

X: Because you fail to understand our need to transcend the dominant discourse, which we take to be an accomplice in the silencing of politically radical voices, you fail to understand our need not to play by the usual rules of your language games.

Y: You haven't transcended anything. As soon as you make any positive claim, you reveal yourselves as either incoherent babblers or expounders of merely personal preferences.

X: We reject grand theory and, instead, advocate a more situational and pragmatic analysis. [Less frequently: acceptance of grand theory accompanied by invocation of a "new method" of analysis.] Remember that we do not share your belief that "correspondence with reality" or, in your less grandiose moments, intersubjective agreement defines "truth" and "rationality." Disagreement can itself be a sign of and part of rationality, while consensus is often a mask for crude majoritarianism and power.

Y: We both agree that the dilemma of objectivism–relativism is a false polarity. [Less frequently: a defense of the dilemma accompanied by a defense of realism and, even less frequently, foundationalism.] But there is still a need to attend to rational methods of justification.

X: Choice of method is choice of determinants. Neither you nor we can transcend our particular manifestations, and, in an important sense, we are both reduced to reiterating our determinants. But that is all that is available. Thus, there is no reason to despair!

Y: There is at least one large problem with all that: your choice of method is grounded only on certain passionate commitments, which themselves will seem either arbitrary or conventionalist. All you seem to have left is "assuming responsibility for self-conscious value choices." Are we starting to hear whispers of "authenticity" from your existentialist chorus?

X: We have no need of foundationalist methods or presuppositions, which themselves are myths. Again, the lack of such foundations as the source of our beliefs does not force us to give up our beliefs about values or mute our expressions of them.

Y: [In the context of legal judgments] But personal choices are one thing and judicial interpretations are quite another. You cannot vindicate or justify the imposition of judicial decisions on those citizens who embrace different value judgments. Personal choices are often merely personal, while judicial choices implicate the coercive powers of the state. Ironically, despite all your bellyaching about the horrors of masking crude majoritarianism and power, it is you who privilege a few (judicial) voices (who will inevitably mirror the dominant discourse) and confer on them the power to dictate the terms of existence to the rest of us, while you simultaneously acknowledge that there is no rational way to reach intersubjective agreement!

X: You, once again, to give your criticisms currency, resort to the very presuppositions that we reject; that is, you beg the question against us by evaluating our claims and methods by precisely those standards from which we have self-consciously distanced ourselves. The alleged maladies of our view, which you so piously and pompously cite, are virulent only if foundational presuppositions are themselves possible and discernible. But they are not. Accordingly, we don't pretend that our views will be acceptable to your outmoded conceptual tools. We are glad they are not! Your criticisms merely restate our claims, contrast them with the dominant discourse, and describe the chasm as *our* weaknesses.

Y: By trying to immunize your position from critical attack you trivialize yourselves. You rejoin to any criticism by claiming that it merely shows the strength of your position as opposition to the dominant discourse. Accordingly, it is *you* who beg the question!

## RHETORICAL STRATEGIES

I have adumbrated a sample of the type of dialogue that is often reflected in the literature. We can extract from such dialogues at least five (somewhat) different rhetorical strategies: the intuitive, analytic, pragmatic, substructuralist, and deconstructive.[2]

*Intuitive.* This strategy rests clearly on tradition, social convention, and faith. It does not interrogate its own starting points but, instead, refers to the authority or "givenness" of institutional practices, established methodologies, and privileged texts. While one might justify an intuitive strategy by using an analytic or other rhetorical strategy, the crux of the intuitive is found in the appeals that constitute its practice.[3] Most of us are eventually pushed to the intuitive in normative (and nonnormative) debate because of the traditional difficulty in bridging the gap between "ought" and "is," and the problematic nature of an Archimedean epistemological point. Accordingly, in such debates we often find proclamations of self-evident principles, axioms, inevitable social convention, and universal practices as the necessary starting points of normative discourse.

*Analytic.* This is the strategy of classical logic and argumentation: deductive, inductive, analogical, and practical. Universal laws of reason are held to govern the validity of argument, while intellectual dullness, distortion, and error are taken as prime enemies of truth. The analytic strategy has supreme confidence in the ability of theoretical structures to explain and (possibly) justify extant social practices. Accordingly, analytics hold "a view of law as a text (as opposed to a practice) that must constantly adhere to the aesthetic requirements of reason."[4]

*Pragmatic.* This strategy privileges community and conversation and is skeptical of totalizing schemes and critiques. It often criticizes analytics for their dualistic tendencies and their proclivity to solidify fluid distinctions into false and inflexible polarities. Pragmatists champion the flux and pluralism of social life and oppose the projects of foundationalism and (almost always) realism.

Pragmatists invoke fallibilism. Emphasis is taken away from the solitary reasoner or an imaginary, ideal reasoning situation and placed instead on "the regulative ideal of a critical community of inquirers,"[5] which has "[an] awareness and sensitivity to [the] radical contingency and chance that mark the universe, our inquiries, our lives."[6]

*Substructuralist.* This strategy refuses to accept the claims of reason at face value. Disparaging analytics as undervaluing experience and practice, substructuralists tend to posit nonrational (often total) explanations for social practices, ideologies, and the core of common sense that constitutes reason. Examples of substructuralist explanations include "contradictions among the means and relations of production (Marx), the advent of bureaucratic organization (Weber), the unconscious (Freud), will to power (Nietzsche), and cultural practice

(Wittgenstein)."[7] The presumed objectivity of many analytic strategists spawns a vision that substructuralists scorn "as a circular arrangement of propositions reflecting the underlying reality unconsciously and in a distorted manner."[8] Accordingly, substructuralists try "to create a community of meaning by replicating the experience of totalizing constructs."[9]

*Deconstructive.* This strategy is most distinguished from the others by its form of presentation: "It puts the unpresentable forward in the presentation itself."[10] Deconstructionists seem to exalt an "anything goes" form, and to advocates of the other strategies their works "seem deliberate (and unnecessary) attempts to estrange, irritate, and offend the reader's sensibilities."[11] Deconstructionists oppose all totalizing ambitions and strive consciously to break the rules of ordinary discourse. Explicitly recognizing that it does not address a universal audience, deconstructionism "abandons the search for common ground altogether, following instead the ironic twists and turns of difference, discontinuity, and disjuncture."[12]

## THE MORAL OF THE STORY

Earlier we experienced a sense of frustration that radical and mainstream theorists reach apparent argumentative impasses. They appear to reach a point where they simply do not share enough common ground to continue in good faith dialogue. In fact, their respective animating assumptions seem so disparate and incommensurate that each seems to end up begging the question against the other. On the other hand, radical and mainstream theorists often do seem to engage each other for at least fleeting moments of genuine debate.

The classification of rhetorical strategies permits us to glimpse a deeper insight into the nature of the problem. Generally, moments of engagement occur when the participants in a dialogue are speaking from within the same rhetorical mode, or possibly, from only somewhat different modes. Generally, the frustration of incommensurability arises when the participants are speaking from significantly different modes. These are generalities, however, because it is possible for incommensurability to arise between participants speaking in the same mode and for engagement to occur between participants speaking in somewhat different modes.

The moral of this tale is that most speakers shift among these different modes.[13] Rarely does any theorist speak systematically and invariably from only one rhetorical strategy. Those who speak from within the analytic mode probably come the closest to achieving complete consistency, because that mode is clearly dominant. But even from those speaking predominantly from within the analytic strategy, we will almost always find invocations of the intuitive and pragmatic modes. For example, notice how Y often assumes that for X to advance valid claims, X must project the same kinds of interpretive and theoretical aspirations and presuppositions as those projected by Y. If X happens to be trying to assert substructuralist claims, the force of X's position will be obscured by Y's reformulation of those claims as analytic, a reformulation that depends on an intuitive strategy. This is because Y's assumption that all valid claims flow from the analytic is itself an implicit reliance on an intuitive commitment that privileges the analytics' own intellectual sources. Moreover, notice how analytics make use of that intuitive commitment to reformulate substructuralist claims as analytic ones in order to employ a pragmatic strategy as Y tells X: "Your rule-skepticism . . . cannot be lived."

I am not claiming here that X or Y is doing anything illicit, illogical, or even undesirable while they both shift among rhetorical strategies. To different degrees, we all tend to use whatever cognitive and rhetorical tools are available to address the instant problem. Rhetorical shifts constitute a clash of paradigms of discourse, a clash that is itself healthy and progressive.[14] Thus, the Janus-faced character of the problem: the extent and degree of rhetorical shifting often results in more immediate incommensurability, but longer-term testing and progress of discourse as the various rhetorical modes refine themselves. This is not to say that we will ever reach the point of everlasting equilibrium, at which rhetorical shifting ceases and discourse stabilizes once and forever. But this observation should not alarm: "Despair is appropriate only if one somehow felt entitled to a discourse system that guarantees communicative transparency in the first place. . . . Once one recognizes the problem of audience fragmentation, such a singular cognitive orientation is no longer rhetorically plausible."[15]

This analysis suggests an interesting way to view law. Rather than seeing law as an unremitting, unarbitrable war of ideologies as do the Critical Legal Scholars, perhaps we can reconceive it as the relentless, often incommensurable, competition of rhetorical strategies. In fact, it has been claimed that the presence of such competition has a salutary effect on the dominant (analytic) legal aspiration of intellectual convergence.[16]

While rhetorical strategies, of themselves, may not seem to have any necessary political implications, they do have a few tenuous contingent connections. Political centrists will most frequently employ analytic and pragmatic strategies, conservatives will most frequently employ intuitive and analytic strategies, leftists will most frequently employ substructuralist and deconstructive strategies. Again, these are generalities that admit of significant variation. At present, there can be little doubt that legal opinions reflect overwhelmingly analytic, intuitive, and pragmatic rhetorical strategies.

The analytic mode is unquestionably the dominant strategy of discourse, in law and generally. It often successfully domesticates and assimilates the apparent insights of the other modes. In this manner, by co-optation and reformulation of the potentially unsettling effects of the other modes, the analytic strategy remains supreme. Whether one views this as a politically pernicious effect of the intellectual rule of philosophers or as a socially necessary hygiene that mediates the dissonance in our life and language will depend itself on an intuitive acceptance of various rhetorical strategies.[17]

To break dialogical impasse, a few preliminary steps are necessary. First, leftist critics and analytic philosophers must acknowledge that they do not speak from alien discourses but rather employ common rhetorical modes to greater and lesser extents. MacKinnon, for example, is as ruthless as any philosopher when she uses the dominant analytic mode to critique her adversaries, while numerous analytic philsophers are not above using substructuralist or deconstructive modes to unsettle the views of their opponents. Thus, it is more than a bit disingenuous for MacKinnon to stigmatize the dominant analytic mode as thoroughly contaminated by male hostility and for analytic philosophers to ridicule as "nonrigorous" the less-dominant rhetorical modes. Second, it should be recognized that once we explicitly abrogate realism and foundationalism—as leftist critics clearly do and as more philosophers are doing—there are no (or at least few) metaphysical trumps of Reason that can be used authoritatively to adjudicate disputes clearly. More is up for grabs than is commonly admitted. Third, both sides should commit to the kind of engaged fallibilistic pluralism that Bernstein endorses.

Thus, I am privileging a type of pragmatism as a way to mediate the apparent cognitive dissonance generated by the clash of mainstream methods and their leftist critics. This program requires an antifoundationalist outlook that abrogates reliance on fixed segments of knowledge and special cognitive faculties. Moreover, despite the way institutions solidify and emit the appearance of naturalness and inevitability, we should appreciate the contingency of current arrangements and the possibilities of transformation. Rather than regretting the loss of fixed foundations and authoritative trumps of Reason, we should revel in increased opportunities for freedom and collective deliberation. Furthermore, we should not assume that convergence of opinion is the necessary goal of rational discussion. Certainly there will be many basic matters on which otherwise divergent ideologies will converge. But where there is a hardened orthodoxy of views on virtually all normative matters we should suspect the presence of stultifying authoritarianism. Finally, our institutions should not strive to eliminate ideological and political conflict; rather, they should rechannel controversy as a way to invigorate social life.

But what grounds support the privileging of the pragmatic mode? Here I can only use an intuitive strategy and appeal to the following considerations on behalf of the pragmatic mode: it best fuses theory and practice and is thus better suited than other modes to a practical enterprise such as law; it more closely tracks an engaged fallibilistic pluralism than do other modes; it can better ameliorate, although not eliminate, cognitive incommensurability; it rejects both extreme foundationalism and simple reductionism; and it offers the best possibilities for transcending the objectivist–relativist polarity.

Still, all this may seem woefully insufficient. After all, the preceding chapters of this book testify that the struggle among rhetorical modes tends to unsettle the claims of all the major classical and contemporary legal theories. Regardless of the kind of legal theory someone concocts by employing one or more of the available modes, critics gleefully assail that theory by using the same mode or the other modes. We seem left with a reenactment of the Tower of Babel, a gaggle of self-contained voices feverishly pursuing but inevitably evading genuine communication.

But, once again, this common first reaction is mistaken. If the source of the worry is the lack of an uncontroversial, transparent, and unifying discourse, then earlier remarks bear repeating: given audience fragmentation, a monolithic cognitive orientation is myth. Perhaps the source of the worry is that the analysis in this section does little to help the problem; it merely underscores our plight. If this is the case, then we should note that this analysis allows us a better understanding of why and how incommensurability occurs[18] and permits us to achieve progress in at least the sense that the supremacy claims of the dominant analytic mode are rendered suspect.[19] Thus, we should be suspicious of claims of universality. Instead, we must evolve a jurisprudence that can give credence to the presence of distinctive, often conflicting rhetorical modes and political ideologies yet not degenerate into abject decisionism and imposition of arbitrary preferences. It is to this task that I now turn.

# CHAPTER 10

## Critical Pragmatism
### *Pluralism, Justification, and Law's Directive Power*

THE LEGAL THEORY that philosophers embrace is related loosely to their political perspective. A theorist who views the fundamental order as corrupt and thoroughly flawed is likely to advocate one of the leftist critiques of law or to propose a libertarian minimalist social order. Those who perceive current institutional arrangements as basically sound and in need only of marginal reform will be more likely to champion a version of analytic jurisprudence. The reason for this connection between legal theory and political perspective concerns the nature of legal language. Legal language generally, and judicial decision making specifically, echo and reinforce existing institutional arrangements because they make extensive use of precedent, received meanings, and antecedent definitions. Accordingly, those who are appalled by existing political conditions and economic distributions will excoriate the methods of legal reasoning that collaborate in wider social injustice. Such theorists will strive to debunk the pretensions of law and to unsettle current understandings as a first step toward desired social transformation. On the other hand, those who acknowledge systemic flaws as marginal and aberrational and who appreciate deeply the benefits of existing institutional arrangements, will hum paeans of praise to the methods of legal reasoning that sustain the enthroned social order. In sum, political centrists have a stake in showing extant law in its best light, while political malcontents have a stake in undermining law's pretensions. Neither theoretical posture—the privileging or the discrediting of law—is demanded by the inherent meanings or logical requirements of interpretation and judgment. Thus, it is virtually impossible to advance a legal theory without revealing at least a portion of one's descriptive and prescriptive view of the world. There is no politically neutral method of assessing a theory of law.

221

As a prelude to advancing and defending Critical Pragmatism, I return to the Rule of Law debate and reexamine the concept of objectivity in law.

## THE RULE OF LAW REVISITED

At least four conceptions of the Rule of Law are contained in the literature: formal, substantive, holistic, and critical.

*Formal.* Much of the debate in legal theory centers misguidedly on a formal notion of the Rule of Law. Apologists for the status quo trot out their most pious and pompous rhetoric when extolling the Rule of Law, while those with revolutionary ambitions ridicule elements of the Rule of Law as accessories in the perpetration of social injustice. Both factions miss the mark. The elements of the Rule of Law—treating like cases alike, providing notice of law's requirements, constructing impersonal and general decrees, and so on—are merely formal requirements that supply no practical guidance.[1] Although such elements implicate notions of objectivity and neutrality, these notions are politically benign in this context. While leftists are fond of stigmatizing them as the conceptual henchmen of the exploitive capitalist system, the incoherent liberal social structure, or the inherently oppressive male order, in the context noted they function merely as harmless logical constraints on decision making.

The proper focus of debate is on issues such as the appropriate criteria of similarity and difference, and of apt treatment for such cases. Here the leftist criticism that standards of "similarity" and "reasonable person" are defined in terms of white, relatively privileged males has considerable merit. The formulation of these standards in that fashion will exclude the claims and experiences of those who are nonwhite, relatively disadvantaged, or female. But such exclusion occurs, not because of invocation of Rule of Law virtues, but because of the substantive standards of similarity and treatment that are adopted. A leftist can consistently embrace Rule of Law rhetoric while simultaneously denouncing judicial decisions that presuppose the flawed substantive standards. Likewise, a political centrist can praise Rule of Law virtues to her heart's content, but that will not redeem flawed substantive standards.

*Substantive* versions of the Rule of Law[2] generally connect formal constraints and process values to a substantive value (e.g., freedom or the facilitation of rights or political fairness), which itself is taken to be necessary for justice. Thus, substantive versions of the Rule of

Law supplement formal versions by connecting Rule of Law virtues to elements of political liberalism such as the primacy of freedom, the dangers of authoritarianism, and the need to ensure social cooperation and by providing for the Rule of Law a justification that goes beyond the alleged requirements of formal logic.[3] Thus, "Someone who stresses [a merely formal notion of the Rule of Law] might affirm that a rule-bound dictatorship evidences the Rule of Law; someone who stresses the substantive aspect would not."[4] The substantive version of the Rule of Law is, however, modest. It claims that a system of the proper kind of legal rules by itself facilitates substantive liberal values such as liberty, autonomy, and fairness. It does not require that a pronouncement, taken by itself, be substantively fair and just to be a legal rule. Thus, adherence to this notion of the Rule of Law does not commit one to the draconian requirement that a legal system must consist only of substantively just rules and decisions. Rather, it would disparage, as deficient due to its substantive violation of the Rule of Law, any system of legality that fundamentally and consistently strayed from liberal values of individual freedom and democratic resolution. Substantive versions of the Rule of Law are often supported by commitments to a separation of governmental powers and to a principled distinction between creating and applying law.

Such notions of the Rule of Law are susceptible to a variety of difficulties. First, the distinction between creating and applying law is not clear: "How do we know the rule is being 'applied'? The skeptic says, 'We can't really tell.' We cannot identify any formal or logical criterion by which we can determine whether or not someone is following a rule."[5] Second, the relationship between the existence of a rule and its "binding-ness" is also unclear: "In what consists the 'binding-ness' of rules? The skeptic says, 'This bond cannot be shown.' We cannot demonstrate any formal or logical nexus between the rule and the rule-follower's behavior in response to it."[6] Third, dependency on antecedently existing rules invites questions of formal realizability: "The skeptic says, 'Traditional formal realizability cannot be shown to exist.' We cannot demonstrate that application of a rule is analytic or deductive. . . . Rules are not logically prior to uniformity of action in response to them; rather, uniformity of action is prior to the existence of rules."[7] Thus, to the extent that substantive versions of the Rule of Law are still tied to the excesses of formalism they are suspect.

Dworkin's non–rule book conception avoids many of these problems but is still susceptible to the difficulties noted in Chapter 3.

Moreover, to the extent that Dworkin's rights conception of the Rule of Law is tied to the existence of antecedently existing right answers to virtually all legal questions it remains implausible.

*Holistic.* Sometimes critics take the Rule of Law to task as a way of stigmatizing holistically the formal processes of legal systems. Rather than committing to the prescriptions of justice under law, these critics may, instead, advocate the end of law (as certain anarchists and Marxists do for different reasons) or propose methods of informal dispute resolution such as arbitration or local citizens' panels (as certain communitarians do). In this context, critics are not merely indicting the formal elements of the Rule of Law but the entire domain of law. I have sketched the problems accompanying "end of law" advocacy in Chapter 6, so I turn now to the reasons communitarians often propose less formal dispute resolution.

Conventional social wisdom holds that there is a connection between the degree of harmony a community achieves and the manner in which it resolves conflicts.[8] The greater the relational distance between parties to a dispute, the more likely is it that they will use the full force of law to settle their conflict. The force of law, it is argued, begins where communal bonds end. The current movement toward neighborhood justice centers, mediation for juvenile offenders, and prison inmate arbitration has historical precursors in the conflict resolution methods used by small, discrete groups in our country. Quakers, Puritans, Mormons, and Jews, among others, believed that adversarial, formal processes of law were antithetical to communal harmony.[9] Courts were perceived as inclined toward sterilizing a dispute by emptying it of its social content and translating it into the abstract, impersonal language of the law.

It is a perplexing, and no doubt unresolvable, question whether our adversary system and our general dependence on law create social disharmony by their combative imagery and confrontations, or whether they merely reflect antecedently existing fragmentation resulting from a pluralistic society. Perhaps the recent movements in our country toward more kinds of alternative dispute resolution signal not only alarm at the rising costs, time, and energy spent in litigation but also a yearning for a deeper sense of community.

It would be, however, both naive and dangerous to embrace alternative dispute resolution wholeheartedly. It seems highly improbable that the elimination of our adversary system and decreased emphasis on pressing legal rights would of itself result in significantly increased communal bonds. The paradox is that a high degree of antecedently existing community and harmony is a precondition of alternative dispute resolution, whose methods are themselves geared toward increasing feelings of community and experiences of harmony. Moreover, alternative dispute resolution may tend to deny already disadvantaged citizens access to formal legal processes. The main determinant to date of who uses such methods has been the poverty line. Accordingly, critics suggest that less reliance on law and legal processes is a way of reinforcing "two-tier" justice, deflecting energy and resources away from political organization and effective litigation strategies for the underclasses.[10] Finally, there is a fear that absent formal proceedings and adherence to Rule of Law virtues, arbitrary and illegitimate appeals to the power, influence, race, and religion of the respective disputants will become paramount.

Thus, the advocates of formal proceedings in an adversarial setting appeal to the traditional notion of the Rule of Law, in both its narrow and broad meanings, while advocates of alternative dispute resolution question our ability to achieve the lofty ideals of the Rule of Law, point out the excessive expense and vast energies required to maintain adversarial litigation, criticize the cult and ideology of legal expertise promulgated by legal insiders, and contend that our present methods are socially divisive and perpetuate the pernicious myths of atomistic, competitive individualism.

*Critical* notions of the Rule of Law emerge from leftist critique. Such notions highlight the role of community practice and champion the loosening of fixed distinctions. Rather than emphasizing the formal characteristics of rules or a logic internal to law, a critical notion of the Rule of Law identifies community agreement and societal practice as the true foundations of rules: "Rules can only be claimed to exist when there is a community agreement in practice. . . . Agreement in action does not follow from there being a preexisting rule; agreement in action is the only basis for claiming that there is a rule."[11] Because the law may lag behind community agreement and practice, this notion of the Rule of Law does not necessarily mirror "black letter" statutes and the allegedly literal rendering of extant doctrine: "A rule will be public whenever strong social agreement exists in practice, regardless of whether a legislature or a court has spoken."[12] Relying on embedded social practices constitutive of rules, the critical notion accepts unsqueamishly that "the law in the statute books is not the real law."[13]

There is here a loosening of fixed distinctions such as rule creators–rule appliers and of rigid appeals to separation of governmental powers. On this view, law does not consist of formally realized

rules: rules are not separate from cases, nor do they logically preex-
ist their application, and thus legal officials cannot pretend to be
mere functionaries who perform their tasks in accordance with carefully circumscribed boundaries: "rules are neither formal in the traditional sense, nor eternal, nor existing independently of us; and so
we know that every application [of legal rules and principles] is a
reinterpretation."[14] The traditional fixed distinctions are inappropriate because "law, as long as it is part of a viable and developing
community, is neither 'found' nor 'made,' but continuously re-inter-
preted. There are still rules. But there are no rules that can be understood apart from their context; nor are there rules that can be understood as fixed in time."[15]

Given that it denies the formal-realizability of rules, embraces
skeptical positions on virtually all the basics of formalism, abrogates
the fixed distinctions often thought preserved by the Rule of Law,
and denigrates the functionalism usually sanctified as the core of
law, one may well wonder why this notion would adhere to Rule of
Law rhetoric at all. The answer is that "we will still find it deeply
normatively appealing to conceive of ourselves as a people governed
by its law rather than by arbitrary individual power, because conceiving of ourselves this way I take to be constitutive of ourselves as
a political community."[16]

What, then, is the judicial role under a critical version of the Rule
of Law? The answer seems purposefully ambiguous:

> To act rightly as a judge is to refuse to use the violence of one's office to
> enforce the law of the state against the law of various dissenting com-
> munities, while at the same time recognizing and taking responsibility
> for the fact that the law of the community of judges can come into con-
> flict with, and is not intrinsically privileged over, the law of other inter-
> pretive communities.[17]

Regarding the traditional judicial virtues of impartiality and independence we are told that "independence and impartiality can refer
to moral autonomy and a commitment to judgment in light of one's
own moral understanding of the nature of community—not just to
formal separation from the interests of the legislature or the litigants."[18] Thus, "judges are an interpretive community conscious of
their obligation to act as independent moral choosers for the good of
a society, in light of what that society is and can become."[19]

At first blush, the critical notion of the Rule of Law seems nothing more than judges recognizing explicitly the vast discretion they

possess because of the alleged impossibility of all formalist aspirations, rendering decisions by self-consciously invoking their descriptive and prescriptive vision of the nation, willingly assuming a (crudely?) instrumentalist perspective, and acknowledging that their interpretive community is not inherently superior to other interpretive communities and the nation as a whole retaining the illusion that it is a system of laws, not people, because doing so has a salutary effect on its self-image. A centrist critic would shudder at its use of the phrase "Rule of Law," and would describe the critical version as an embodiment of pernicious abuse of official power coupled with self-deception.

Clearly, there is much persuasive force to the centrist's charges. The judicial imperatives offered by the critical notion of the Rule of Law—to act as independent moral choosers, to acknowledge that the decisions of the judicial community are not intrinsically privileged over the law of other interpretive communities, and to refuse to use the coercive power of one's office to enforce the law of the state against the law of various dissenting communities—neither coexists easily or admits of adequate specification. Furthermore, appeals to the rules embedded in societal practices may implicate precisely the sort of arid conventionalism that advocates of the critical notion of the Rule of Law otherwise disparage. Harboring leftist ambitions, the proponents of the critical notion may find themselves stuck ironically with the conclusions of routine, centrist politics. Finally, given a radical unsettling of all formalist presuppositions, the continued appeal to Rule of Law rhetoric is redolent of manipulation and duplicity.

Advocates of the critical notion could rejoin that they do not propose an unbridled judiciary. After all, judges would be constrained by a conception of rules that incorporates community agreements and practices. Moreover, judges would pay homage to their wider community and thus would not be free to impose conclusions arbitrarily.

Without additional determinate content it is difficult to assess fairly the relative merits of the critical notion of the Rule of Law. At first glance it needs considerable refinement. But it is already an important contribution to the literature because it reminds us that the Rule of Law is a contested concept and because it challenges leftist politics to reconceive a principled version of judicial decision making, while at the same time abrogating formalist assumptions and unconvincing legal distinctions.

## OBJECTIVISM AND RELATIVISM

There are several different notions of "objectivity," a few of which I examine and explain.

Metaphysical objectivity contends that the structure of reality, independent of and external to all individual perceivers, provides the basis for determining correct judgments. On the moral level, correct judgments are those corresponding to the reality of the impersonal nature of the universe, the nature of humans, or the imperatives of a supernatural being. Metaphysical objectivity would provide the security of truly authoritative principles only if it were a comprehensible metaphor in normative matters. Once discerned, such principles would be beyond revision, at least as long as the corresponding reality remained unchanged. But it is not clear that metaphysical objectivity is a comprehensible metaphor in normative matters. First, humans cannot ascend to an Archimedean point and compare reality to our normative judgments to assess the truth of those judgments, that is, we cannot transcend our context within reality and view reality from the outside. Second, it is unclear how and why nonnormative facts about the universe or human nature translate into specific normative principles. We would need a bridge—a first principle, an axiom, a self-evident starting point—to connect those facts to a moral order. But it is precisely such a bridge that metaphysical objectivity is supposed to provide, not require. Third, it is doubtful that requisite facts about the universe or an inherent human nature exist. Both of these concepts are themselves centers of dispute. Fourth, even if an omnipotent, omnibenevolent supernatural being exists, that being cannot be used to free us from our fallible use of human judgment. Plato's dilemma in the *Euthyphro* still stands: Are God's decrees morally correct because God perceives accurately an indepencent standard of the Good? Or are God's decrees morally correct because they are God's decrees? If the former, then God is unnecessary for metaphysical objectivity.[20] If the latter, then how do we know independently that God is Good, rather than merely powerful enough to command our allegiance? Finally, even if there is metaphysical objectivity in normative decision making, can we ever know when we have achieved it?

On the level of judicial decision making, metaphysical objectivity resonates in a crude formalist vision. Correct judgments are those corresponding to the reality of a completely coherent set of legal materials that, when applied by rational officials using appropriate methods of reason, ensures (at least in principle) a logically correct result for virtually every case. Such a process need not be mechanical, at least not in hard cases, as judges would still have to discern the proper materials to apply to the fact pattern at bar. But presumably, a judge's own prejudices, political beliefs, and ideological perspective would be irrelevant to the decision. A judge must reason as follows: "I realize that I possess perspective X, but X is irrelevant to my decision making. I am constrained by antecedently existing legal materials and impersonal logic, which fully determine the results of my decisions. I recognize that judicial decision making is not politics and that my role is one of dispassionate inquiry toward the correct result that I discover and do not invent."

We have already examined the overwhelming problems of this view of judicial decision making. To reiterate, the notion of metaphysical objectivity, at least in the enterprises of morality and law, is either inaccessible to humans or is an incomprehensible metaphor.

Communal or intersubjective objectivity may be of two sorts. Societal consensus reflects the actual conventions the society embodies. In the realm of law, the moral and legal beliefs of the community ultimately confirm or nullify the conclusions judges reach. Insofar as community consensus varies from a judge's personal political and moral beliefs, it imposes an objective, external constraint on her. Under communal objectivity, a judge must reason as follows: "I realize that I have perspective X, but X is irrelevant to my decision making. I am constrained by legal materials and impersonal logic, as well as the moral and legal beliefs of the community. I cannot decide on the basis of my perspective and then buttress such decisions by the use of a merely plausible legal argument. Rather, I must decide on the basis of legal materials and objective community standards that should reflect the best legal argument."

Societal presuppositions are not necessarily principles that society considers true by actual consensus, but those presupposed by the institutions, prior decisions, and constitution of that society.[21] To illustrate, it is conceivable that a majority of Americans would today reject a number of guarantees ensured by our Bill of Rights. Nevertheless, these guarantees reflect principles objectively presupposed by our governmental institutions and may thus be considered communally objective. Likewise, the principles presupposed by clear judicial precedents may not be in full accord with current societal consensus, but they may still be considered objective constraints on judicial decision making. The discovery of such presuppositions will often require interpretation based at least partly on judges' ideological perspectives. In a limited way, under this view, judicial decision making implicates politics.

Although they will sometimes conflict, societal consensus and societal presuppositions do not necessarily reflect belief in timeless truths or the authoritative structure of reality. Proponents of communal objectivity claim only that judges are engaged in reasoning of a public nature with society, and that public standards ultimately verify or invalidate judicial opinions. Thus, these standards are objective constraints on judicial decision making.

Criticism of communal objectivity centers on its conventionalism. Societal consensus is better understood as intersubjective agreement, the shared values of a group. But such values, even if they could be identified confidently, are objective only in that they are not necessarily identical with a judge's personal convictions, not because consensus confers added moral or legal credentials on beliefs. Alternatively, if societal consensus is taken to mean only that judges are engaged in a continuing reasoned dialogue with society, it differs little from the recognition that political prudence is a genuine constraint on judges. To call such a constraint "objective" may confuse principled dialogue with mere political expediency.

So, too, societal presuppositions may seem elusive. Our institutions are so complex that many different sets of principles can explain and justify them equally well. Under these circumstances, to claim one and only one set of principles as their unique explanation seems presumptuous. Even if such a venture could be completed successfully it would result in a morass of conflicting principles that would need to be considered in relation to one another. Some will argue that societal presuppositions are either a set of fictions, or, if discernible, still require judges to invoke their subjective ideologies during the process of relative weighting.[22] Thus, the extent to which societal presuppositions are truly external constraints on judges, as opposed to mere reflections of judges' personal preferences, remains highly contestable.

Perspectival objectivity consists of certain requirements of the judicial point of view. Formal imperatives of impartiality, attentiveness, disinterestedness, and rationality mark the bounds of justified judicial latitude in decision making. Thus, judges are required to attend the Rule of Law virtues, to avoid conflicts of interest and favoritism, to attend carefully to the legal materials applicable to the case, and to arrive at the best decision. Unlike metaphysical objectivity and communal objectivity, perspectival objectivity contends that formal requirements of the judicial frame of mind have a sufficiently objective character to restrain judges from justifiably deciding cases on the basis of personal ideology.

The force of perspectival objectivity is assailed for lacking content. Judges must fill in the meaning of "attentiveness," "impartiality," and "disinterestedness" from their own subjective ideologies. Leftists complain that such phrases are failed attempts to shroud judicial manipulation with a cloak of ersatz justification. Formal requirements, they charge, are too vague and open to interpretation to serve as substantive constraints on judges.

## IS THERE OBJECTIVITY IN LAW?

There are at least two important observations regarding the foregoing discussion. First, two questions are sometimes conflated: Are there external constraints on judicial decision making? and, Are there objectively correct answers to legal questions? The answers to these questions need not be the same. For example, there may be external constraints on judicial decision making that are themselves merely conventional. Such constraints will not fulfill the rigorous demands of metaphysical objectivity. Second, most of the criticism of objectivity in law acknowledges the inaccessibility or incomprehensibility of metaphysical objectivity but then assumes the standard of metaphysical objectivity when undermining the claims of other forms of objectivity. In other words, criticism of communal objectivity and perspectival objectivity often centers on their inability to meet the criteria constituting metaphysical objectivity. Because of all this, answers to the question, Is there objectivity in law? are often muddled.

*External Constraints.* Judges feel constrained by communal objectivity. Any legal system needs stability, both to satisfy the legitimate expectations of citizens and to provide notice of what actions are illegal. For example, if the doctrine of *stare decisis* were abandoned, citizens could not depend on the force of prior decisions, the boundary line separating illegal from legal conduct would be obscured, and public anxiety could increase significantly and dangerously. Thus, judges often justifiably rely on forms of communal objectivity to ensure public expectations and to provide notice of law's requirements. Acknowledgement of communal objectivity's role in decision making does not eliminate the need for judgment but recognizes that the judiciary lacks unbridled powers. Citizens have a right to good faith judicial efforts that apply consistently the principles that ground governmental institutions. The controversial nature of such principles does not of itself render them indiscernible. The existence of competing claims or principles does not imply that all claims and all principles are equally persuasive and well established. In each case, judges must make their best judgment concerning the imperatives of the public standards that they must use in deciding. Judges are not free to advance their own views as such but must recognize elements of communal objectivity and maintain perspectival objectivity in weighing competing claims.

Moreover, although formal requirements constitute perspectival objectivity, it does not follow that these requirements are so devoid of content that judges may fill in meanings from their own ideological biases. Formal requirements furnish citizens a set of prejudgment conditions that judges must meet to exercise their function properly and to avoid ad hoc decision making. Public opinion excoriates any judge who ignores these restraints. The power of these restraints is also reinforced by professional socialization, the practices constituting legal education and experience. Thus, the requirements of perspectival objectivity go beyond the constraint of political prudence. They serve instead as minimal duties that judges knowingly assume on becoming members of the judiciary. In sum, they partly define what it means to be a judge.

We must note, however, that this notion of external constraint, depending as it does on institutionalism, professionalism, and established practices, has serious limitations. First, it relies almost entirely on social and professional conventions that are not prescriptively self-ratifying. Second, it thus cannot by itself provide a justification of judicial decisions or an account of law's directive power. Third, the answers forthcoming from this context cannot secure foundational legal truths, nor are these answers immune to revision. Accordingly, we must be wary of the influences of power and privilege in the formation of our professional practices and social conventions. Although they tend to obscure the sources of our conventions, regularity and habit cannot confer additional prescriptive force on that which emerges from contingent power.

*Objectively Correct Answers?* To address the question of whether there are objectively correct answers to legal disputes we must explore the meaning of the question itself. It could mean that correct answers are somehow "just out there" in a self-executing text; are required by brute, noninterpretive facts; or are given by the inherent order of a cognitively transparent universe. This notion of "objectively correct" takes legal answers to be reports of "ontologically independent meanings scattered among the furniture of the universe."[23] Such a meaning is seductive but ultimately unhelpful. It is seductive because, if achievable, it would realize the formalist vision of fully authoritative answers not dependent on human vicissitudes and fallibilities. It is unhelpful, however, for precisely the reasons given earlier to show that metaphysical objectivity is an incomprehensible metaphor.

Much of the debunking of objectively right answers in law consists of commonplace observations that impugn metaphysical objectivity. But this issue, at least in jurisprudence, is a red herring because usually those who argue for the existence of right answers do not subscribe to metaphysical objectivity. Even natural law theorists, who do contend that there are ontologically independent moral facts and meanings underlying the universe, do not claim that metaphysically objective meanings can be applied straightforwardly to the practical enterprise of judicial decision making.

## CRITICAL PRAGMATISM

A Critical Pragmatism, one capable of halting degeneration into rabid skepticism, should not rely on the suppositions of metaphysical objectivity. Rather, it should begin with an insight from the phenomenology of normative discourse: once inside the enterprise of normative debate, once we are actually arguing for and evaluating moral and legal conclusions, we all presuppose that "some claims are better than others, that some are right and others wrong."[24] The arguments we advance to support our favored normative conclusions are not supported by different esoteric arguments that claim that our conclusions are objectively correct. As Dworkin points out: "But now suppose someone, having heard my arguments [that slavery is unjust], asks me whether I have any different arguments for the further view that slavery is objectively or really unjust. I know that I do not because, so far as I can tell, it is not a further claim at all but just the same claim put in a slightly more emphatic form."[25]

Unlike discussions about matters involving only subjective preferences—Which food is superior, Italian or Chinese? Which color is more attractive, red or violet?—the phenomenology of normative discourse necessarily implicates an intricate network of beliefs, attitudes, and social practices that themselves generate internal theoretical constraints on judgments. Normative discourse is characterized by argument in a strong sense: defending one's position with nonarbitrary reasons, which at some point implicate concepts of human interests. This process, although constituted by numerous historically shaped criteria, is a structured and rule-governed enterprise. The experience of robust argument distances normative discourse from disagreements over matters of merely subjective preferences but does not necessarily commit us to strong and implausible foundationalist assumptions.

The aim of normative discourse so conceived is not necessarily the end of disagreement and the solace of objective final answers, but rather a commitment to political disputation in its most zestful form: the liberating recognition that more is up for grabs than habit and convention generally permit; that creativity and experimentation not only always have a place in, but are at the center of, social deliberations; and that the historical forces of class oppression cannot be justified by appeals to ahistorical entities, such as inherent human nature, which themselves lack independent justification. Under such a conception, we seek a deeper understanding of disagreement and incommensurability, and a profound comprehension of the connection between the people we are and the disputes in which we engage.

The aim here, however, is not to denigrate but to clarify the possibility of moral assessment or moral insight.

> A moral vision may contradict, for example, what we know or think it rational to believe on other grounds, be they logical, metaphysical, or empirical. But we cannot any longer hope that these kinds of criticisms will leave just one moral vision intact. Ultimately, there is still a point at which one has to say: "This is where my spade is turned."[26]

Accordingly, we do not begin with aspirations for an ideal vantage point or an abstracted universal human chooser. Rather, we start with the values we presently embody and the social world that is our context: our traditions and conventions have currency because they partly constitute who we are. This does not counsel an arid conventionalism, because social transformation is necessary, among other reasons, to close the gap between our political expectations and our institutional outcomes. Once we self-consciously abrogate the search for certainty and fixed foundations, our normative inquiries can attend to the social contexts in which we participate in the process of acquiring understanding and knowledge.

In fact, this conception of moral assessment is compatible with

Marxist versions of immanent critique:[27] examining a normative theory's classifications, premises, reasoning, and conclusions to unmask its internal deficiencies, including logical contradictions and errors, unexamined or indefensible premises, scope limitations, and gaps between theoretical goals and practical achievements; scanning and interrogating social institutions to discover the reasons theoretical deficiencies exist; clarifying and restructuring social reality by positing alternative theories, and thus recognizing that current social reality prefigures the future; and subrogating the deficient theoretical structure, not by eliminating or ignoring the past, but by invoking superior theoretical constructs dependent on critical insights emerging from serious inspection of current practice.

This conception of normative discourse, which supports Critical Pragmatism in jurisprudence, assumes that "we cannot isolate 'the world' from theories of the world, then compare these theories of the world with a theory-free world. We cannot compare theories with anything that is not a product of another theory."[28] Normative justification is thus constituted by theoretical explanation. A normative project is rational "not because it has a foundation but because it is a self-correcting enterprise which can put any claim in jeopardy, though not all at once."[29]

Moreover, a different notion of objectivity, one based on practice and behavior, emerges here: "If we find that we must take a certain point of view, use a certain 'conceptual system,' when we are engaged in practical activity . . . then we must not simultaneously advance the claim that it is not really 'the way things are in themselves.' "[30] This conception of objectivity, however, does not force us to relinquish the pluralism and fallibilism urged here: "one does not have to believe in a unique best moral version, or a unique best causal version, or a unique best mathematical version; what we have are better and worse versions, and that is objectivity."[31]

Thus, Critical Pragmatism rejects the view that facts and reasoning must be either metaphysically objective or abjectly conventional. The facts and reasoning indigenous to normative enterprises often involve both objective factors and human choices. The social decisions pertain to the classification and categorization of the objective factors. These factors and practical activity themselves constrain the range of permissible classifications but generally do not ordain any particular classification. This, underscoring as it does the themes of pluralism, fallibilism, and experimentation, has a salutary effect on the human inclination to identify current practice as the only natural or the one correct mode of being.

Much of the paradigm for Critical Pragmatism in jurisprudence emerges from a contemporary version of philosophy of science: "none of the beliefs we have, about the world and what is in it, is forced upon us by a theory-independent recalcitrant reality. . . . There is no paradox in the proposition that facts both depend on and constrain the theories that explain them"[32] and:

> A hypothesis or a statement may be warranted, may be reasonable to believe, in an objective sense of the words "warrant" and "reasonable," even though we cannot specify an experiment (or data) such that were we to perform it (or were we to collect them) we would be able to confirm or disconfirm the hypothesis to an extent which would command the assent of all educated and unbiased people.[33]

Other elements of the paradigm for Critical Pragmatism in jurisprudence emerge from a vigorous conception of praxis, which holds that cognitive forms emerge from historical development and immanent critique, that such emergence is influenced by and reflected in the social institutions of labor and production, and that particular cognitive forms and ideologies are offshoots of and may modify socially dominant practices. Still other elements of the paradigm for Critical Pragmatism flow from fallibilistic, pluralistic themes adumbrated previously. The power of certain propositions and conclusions is grounded, not in abstract cognition, but in societal practices and activities: "Giving grounds . . . justifying the evidence, comes to an end; but the end is not 'certain propositions' striking us immediately as true, i.e., it is not a kind of seeing on our part; it is our acting, which lies at the bottom of the language-game."[34]

Critical Pragmatism holds that normative discourse in the legal sphere is more like these conceptions of philosophy of science and of praxis than it is like discussions about matters only of subjective preferences. But it must also acknowledge that the network of theoretical structures accepted in the scientific community converge more than those contending for dominance in the moral, political, and legal arenas. Understanding that contestability and disagreement are part of a robust conception of rationality and that convergence of conclusions is neither guaranteed nor always desirable, the Critical Pragmatism urged here softens Dworkin's right answer thesis.

Critical Pragmatism insists that there are right answers in law in at least three senses of that phrase. First, there are right answers in the sense that the internal constraints and theoretical presuppositions of a particular ideology will demand certain specific answers to numerous legal questions.[35] Such answers are correct in the relativized sense that once one adopts the requisite presuppositions and recognizes the internal constraints of a particular ideology, certain conclusions will follow in concrete legal situations. Second, there are also right answers in the sense that otherwise divergent ideologies will nonetheless converge on some matters. Although Marxism, feminism, liberalism, conservatism, and economic analysis are unquestionably distinct, they still share some common prescriptive presuppositions, they agree on the validity of numerous legal rules and extant doctrine, and thus their conclusions converge on many issues. Third, there are right answers in the sense that antecedentally existing doctrine on a specific legal question may overwhelmingly reflect one particular legitimate legal ideology.

It must be admitted, however, that these are limited senses of right answers and that they will strike some as odd or inadequate. These right answers are not demanded by Reason itself, or immune to revision, or uncontaminated by conventionalism, or incontestable, or fully required by the one proper interpretation of extant legal doctrine, or demonstrably correct from a neutral vantage point. Critical Pragmatism acknowledges that the cat is out of the bag: law and judicial decision making are political in that judicial interpretations implicate descriptive and prescriptive world visions. But, as we shall see, not just any world vision passes the tests for a legitimate legal ideology, nor are we committed to the simple-minded proposition that one vision is no better or worse than any other. Recall also that the very distinction between easy and hard cases suggests that the phenomenology of judicial decision making includes more convergence than divergence. Indeed, such convergence is contingent: largely a result of the selection, education, and professional socialization of lawyers and judges, and on areas of agreement among otherwise disparate ideologies. Moreover, as an empirical matter, members of the legal profession and elected government officials, perhaps reflecting the dominant views of wider constituencies, are overwhelmingly political centrists.

There is still, however, currency in making this modest right answer claim. First, it allows us to stigmatize as mistakes those judicial decisions that incorrectly apply the presuppositions, or incorrectly ignore the internal theoretical constraints, of a particular ideology. Second, it permits us to account for the distinction between easy and hard cases, the predictability of most legal outcomes, and the convergence of otherwise divergent ideologies. Third, it grants us a way to fashion a deeper notion of the institutional and social constraints on judicial decision making. Fourth, it is compatible with the formal aspirations of the Rule of Law. Fifth, because it incorporates a merely modest formalism it is able to recognize concrete social reality: the contingency and political sources of legal conclusions; the continuing presence of class, gender, and racial oppression; and the economic and social pressures from which the judiciary is not excluded.

## CRITICAL PRAGMATISM AND JUDICIAL DECISION MAKING

The power of Dworkin's method rests on the constructive model of moral and legal reasoning and its notion of the external constraints on the judiciary. The power of leftist critique rests on its apprehension that more than one normative structure can fulfill the requirements of explaining most and criticizing the rest of the extant law, and on its understanding of the historical sources of political domination and oppression. Stripped of their exaggerated claims, both of these views can serve as a basis for building a more reasonable view of judicial decision making. Critical Pragmatism recognizes a measure of objectivity emerging from internal theoretical constraints, from community agreements and practices, and from behavioral restraints, but it spurns arid conventionalism because it does not take societal conventions as timeless givens or as incorrigible foundations. We must test extant societal conventions by internal criteria of coherence with other conventions, compatibility with fundamental theories of the person, and the role of morality in a diverse society; by the methods of immanent critique; and by their ability to facilitate our professed principles and goals.

## METHOD OF LEGAL REASONING

### PLATEAU 1: In Search of Legitimate Legal Ideologies

*Stage A:* A set of principles and policies that explain and justify extant constitutional provisions must be established by means of coherence methodology. After different sets are generated, they are tested by more general political institutions and principles (e.g., separation of powers). Finally, elaboration of the contested concepts such sets employ must be undertaken.

*Stage B:* A set of principles and policies that explain and justify United States Supreme Court decisions must be established by means of coherence methodology. A theory of mistakes is essential.

Examples of principles are conscionability, punitive desert, justified reliance, restitution for unjust enrichment, comparative blame, due care, relational duties, proportionality of remedy. Obviously, no exhaustive list is intended by these examples.

Examples of policies are general safety, community welfare, facilitation of democracy, public health, wealth maximization, promotion of family harmony, and so on.

*Stage C:* In accordance with coherence methodology, a set of principles and policies that explain and justify legislative enactments must be established by discerning which arguments might have and should have persuaded the legislature to enact particular statutes. If equally appropriate sets of principles and policies are generated, then look to the actual motivations of the legislators.

*Stage D:* Establish by means of coherence methodology a set of principles and policies that explain and justify lower-court decisions. Earlier decisions exert a controlling force on later ones, and if prior decisions D are explained and justified by principles and policies P, and P dictates a certain conclusion C in the instant case I, and P has neither been recanted nor institutionally regretted, then conclusion C in I.

*Stage E:* Establish by means of coherence methodology a set of principles and policies that explain and justify all prior stages taken as a whole. Better explanations of legal materials will stigmatize relatively few decisions and statutes as mistakes and will fit consistently with extant materials. In a reasonably moral legal system, better justifications of legal materials should correlate with better accounts of background morality. Appeals to background morality are implicated at each stage of the method of legal reasoning because the process of discerning the requisite principles and policies requires, and the principles and policies themselves embody, various normative commitments.

*Stage F:* A variety of plausible legal theories are produced from the earlier stages.

*Stage G:* Summary of the tests of the earlier stages and introduction of a few additional tests that a legal theory must pass: it must account for a significant amount of legal doctrine and criticize the rest; it must be compatible with certain formal elements of the Rule of Law such as treating like cases alike and providing notice and predictability; it must exercise significant rational constraint on judges; it must recognize concrete socioeconomic reality; it must be articulable; it must be viewed, when evaluated by extant social rules and practices, as plausible by significant segments of the wider society; it must accord with the phenomenology of law as experienced by judges and ordinary citizens; it must cohere with nonmoral, moral, and nonlegal facts; and it must not degenerate into a crude instrumentalism. In fulfilling these tests, no independent assessment of the judicial role itself is required.

*Stage H:* Fewer legal theories survive. These are "legitimate legal ideologies," which roughly reflect general political philosophies such as centrist–liberalism, centrist–conservatism, socialism, economic–libertarianism, and so on. Trying at this stage to forge "master legal theories," by taking principles and policies from each legitimate legal ideology and assigning relative weights in accordance with their embodiment in extant legal doctrine, is unlikely to be successful. Except in relatively homogeneous societies, such a project is doomed to interminable confusion and conflict. Thus, no single, demonstrably best, legal ideology is likely to emerge from Plateau 1 analysis—but the field has been narrowed.

## PLATEAU 2: Deciding Individual Legal Cases

*Stage A:* The legitimate legal ideologies emerging from Plateau 1 analysis will often be in conflict. So, we must discern legal decisions for which the competing values reach similar conclusions and extract general principles from such cases. A limited common framework of shared commitments and data is thus produced.

*Stage B:* Those legal judgments still in conflict are refined by drawing out the implications of the shared framework; arguing by analogy with and disanalogy from the agreed-upon decisions; and exposing internal inconsistencies, unnoticed consequences, and poorly defined or unclear concepts in the unshared frameworks of the competing ideologies. Particular attention must be paid to the future applications of possible decisions.

*Stage C:* The analysis of the previous stages will generate "right answers" to numerous legal questions. These right answers pertain to easy legal questions where the conclusions of legitimate legal ideologies converge because of the (limited) common framework the ideologies share. There will be other right answers that pertain to legal questions that are easy because prior decisions overwhelmingly reflect one specific legitimate legal ideology.

A judge is obligated to decide easy cases in accord with their respective right answers, but the scope of this obligation is bounded. Judges are justified in not applying settled law only after making the determination that inordinate substantive injustice would occur if the settled law is applied; no other institutional justifications (e.g., the rules, principles, and policies that support the settled law are themselves morally justified and ignoring them in the extraordinary instant cases will do them significant damage; or the legal system as a whole is morally justified and will be damaged more by ignoring the law's requirements than the good that is produced, or harm prevented, in the instant case) can be persuasively offered for applying the law; and there is no less drastic means of resolving the problem (e.g., negotiated compromise or alternative dispute resolution).

*Stage D:* Some legal questions, however, will admit of no right answer from this process. In such hard cases, a judge should acknowledge the values of fallibilistic pluralism: recognizing the presence of and remaining open to normative perspectives different from her own; granting the partiality and limitations of her own perspective; admitting the insights of alternative perspectives; attending more carefully to the particulars of the instant case; invoking elements of immanent critique—interrogating social institutions to discover the reasons theoretical deficiencies are present in hard cases; clarifying and restructuring social reality by paying attention to the presence and historical sources of political oppression; and assiduously cultivating an understanding of the experiences of politically subordinated groups. In such cases, a judge has the discretion to apply directly the answer suggested by a legitimate legal ideology but lacks the discretion to introduce justifiably an answer suggested by or reasoning emanating from a worldview not previously recognized as a legitimate legal ideology. Judicial discretion is thus constrained by the judge's need to persuade other legal insiders of the plausibility of her conclusions and to attend generally to Plateau 1, Stage G requirements.

The Critical Pragmatism in jurisprudence sketched here implies the following: (1) legal theory yields a rational, although not fully determinate, structure to open-ended legal concepts; (2) in a pluralistic culture the presence of several legitimate legal ideologies will preclude any single all-embracing theory from being able to account for the complex set of legal materials; (3) despite the lack of an all-embracing theory, the legitimate legal ideologies presuppose at least a thin, common normative framework; (4) this common framework prevents unarbitrable, unremitting ideological conflict; (5) right answers (in the senses explicated previously) exist to most legal questions; (6) hard cases should be subject to a judicial discretion bounded by the values of fallibilistic pluralism and by the independent tests a justified legal theory must pass; and (7) judicial decision making implicates ideological vision and is thus political all the way down, but it does not follow that it is irrational, merely subjective, or unconstrained.

Critical Pragmatism in jurisprudence, although influenced greatly by Legal Idealism, Critical Legal Studies, and the general leftist critique of law, is in numerous ways distinct from those views. Unlike Legal Idealism, Critical Pragmatism softens Dworkin's thesis by denying that hard cases have right answers in any strong sense; does not a priori privilege the principles of centrist–liberalism; admits a wider range of judicial discretion; does not assume that one uniquely correct legal theory can emerge from coherence methodology; and addresses, in at least a limited way, the presence and historical sources of political oppression. Unlike Critical Legal Studies, Critical Pragmatism accepts a modest version of formalism; recognizes that legal reasoning and theory can constrain judges to some degree; accounts for both the experience of convergence and the experience of conflict in law; and allows for right answers in a limited but nontrivial sense. Moreover, Critical Pragmatism eludes the charges Dworkin levied against pragmatism. Unlike pragmatism as characterized by Dworkin, Critical Pragmatism attends to antecedently existing doctrine and thus does not degenerate into a crude instrumentalism, it involves no disingenuous manipulation of the judicial role, and it acknowledges theoretical and doctrinal constraints that preclude ad hoc, case-by-case decision making.

## RECURRING QUESTIONS

*Is Plateau 1 Analysis a Sham?* It may be argued that the Plateau 1 analysis of Critical Pragmatism is a sham. After all, judges are not philosophers or theoreticians who conjure elaborate conceptual edifices in order to decide a case at bar. Rather, they decide legal questions by looser techniques of practical reason: attending to the arguments of respective counsel, deliberating, making a series of specific interpretive judgments, respecting established authority and settled law, relying on the tacit knowledge they have gained from their experiences and professional socialization, and so on. Furthermore, a critic may add that even if judges did engage in the baroque analysis of Plateau 1 their time would be wasted because at Stage H they are merely reiterating their political philosophies. Therefore, Plateau 1 analysis is either irrelevant or duplicitous.

The critic is undoubtedly correct that only the most philosophically inclined and sophisticated jurists could undertake Plateau 1 analysis in its fullest form. But Critical Pragmatism does not claim to be a merely descriptive account of what appellate judges do. It aspires instead to a philosophical justification for judicial decision making. Just as Dworkin posited his ideal (and philosophically inclined) jurist, Hercules, "a lawyer of superhuman skill, learning, patience, and acumen,"[36] Critical Pragmatism advances its superhuman judge, call her "Vittoria." She takes extant legal doctrine seriously, but she also understands the frailties of our language and logic. She respects consistency with the past as one of the imperatives of her role, but she also refuses to ignore the flux and tensions in law. Vittoria brings an antecedent commitment to the values of fallibilistic pluralism and refuses to see law as inherently neutral, yet she has faith in reasoned discourse and the directive power of law. She is not so naive as to think that her descriptive and prescriptive world vision is irrelevant to her decision making, yet she is not so cynical as to think that the results of legal reasoning are extensionally equivalent to her subjective preferences. Vittoria attends to the historical context, including the vestiges of past oppression, in which she is situated, but resists the temptations of crude instrumentalism. She is engaged in a good faith enterprise to understand and evaluate the force of law. In sum, Vittoria employs Plateau 1 analysis as the best way, given her considerable powers, to discern the law's requirements and limitations.

Several rejoinders to the critic are now available to Critical Pragmatism. First, Plateau 1 analysis does not hold itself out as a merely descriptive account of the way judges operate; rather, it strives for a philosophical justification of the enterprise of judicial decision making. Second, the majority of judges, employing numerous elements of practical reason, still make Plateau 1 type calculations although in a somewhat less refined fashion than Vittoria. Third, even those judges who lack the temperament and antecedent commitments of Vittoria will be affected by the theoretical and prudential constraints partially constituting Plateau 1 analysis. Fourth, Plateau 1 analysis has currency in narrowing the field of legitimate legal ideologies in particular legal systems. Fifth, in any complex legal system no single world vision will stand as the only legitimate legal ideology; thus, it is not true that Plateau 1, Stage H analysis is a sham because judges must end by merely reiterating their own political philosophies. Accordingly, Plateau 1 analysis is neither irrelevant nor duplicitous.

*Distinction Between Easy and Hard Cases?* The leftist critique of law challenges the distinction between easy and hard cases. Given the radical indeterminacy of language, logic, and normative reasoning, the leftist critique concludes that easy cases are comforting illusions. Easy cases are comforting because they provide the security of seemingly fixed points of authority, but they are illusions because their conclusions can be quickly unsettled when the will to do so exists. Moreover, at their worst, easy cases have the effect of solidifying received (and politically repressive) notions of difference–sameness, legal neutrality, and universality. In this fashion, law creates meaning through differentiation as the experiences and interests of the politically powerful—who are overwhelmingly white, privileged males—become the prisms through which judges interpret liabilities and rights. Consequently, rigid adherence to easy cases results in the marginalization of the experiences and values of relatively powerless groups. Therefore, any justification of judicial decision making that recognizes the imperatives of easy cases has reintroduced pernicious formalism into legal theory and is thereby an accomplice in the continued subjugation of oppressed people. Critical Pragmatism, it may be argued, may better serve the powerless by resuscitating the deviant strains of legal doctrine. In sum, by recognizing easy cases, Critical Pragmatism tacitly reiterates an inaccurate view of legal language, logic, and normative reasoning, as well as inadvertently contributes to a political perspective that is one-sided and biased.

In one sense the critic is correct. By counseling the existence of easy cases, Critical Pragmatism does recognize and reinforce a limited conservative (status quo preserving) bias in judicial decision making and has accepted a modest formalism. But this need not result in wholesale conservatism or in mechanical jurisprudence. Recall that Critical Pragmatism states that as a contingent reality legitimate legal ideologies will converge on numerous legal questions. The majority of legal questions are settled so firmly that they are not even litigated.[37] Only interesting hard cases comprise the law texts that preoccupy legal academics. Usually, disparate ideologies agree on the appropriate legal doctrine that decides legal questions and on its proper application. To agree, as Critical Pragmatism does, that legal language, logic, and normative reasoning are not fully determinate does not imply that easy cases are fictions.

As an example, one of the seemingly easiest legal questions is, How old must a person be in order to be eligible to the Office of President? The answer provided by Article II, Section 1 of the Constitution, is "at least thirty-five years old." Yet it is possible here to lodge an argument that the framers did not intend thirty-five years of age as a magical number that forever signifies the acquisition of a presidential potential previously lacking, but that when they ratified Article II, thirty-five years of age signified to the framers in the eighteenth century a certain standard of life experience and judgment that is in the twentieth century signified by age X. Thus, Article II, Section 1 should be interpreted not by rigid adherence to a specific number but by "the evolving standards of maturity that characterize a progressing society."

Now, it is clearly empirically possible to make the argument of the previous paragraph. In this sense, the critic is correct in thinking that legal language is radically indeterminate. But the problem is that given the other values of law—striving for settled expectations; a measure of efficiency, consistency, and predictability; simplification of the moral universe that forms the context for dispute resolution; and so on—it is virtually impossible that the argument will be found persuasive. Moreover, the values of law just cited are not merely those embodied by our particular legal system; rather, they are essential attributes of all legal orders. Without numerous bright-line rules, such as the age-limit provision, these legal values would always be hostage to the exigencies of the moment.

We must also remember that judicial decision making, although a preoccupation of academics, is not the whole of law. There are other and clearer ways of changing the law. Critical Pragmatism appreciates easy cases as part of the phenomenology of judicial decision making and as speaking to certain essential legal values. Furthermore, easy cases, insofar as they reflect convergent conclusions of disparate ideologies in a pluralistic society, are unlikely to be a prime source of political repression. Easy cases become politically pernicious when they reflect the conclusions of one ideology that is itself morally suspect. The critic should reformulate his claim: "I admit there are cases that have hitherto been viewed as easy. But that is true because one (morally suspect) ideology is prevalent in law. The introduction of additional ideologies will unsettle the line between hard and easy cases, and I view this as morally desirable insofar as the relatively powerless are thereby enfranchised."

There is much in this reformulated claim that is compatible with Critical Pragmatism, which provides the possibilities for some experimentation and change in its view of the adjudication of hard cases. But those who deny the presence of easy cases misperceive the reality of law. The substantive issues here, all of which Critical Pragmatism addresses, are the number and nature of easy cases, their relationship to hard cases, and the manner and extent to which easy cases can contribute to political repression.

*When Are Judicial Decisions Justified?* Critical Pragmatism accepts several tenets of analytic jurisprudence: judges are required to address cases cognitively, by rational persuasion formulated in arguments that are available to the public; judges are to avoid case-by-case decision making, by classifying cases in accordance with classes of received legal doctrine; judges must use general norms embodying rules, principles, and policies, as part of their cognitive approach; judges must recognize a distinction between merely instantiating their own subjective preferences and deciding cases in accord with what the law requires; judges must experience, and not simply posit, an (unfixed) distinction between easy and hard cases; there are right answers, in the senses adumbrated previously, to numerous legal questions; these senses of right answers, although limited, are not trivial; the answers to most legal questions are predictable mainly because of the convergence of otherwise disparate ideologies, and judicial habits of analogy and categorization emerging from common institutional socialization and intellectual background; and our normative vision is always constrained by our context such that the most viable alternatives to existing arrangements will always appear to be marginal adjustments and incremental changes.

Consequently, Critical Pragmatism cannot accept the view, often proclaimed by leftist critics, that judicial decision making is merely "choice." In fact, the judgments required in answering legal questions implicate rationality and cognition all the way down.[38] But Critical Pragmatism also admits the contingency and contestability of judicial arguments and legal conclusions; the presence of several legitimate legal ideologies in extant doctrine; the undeniable experience that the outcomes of hard cases usually depend in one way or another on the ideological perspective of the particular judge(s) deciding the cases; that judges internalize law's institutional history and possess tacit knowledge of how to decide; that legitimate legal ideologies are partial and not general vantage points about which everyone who is rational must agree; that political conflict is unavoidable in a pluralistic society; that convergence of moral outlook is neither necessary nor always desirable; and that communicative transparency in normative debate is both hindered (in some ways) and facilitated (in other ways) by the presence of several different rhetorical modes.

Critical Pragmatism's general answer to the question of whether judicial decisions are justified is that these decisions are justified if the reasons and arguments advanced by the judge are adequate to establish the answer to the case at bar. Moreover, "the soundness of judicial justifications of decisions on questions of law should not be sharply distinguished from what socially passes for acceptable legal arguments, and the correctness of propositions of law is, in part, determined by whether sound legal justifications can be given for them."[39]

But this general answer requires greater specificity. First, Critical Pragmatism recognizes a distinction between what the law requires and what justifies a judicial decision. Sometimes the answer the law requires in easy cases cannot be justified. This occurs when extant legal doctrine is relatively clear, but the answer it provides would result in inordinate substantive injustice that cannot be rationalized on other institutional grounds. Moreover, sometimes an answer to a legal question is justified although it is not required by law. This occurs in hard cases where a range of plausible rationales and answers are available, all of which are reasonable when judged by background morality and other institutional grounds. Finally, Critical Pragmatism holds that in cases where the law's requirements are clear but its answer is unjustified, a decision known by the judge to be contrary to the law's requirements may be the only justified decision.

Recall my earlier remarks in Chapter 2 about the Hart–Fuller debate when we considered this issue in the context of a judge's role. The problem was this: What must a judge do when she perceives the requirements of law clearly but also perceives clearly that these requirements will result in inordinate substantive injustice, and they cannot be otherwise justified on institutional grounds? The extreme formalist says that once a judge discerns accurately what the law requires she is obligated to decide in accord with the law "come hell or high water." Under this view, that the law requires X is a sufficient reason for a judge to apply X. Natural Law theory agrees with this view but adds that if the decree in question is in violation of Natural Law then the decree is not truly law and cannot justifiably bind a judge.

Both answers are deficient. Extreme formalism degenerates into a rigid fanaticism that becomes implausible in much the same way any

absolutist position does: by constructing examples in which the social and moral consequences of deciding a legal question become
more and more disastrous we will become less and less inclined to
think that the judge is justified in applying the law, regardless of the
clarity of extant doctrine. The Natural Law theorist avoids this problem, but at the cost of ignoring the pedigree of legal doctrine by
making "law" necessarily morally sound. Thus, by semantic fiat,
Natural Law theory can declare that well-settled doctrine is not truly
"law" and is thus unable to generate judicial obligations.

Critical Pragmatism, on the other hand, bites the bullet: a judge
is obligated to decide easy cases in accord with their respective right
answers, but the scope of this obligation is bounded. Judges are under the relevant obligation if and only if affirming the right legal
answer would not generate inordinate substantive injustice that cannot be justified on other institutional grounds.[40] The acknowledgment that the judicial obligation to apply what are clearly the law's
requirements is bounded does not open the doors to wholesale judicial civil disobedience. Judges are justified in not applying the
law only after making the determination that substantive injustice
would occur; that no other institutional justifications could be persuasively offered for applying the law (e.g., that the rules, principles, and policies supporting applying the law are morally justified
and that ignoring them in the extraordinary instant case will do
them significant damage; that the legal system as a whole is morally
justified and will be damaged more by ignoring the law's requirements than the good that is produced, or harm prevented, in the
instant case); and that there are no less drastic means of resolving
the problem (e.g., negotiation, alternative dispute resolution) available.

Just as carefully circumscribed civil disobedience on the part of
citizens need not signal the onset of political anarchy, so, too, admitting limitations to the judicial obligation to apply the law's requirements need not be the first step to subjective, arbitrary decision
making. Thus, Critical Pragmatism denies judges automatic use of
the functionalist excuse "I was just doing my job." Only an uncompromising and unconvincing absolutist allows job holders to avoid
personal responsibility and to hide behind unbounded obligations to
fulfill occupational roles. Critical Pragmatism insists that job holders
cannot incur moral obligations to do that which is, on balance, demonstrably and substantially morally wrong.

Accordingly, Critical Pragmatism holds that a clear showing that
Y is demanded by law is insufficient to establish that Y is justified

and should be applied by judges. There is always a further question with three dimensions: Can Y be justified either on its own moral merits; or because Y is supported by morally justified rules, principles, and policies that would be damaged significantly if Y were ignored in the instant case, or because the morally justified legal system will be damaged more by ignoring Y in the instant case than the good that is produced or harm that is prevented? Such tests will not generate the wholesale overturning of settled legal doctrine but will allow judges a principled exception in extraordinary cases.

If law is to have a directive function that is at least somewhat independent of its coercive function, then judicial decision making must trigger moral assessment—not in the Natural Law sense that a decree must necessarily be morally sound to be a "law"; not in the crudely instrumental sense that each decision must be justified by its own substantive moral merits; not in the sense of leftist critique that each decision must be taken as a unique particular within its own special context that eludes classification; but in the minimalist sense embodied by Critical Pragmatism. Settled doctrine is not morally self-ratifying but is instead subject to the further three-dimensional question of moral justifiability. The position urged here takes institutional or strictly legal justification as inadequate to support law's directive function.

Appeals to the necessity of moral assessment in judicial decision making, however, are sure to arouse the curiosity of critics. Whose morality is the relevant standard here? What sources, if any, is a judge required to consult? How is such an appeal different from instantiating the merely subjective preferences of judges?

Critical Pragmatism counsels the use of background morality, not use of the constructive morality presupposed by legal doctrine taken as a whole. This constructive morality can yield only an institutional morality, which, although almost always similar to, is not necessarily identical to background morality. Background morality, although affected by and usually reflected in legal material, makes no direct appeal to legal doctrine or institutions. It is this "morality" that salvages law's directive function, yet remains conceptually distinct from "legality." Law will be perceived by legal outsiders as having a normative force beyond its coercive force only if legal requirements are generally consistent with the background morality embraced by large segments of society. If legal requirements are merely internally coherent with the constructive morality presupposed by legal institutions, then that holds open the possibility of a dictator who oppresses the majority of the people through means of his (philosophically consistent) legal system. Such a dictator would exercise the coercive force of law, but if his system varied significantly from his society's background morality then his law would lack directive force even though there was general compliance with the dictator's decrees.

When developing acceptable versions of background morality, special care must be given to understanding the presence and the historical sources of political oppression, the role of immanent critique, and the values of fallibilistic pluralism. For reasons stated earlier, the resultant version of background morality will be more than a mere reflection of a particular's judges subjective preferences: moral reasoning itself is distinct from a compilation of subjective preferences; there is an unavoidable social aspect to moral theory; and moral reasoning implicates a whole series of other fundamental theories that are to significant degrees distinct from merely subjective preferences.

There is another aspect of justification, that of the process of judicial decision making itself, that bears mention. There is no necessary connection between the justification of a judicial decision and the justification of the process by which that decision was reached. We can imagine Judge Russo deciding a case in the following way: Russo calls his friend Rossi, who has been institutionalized for the past five years for mental incompetence. As a lark, Russo poses a "hypothetical" legal question to Rossi. The question, which carefully sanitizes names and specific confidential facts, closely tracks the case Russo is currently contemplating. Russo, completely fatigued by the actual case, decides to trust the judgment to Rossi's whim. Rossi, not having a clue as to proper legal procedure or method, throws a pair of dice, and says, "Plaintiff wins." Russo then finds for the plaintiff. It turns out that a judgment for the plaintiff is a justified decision when tested by Critical Pragmatism's method of legal reasoning. But, obviously, the process of judicial decision making in this case is unjustified.

We can also imagine a situation in which Judge Rapone attends carefully to the instant case, maintains the perspectival attitude required by Critical Pragmatism, respects the values of fallibilistic pluralism, applies the appropriate tests of legal theory, diligently employs coherence methodology, and complies generally with Critical Pragmatism's method of legal reasoning. The process of Rapone's decision making in this case is justified. Yet, it turns out that the decision itself is unjustified when tested by the three-dimensional justification question: Rapone has in good faith made some errors during his deliberations.

Thus, there are always at least two questions of justification inherent in judicial decision making. First, Is the process of decision-making justified? Second, Is the decision itself justified? The first question can be answered only by appeal to a theory of how judges ought to decide cases in their institutional role. Critical Pragmatism provides one, but not the only plausible, such account. The second question can be answered by appeal to Critical Pragmatism's three-dimensional justification test.

*Too Much Discretion? Not Enough?* Both proponents of (several versions of) analytic jurisprudence and proponents of a leftist critique will find Critical Pragmatism's Plateau 2 analysis inadequate, but for different reasons. Analytic jurisprudence will criticize as too broad the judicial discretion attending hard cases, while a leftist critique will criticize that discretion as too narrow. Analytic jurisprudence will be concerned that such discretion cannot be reconciled with the unelected status of the most important judges, while the leftist critique will question whether relatively powerless groups will be further disenfranchised by a judiciary in which those groups are radically underrepresented from the outset. Moreover, a leftist critique will disparage the general allegiance to law counseled by Critical Pragmatism in easy cases.

In one sense this cross-fire is comforting, for it suggests that Critical Pragmatism has accomplished one of its goals: a theory of judicial decision making that is distinct from mainstream analysis, yet one that is not a replica of knee-jerk leftist reaction. The type of discretion suggested by Critical Pragmatism for hard cases is the result of numerous factors: (1) the presence of several legitimate legal ideologies in legal doctrine, a presence that is experienced by judges and not merely posited by academic theorists; (2) the degrees of indeterminacy in our logic, language, and normative reasoning; (3) the difficulty of reaching firm, clear answers to complex moral questions with numerous conflicting considerations; (4) the need to recognize the values of fallibilistic pluralism; (5) an appreciation of the institutional values served by the judiciary; (6) an understanding that in the presence of several plausible alternatives, judges must still render fair consideration and a reasonable decision; (7) a respect for the judge's role in our system of justice, a role that should not permit automatic use of the functionalist excuse "I was just doing my job" but that also precludes crude instrumentalism; and (8) the recognition that human reason is not helpless and does not yield to an independent faculty called "choice" in the face of all this.

To the extent that other theorists disagree with some or all of these eight factors, they will repudiate Critical Pragmatism's notion of judicial discretion. The arguments for the eight factors have been advanced earlier. Their persuasiveness, in the face of attacks from the political center that Critical Pragmatism goes too far and from the political left that it does not go far enough, must now be evaluated by the reader.

*Can the Judicial Role Be Justified?* The most important federal judges in our system are unelected. The rationale for this is the perceived need to insulate such judges from the vagaries of recurrent political pressures: judges must make principled decisions without fear of reprisals from outraged constituents. Thus, judges comprise an elite corp who are able to exercise amplified power with no apparent accountability. At first blush, this seems dangerously aberrational in our democratic republic. Formalist visions justify the judicial role by distinguishing clearly between legislative functions, which are beyond the judiciary's rightful powers, and interpretive functions, which constitute the application of preexisting doctrine. This justification, however, rests on dubious assumptions about legal decision making and the nature of language, logic, and normative reasoning, assumptions that have been examined and rejected earlier.

Critical Pragmatism offers a different sort of justification for the judicial role. First, it highlights the institutional values served by our judiciary: preserving social tranquility by peaceful dispute resolution, achieving a measure of administrative efficiency by keeping the amount of litigation manageable, striving for reasonably settled expectations by achieving a measure of consistency and predictability, simplifying the moral universe that forms the context for dispute resolution, acting as part of governmental checks and balances, and respecting some degree of separation of governmental powers. Second, it admits the imperfect knowledge of judges and the limitations of our language, logic, and normative reasoning. Third, it rejects crude instrumentalism: judges cannot decide on a case-by-case basis because doing so undermines the institutional values presumably served by the judiciary.

Critical Pragmatism thus does not find the justification of judicial power in the ability of judges to find relevant legal doctrine and apply to it appropriate legal cases. The ability cited is relevant to the justification of particular decisions and of the decision-making process, but it leaves unsettled the legitimacy of the judiciary as an institution. Consequently, pointing out the weaknesses of formalist visions is insufficient to undermine the legitimacy of the social power that judges exercise. Such legitimacy must be based on a deeper political theory of institutional arrangements.

Critical Pragmatism, accepting a role for social vision in judicial decision making, offers a pragmatic "justification" for the legitimacy of judicial power. Given that the institutional values served by our judiciary are important and necessary; that current legal arrangements are reasonably successful in sustaining these institutional values; that there is, all moral ramifications considered, no demonstrably superior way of achieving these values; that there are significant transition costs—in terms of human effort, resulting confusion and anxiety, loss of tradition, and so on—in replacing the judicial role with some other mechanism that could achieve the relevant institutional values; that there is independent value in insulating judges from constituencies, we should retain the general imperatives of the judicial role in our system, even after repudiating the strong claims of formalist visions.[41]

This argument does not establish a powerful independent justification for our judiciary as the only and necessarily the best form of institutional arrangement. Such a justification can be provided only by defending a highly developed political theory, a project that is beyond the scope of this work. Critical Pragmatism simply offers some practical reasons for retaining the general contours of the present model while rejecting the excesses of extreme formalism.

It would be disingenuous, however, to claim that these practical reasons are nonideological.[42] Critical Pragmatism does not present itself as the only plausible explanation and justification of judicial decision making, nor does it gloss over the tensions and uncertainties humans embody. It aspires to survey critically mainstream methods, to take seriously the leftist critique of law, to illustrate how traditional philosophical problems plague legal theory, to demonstrate the impasses to which our argumentational strategies lead, and to suggest ways we might transcend pragmatically those dead ends. But it begins from the vantage point that there is much worth preserving in current social practices. It is difficult for those of us still close enough to, but far enough away from, the immigrant experience to think otherwise.

Clearly, those who do not share this antecedent commitment, those who are convinced that our judiciary is a prime collaborator in a fundamentally corrupt and thoroughly despicable social order, will question sharply each step of the pragmatic justification. Are the cited institutional values truly that important? Do judges actually serve important and necessary institutional values? Must transition costs necessarily be high? Would they be offset by moral and political gains generated by a new social order? Might there be a conception of the judicial role demonstrably superior to current practice? Does Critical Pragmatism itself merely echo and legitimate the flaccid eclecticism of the hopelessly conflicted?

The quest to understand extant legal theory, a pursuit born in awe of law's majesty, compels the interrogation of my own creation. In jurisprudence, final serenity is neither conceptually possible nor viscerally felicitous.

# NOTES

## INTRODUCTION

1. It is unclear whether any legal theorist has held so uncompromising a view. The following come close: C. C. Langdell, "Preface to the First Edition," *Selection of Cases on the Law of Contracts* (1879); Joseph H. Beale, *A Treatise on the Conflict of Laws* (1935), secs. 3.2, 3.4, 4.12; and Max Weber, "The Categories of Legal Thought," in *Economy and Society*, ed. G. Roth and C. Wittich (1922).

2. See Ernest J. Weinrib, "Legal Formalism: On the Immanent Rationality of Law," 97 *Yale Law Journal* 949, 953–957 (1988).

3. See the criticisms raised in Part Two.

4. See Mark Kelman, *A Guide to Critical Legal Studies* (Cambridge, Mass.: Harvard University Press, 1987), 215.

5. Critics allege here that Legal Formalism is necessarily allied with belief in Metaphysical Realism. Metaphysical Realism is the view that numerous truths about the world are mind-independent: such truths are embedded in the universe and they can be discovered, but not created, by humans. Notice that the term "realism" is used in the literature in several confusing ways: a Legal Realist is a kind of skeptic and somewhat of a non-cognitivist, while a Metaphysical Realist is the ultimate cognitivist and objectivist.

6. For the full range of the history of the Legal Realist movement, see Edward Purcell, *The Crisis of Democratic Theory* (Lexington: University Press of Kentucky, 1973), 74–94.

7. See Karl Llewellyn, "The Rule of Law in Our Case Law of Contracts," 47 *Yale Law Journal* 1243 (1938), and "On Warranty of Quality and Society," 36 *Columbia Law Review* 699 (1936); Jerome Frank, *Law and the Modern Mind* (1930); Walter Cook, "The Logical and Legal Bases of the Conflict of Laws," 33 *Yale Law Journal* 457 (1924); and Wesley Sturges and Walter Cook, "Legal Theory and Real Property Mortgages," 37 *Yale Law Journal* 691 (1928).

8. Frank, *Law and the Modern Mind*, gives the clearest statement of this.

9. See note 7.

10. Purcell, *Crisis of Democratic Theory*. Some Legal Realists bit the bullet and accepted nihilism as the consequence of their attacks. See, for example, Wesley Sturges, *Cases and Materials on the Law of Credit Transactions* (1930);

Underhill Moore, "Rational Basis of Legal Institutions," 23 *Columbia Law Review* 609 (1923); and Cook, "Logical and Legal Bases."

11. See note 10.

12. Ibid.

13. See, for example, Thomas Kuhn, *The Structure of Scientific Revolutions*, 2d ed. (Chicago: University of Chicago Press, 1970); Paul Feyerabend, *Against Method: Outline of an Anarchistic Theory of Knowledge* (London: New Left Books, 1975).

14. See, for example, Martin P. Golding, "A Note on Discovery and Justification in Science and Law," 28 *Nomos* 124, 140n. 21 (1986) (citing even the noted Legal Realist Oliver Wendell Homes as an example).

15. Plato held the view that the changeable objects and events in our world were classifiable because of the existence of Universals or Forms in a higher, unchanging world. Various particulars are mere instances of general essences in which they participate. See, for example, his *Republic*, *Theaetetus*, and *Meno*.

16. This view is described and challenged by Frederick Schauer, "Formalism" 97 *Yale Law Journal* 509, 522–524. (1988).

17. For a description of the elements of the liberal notion of the Rule of Law employed in this book, see A. V. Dicey, *Introduction to the Study of the Law of the Constitution* (London: Macmillan, 1968), 188–196; Roberto Unger, *Law in Modern Society* (New York: Free Press, 1976), 52–54, 273–274; Hugh Collins, *Marxism and Law* (Oxford: Oxford University Press, 1984), 135–137; Friedrich Hayek, *The Road to Serfdom* (Chicago: University of Chicago Press, 1944), 124–129, and *The Constitutional Liberty* (Chicago: University of Chicago Press, 1960), 210–215; Franz Neumann, *The Democratic and the Authoritarian State* (Glencoe, Ill.: Free Press, 1957); and H. W. Jones, "The Rule of Law and the Welfare State," 58 *Columbia Law Review* 143 (1958). For a description of linguistic conventionalism, see the articles by Stanley Fish cited in Chapter 5, notes 11, 17, 20, 22, and 27.

18. See, for example, Richard J. Bernstein, *Beyond Objectivism and Relativism: Science, Hermeneutics and Praxis* (Philadelphia: University of Pennsylvania Press, 1983). Bernstein argues that we are still prisoners of the belief that the only alternatives open to us are either some form of objectivism and foundationalism or relativism, skepticism, historicism, and nihilism. Here "objectivism" is the conviction that there is a permanent, ahistoric matrix to which we ultimately appeal to determine the nature of rationality, knowledge, and truth. "Relativism" is the conviction that all such concepts must be understood as relative to a specific conceptual scheme, theoretical framework, paradigm, or form of life. Because there is a nonreducible plurality of such conceptual schemes, the relativist denies that these concepts have a determinate and univocal significance. By exposing new continuities among science, hermeneutics, and praxis, Bernstein argues that we are now witnessing and participating in a movement beyond objectivism and relativism. He claims that what is now emerging is a "new conversation" about human rationality (227–230). The movement beyond objectivism and relativism is

not just a theoretical problem but a practical task motivated by a moral concern: to nourish the type of solidarity, participation, and mutual recognition that is grounded in dialogical communities. See also Richard J. Bernstein, *The Restructuring of Social and Political Theory* (Philadelphia: University of Pennsylvania Press, 1976); Alasdair MacIntyre, *After Virtue* (Notre Dame, Ind.: University of Notre Dame Press, 1982).

## CHAPTER 1

1. The explanatory portions of this section owe much to Lloyd L. Weinreb, *Natural Law and Justice* (Cambridge, Mass.: Harvard University Press, 1987); and Edwin W. Patterson, *Jurisprudence: Men and Ideas of the Law* (1940. Reprint. Brooklyn, N.Y.: Foundation Press, 1953).

2. See, for example, Gregory Vlastos, "Equality and Justice in Early Greek Cosmologies," 42 *Classical Philology* 156–178 (1947); Francis M. Cornford, *From Religion to Philosophy* (New York: Harper, 1957).

3. See G. B. Kerferd, *The Sophistic Movement* (Cambridge: Cambridge University Press, 1981), 111–130; W.K.C. Guthrie, *History of Greek Philosophy*, vol. 2, *The Presocratic Tradition from Parmenides to Democritus* (1965) (Cambridge: Cambridge University Press, 1962–1981), 344.

4. See, for example, E. R. Dodd's commentary on the *Gorgias* (Oxford: Clarendon Press, 1959).

5. Guthrie, *History of Greek Philosophy*, vol. 4, *Plato: The Man and His Dialogues: Earlier Period* (1975), and vol. 5, *The Later Plato and the Academy* (1978); Frederick Copleston, *A History of Philosophy*, vol. 1, pt.1 (1946) (Garden City, N.Y.: Doubleday, 1946–1962), 188–231.

6. Weinreb, *Natural Law and Justice*, 32.

7. See, for example, Guthrie, *History of Greek Philosophy*, vol. 6, *Aristotle: An Encounter* (1981); Copleston, *History of Philosophy*, vol. 1, pt. 2 (1946), 56–61.

8. Weinreb, *Natural Law and Justice*, 33.

9. See note 7.

10. See note 7.

11. Aristotle, *Nichomachean Ethics* 1094b, trans. W. D. Ross, *The Complete Works of Aristotle*, rev. Oxford trans., vol. 2 (Princeton, N.J.: Princeton University Press, 1984), 1729.

12. Diogenes Laertius, *Lives of Eminent Philosophers* 7.135, trans. R. D. Hicks (1925); J. M. Rist, *The Stoics* (Berkeley: University of California Press, 1978), 137–160.

13. Cicero, *De re publica* 3.22.33, trans. Clinton W. Keyes (1928), 211.

14. Gaius, *Institutes* 1.1, trans. Francis de Zulueta, *The Institutes of Gaius*, pt. 1 (Oxford: Clarendon Press, 1946), 3.

15. Barry Nicholas, *An Introduction to Roman Law* (Oxford: Clarendon Press, 1962), 55; Patterson, *Jurisprudence*, 343–344.

16. Patterson, *Jurisprudence*, 344.

17. Justinian, *Digest* 1.1.4, trans. T. Mommsen, P. Krueger, A. Watson, *The Digest of Justinian*, vol. 1 (Philadelphia: University of Pennsylvania Press, 1985).

18. *Summa Theologica*. All references from *Fathers of the English Dominican Province* (trans.), 3 vols. (New York: Benziger, 1947).

19. Ibid., 1–2, question 90, arts. 1–4.

20. Ibid., 1–2, question 91, art. 2.

21. This criticism usually springs from a Legal Positivist and is explained in Martin P. Golding, *Philosophy of Law* (Englewood Cliffs, N.J.: Prentice-Hall, 1975), 33.

22. See note 18, 1–2, question 91, art. 1.

23. Ibid., arts. 4–5.

24. Ibid., question 94, arts. 3, 5.

25. Ibid., question 95, art. 2.

26. Ibid.

27. Ibid., question 94, art. 3.

28. Ibid., art. 2.

29. Ibid., arts. 4, 6.

30. Ibid.

31. This phrase is used by John Mackie in *Ethics: Inventing Right and Wrong* (Harmondsworth, England: Penguin, 1977), chap. 1.

32. Ibid.; see also Part Two.

33. See, for example, Ruth Benedict, "Anthropology and the Abnormal," 10 *Journal of General Psychology* 59 (1934).

34. See note 29.

35. Ibid., 1–2, question 96, art. 4.

36. John Finnis, *Natural Law and Natural Rights* (New York: Oxford University Press, 1980), 90.

37. Ibid., chap. 5.

38. Ibid., 103, 126.

39. Ibid., 67–70.

40. Ibid., 85–86.

41. This criticism is explained in Golding, *Philosophy of Law*, 32–33.

42. Finnis, *Natural Law and Natural Rights*, 125–127.

43. Ibid., 127, 281.

44. Ibid., 86.

45. Ibid., 95–96, 102–112.

46. Ibid., 86–90.

47. Ibid.

48. Ibid., 65–66, 68–69.

49. Ibid., 65, 70.

50. Ibid., 66.

51. Ibid., 105.

52. Ibid., chap. 5.

53. Ibid., 121, 126; William H. Wilcox, "Essay Review: Natural Law and Natural Rights," 68 *Cornell Law Review* 408, 415–417 (1983).

54. See, for example, Wilcox, "Essay Review," 416–419.

55. Ibid., 419.

56. Finnis, *Natural Law and Natural Rights*, 127.

57. Ibid.

58. Ibid., 289.

59. Ibid.

60. See, for example, Weinreb, *Natural Law and Justice*, 113–115.

61. John Finnis, "On Reason and Authority in *Law's Empire*," 6 *Law and Philosophy* 357, 371 (1987).

62. Ibid.

63. Among others, Finnis points this out in *Natural Law and Natural Rights*, 33–34. See also Patterson, *Jurisprudence*, 351; Weinreb, *Natural Law and Justice*, 58.

64. See Part Two.

65. This is a Legal Formalist and, often, a Legal Positivist criticism.

66. Finnis tells us that obligations are imposed by the requirements of practical reasonableness. While moral obligations have variable normative force—they can be overridden by numerous countervailing reasons—legal obligations have invariant normative force: they are equally obligatory and are under the domain of legal norms. Finnis is not thereby committed to docile compliance with all laws. He provides that citizens may, under certain circumstances, reject the imperatives of law and honor overriding moral obligation. See Finnis, *Natural Law and Natural Rights*, 308–316, 318–320, 351–366.

67. Michael S. Moore, "A Natural Law Theory of Interpretation," 58 *Southern California Law Review* 279 (1985).

68. Ibid., 281.

69. Ibid., 286.

70. Ibid.

71. Ibid.

72. Ibid., 283.

73. "Imagine a judge deciding . . . whether a frozen, eviscerated chicken is or is not a 'manufactured product' for purposes of granting an exemption from Interstate Commerce Commission certification for the interstate carriers of such items. Suppose that the judge decides that no certificate is required. . . . [The three premises] in the example just given would be respectively: 1. (Statement of Law): If an item is not a manufactured product, then its carriage does not require a certificate. 2. (Statement of Fact): These items were frozen, eviscerated chickens. 3. (Interpretive Statement): If an item is a frozen, eviscerated chicken, then it is not a manufactured product" (ibid., 282–283).

74. Ibid., 283.

75. Ibid.

76. Ibid.

77. Ibid., 284.

78. Ibid., 287–288.

79. Ibid., 294.
80. Ibid.
81. Ibid.
82. Ibid.
83. Ibid.
84. Ibid.
85. Ibid.
86. Ibid., 296–297. "We can disagree with others because our conventions are not necessary truths about the meaning of [terms]. Rather, their conventions and ours are scientific theories about the true nature of [natural kinds of events]. As scientific theories about the same thing, they can compete with one another. We can claim, as we surely do, that our theory is better than theirs, something we could not claim if we were simply comparing our arbitrary conventions . . . with their [arbitrary conventions]" (298).
87. Ibid., 307–308, 320–321.
88. Ibid., 311–312. In support of his first observation, Moore tells us that "the very language we employ commits us to a realist metaphysics: we use singular terms to pick out ('rigidly designate') real objects that exist and would exist 'through all possible worlds,' and we use general predicates to 'indexically refer' to natural kinds of things or events, whatever their hidden natures might turn out to be" (311).
89. Ibid., 312. In support of his second observation, Moore tells us that "a skeptic needs [a vantage point that is free of all conventions] if, *by his own metaphysics*, he can assert the truth of his skepticism. He needs to be able to step out of the human condition for just a peek at the universe to be able to say how it is. . . . Yet no skeptic can do this, for no one can. . . . A realist's conceptual categories are not distorting lenses through which to see an undistorted world; rather, they constitute a *theory* as to how that undistorted world really is" (312).
90. Ibid., 314–320.
91. Sanford Levinson, "What Do Lawyers Know (and What Do They Do with Their Knowledge)?" 58 *Southern California Law Review* 441, 452 (1985).
92. Ibid.
93. Ibid.
94. Arnold Rothstein was a notorious gambler and racketeer who is alleged, among other things, to have fixed the 1919 World Series of Baseball.
95. Moore, "Natural Law Theory," 371.
96. Ibid.
97. Ibid.
98. Ibid., 376.
99. It seems a victory, if at all, of theoretical significance only. Stephen Munzer makes a further point about the identification of real values, their application, and legislative authority: "[Moore] underestimates how difficult it is to identify 'real values.' Sometimes the attempt to identify them may

lead to great disagreement and consequently to great unpredictability. Furthermore, while a certain value might be best for a statute in an ideally just and well-ordered society, it does not follow that that is necessarily the most appropriate value for the actual statute in the actual society in question. Finally, Moore ignores the point that the legislature transmits authority as well as meaning. It transmits an authorized set of values. Ordinarily, it is not for the judge to override this set of values." Stephen R. Munzer, "Realistic Limits on Realist Interpretation," 58 *Southern California Law Review* 459, 472 (1985).

100. Moore, "Natural Law Theory," 376.

101. Ibid., 376–377.

102. Ibid., 377.

103. Ibid.

104. Ibid., 378.

105. Ibid.

106. Ibid., 388.

107. Ibid.

108. Ibid.

109. Ibid.

110. Ibid., 389.

111. Ibid., 390–391.

112. Ibid., 391.

113. Ibid.

114. Ibid. "The justification for judicial review is simply that people really have rights, and no consensus of the majority, even when embodied in a statute, should be allowed to trample on them. A realist can concede the antidemocratic nature of judicial review because he can justify it with higher values. . . . [Moreover] it makes little sense to use the majority's (consensus) values in determining the minority's rights against that very majority" (395).

115. Ibid., 396.

116. Ibid., 397.

117. Ibid., 398.

118. Levinson, "What Do Lawyers Know?" 454.

119. Ibid., 455

120. Ibid.

121. Having addressed this topic at length elsewhere, I will not canvass again the various rationales offered in the literature. See Raymond A. Belliotti, "Our Adversary System: In Search of a Foundation," 1 *Canadian Journal of Law and Jurisprudence* 19 (1988).

122. Munzer, "Realistic Limits," 463.

123. Ibid.

124. Ibid.

125. Ibid., 465.

126. Moore, "Natural Law Theory," 379–381.

CHAPTER 2

1. John Austin, *The Province of Jurisprudence Determined* (1832. Reprint. London: Noonday Press, 1954), chap. 1.

2. Ibid., 126–140.

3. Ibid., chap. 1.

4. Ibid., 193–212.

5. Ibid.

6. Ibid., chap. 1.

7. Ibid., 193–212.

8. H.L.A. Hart, "Legal and Moral Obligation," in *Essays in Moral Philosophy*, ed. A. I. Melden (Seattle: University of Washington Press, 1958), 82–107.

9. Ibid.

10. Lon L. Fuller, *The Morality of Law*, rev. ed. (New Haven, Conn.: Yale University Press, 1969).

11. Ibid.

12. Hart, "Legal and Moral Obligation," 82–107.

13. H.L.A. Hart, *The Concept of Law* (Oxford: Clarendon Press, 1961), chap. 1. For a concise, excellent account of Hart's work, see Martin P. Golding, *Philosophy of Law* (Englewood Cliffs, N.J.: Prentice-Hall, 1975), 43–50. For a fuller critical examination see Michael Martin, *The Legal Philosophy of H.L.A. Hart: A Critical Appraisal* (Philadelphia: Temple University Press, 1987).

14. Hart, *Concept of Law*, chaps. 1, 5, 6.

15. Ibid., 114 and chaps. 1, 5, 6 generally.

16. Ibid.

17. Ibid.

18. Ibid.

19. Ibid., 97 and chap. 5 generally.

20. Ibid., 41, 90–92, and chap. 5 generally.

21. Ibid., 98 and chap. 5 generally.

22. Ibid.

23. Ibid.

24. Ibid.

25. Ibid.

26. Neil MacCormick, *H.L.A. Hart* (Stanford, Calif.: Stanford University Press, 1981), 109.

27. Hart, *Concept of Law*, 119–120 and chap. 6 generally.

28. Ibid., 126 and chap. 5 generally.

29. Ibid.

30. See, for example, Martin, *Legal Philosophy*, 59–60.

31. Hart, *Concept of Law*, 126–127.

32. Ibid., chap. 5.

33. Ibid., 132 and chap. 5 generally.

34. Ibid.

35. Ibid., 189–195; Golding, *Philosophy of Law*, 33–34.

36. Golding, *Philosophy of Law*, 33.

37. H.L.A. Hart, "Problems of Philosophy of Law," in *The Encyclopedia of Philosophy*, vol. 6, ed. Paul Edwards (New York: Macmillan, 1967), 271.

38. Martin, *Legal Philosophy*, 56.

39. Golding, *Philosophy of Law*, 49–50; H.L.A. Hart, "Positivism and the Separation of Law and Morals," 71 *Harvard Law Review* 593 (1958); Lon L. Fuller, "Positivism and Fidelity to Law—A Reply to Professor Hart," 71 *Harvard Law Review* 630 (1958).

40. Hart, "Positivism and the Separation of Law and Morals."

41. Fuller, "Positivism and Fidelity to Law."

42. See, for example, Joseph Raz, *The Authority of Law* (Oxford: Clarendon Press, 1979), 150–151.

43. Hans Kelsen, *The Pure Theory of Law*, trans. M. Knight (Berkeley: University of California Press, 1967); Kelsen, *General Theory of Law and State*, trans. A. Wedberg (Cambridge, Mass.: Harvard University Press, 1946). For a concise, critical account of Kelsen's work, see Golding, *Philosophy of Law*, 39–43.

44. See, for example, Cornelius F. Murphy, Jr., *Modern Legal Philosophy* (Pittsburgh, Pa.: Duquesne University Press, 1978), 85–89.

45. Ibid., 104–106.

46. Ibid., 90, 108; Golding, *Philosophy of Law*, 39–41.

47. Kelsen, *Pure Theory of Law*, 199.

48. Ibid.

49. Murphy, *Modern Legal Philosophy*, 86, 103.

50. Ibid., 91–92; Golding, *Philosophy of Law*, 41–42.

51. See, for example, Murphy, *Modern Legal Philosophy*, 98–99; Hart, in this chapter; Dworkin, in Chapter 3.

52. Raz, *Authority of Law*.

53. Ibid., 37–40.

54. Ibid.

55. Ibid., 47–50.

56. Ibid.

57. Ibid., 49. The "strong social thesis" is later renamed the "sources thesis." Note that the two names are often used interchangeably.

58. Ibid.

59. Ibid., 146–150.

60. Ibid., 44–45.

61. Ibid., 44–47.

62. Ibid., 47–50.

63. Ibid., 50–52; Joseph Raz, "Authority, Law, and Morality," 68 *Monist* 295, 299, 310 (1985).

64. See note 63.

65. Raz, *Authority of Law*, 44–45, 48–49.

66. Ibid., 49–50.

67. Ibid., 50–52.

68. Ibid.
69. Raz, "Authority, Law, and Morality," 298.
70. Ibid.
71. Ibid., 305–310.
72. Ibid., 305.
73. Raz, *Authority of Law*, 234.
74. See Dworkin, in Chapter 3.
75. Ibid.; see also Jules Coleman, "Negative and Positive Positivism," 11 *Journal of Legal Studies* 139 (1982); David Lyons, "Principles, Positivism, and Legal Theory," 87 *Yale Law Journal* 415 (1977); John Mackie, "The Third Theory of Law," *Philosophy and Public Affairs* 3 (1977); C. L. Ten, "The Soundest Theory of Law," 88 *Mind* 352 (1979).
76. See Dworkin, in Chapter 3.
77. See note 75.
78. Raz, *Authority of Law*, 50–51.
79. W. J. Waluchow, "The Weak Social Thesis," 9 *Oxford Journal of Legal Studies* 23, 38 (1989).
80. Ibid., 38–39.
81. Philip Soper, *A Theory of Law* (Cambridge, Mass.: Harvard University Press, 1984), 7, 8–12, 91–100.
82. Ibid., 51.
83. Ibid., 59.
84. Ibid., 75–79.
85. Ibid., 55, 80.
86. Ibid., 131.
87. Ibid., 119.
88. Ibid., 84.
89. Ibid., 126–130.
90. Ibid.
91. Ibid., 134–143.
92. Ibid., 126–130, 134–143.
93. See, for example, Steven J. Burton, "Review Essay: Law, Obligation, and a Good Faith Claim of Justice," 73 *California Law Review* 1956, 1974–1977 (1985); John M. Fischer, "Book Review: Obligation and Mutual Respect," 95 *Yale Law Journal* 437, 447–450 (1985); Joseph Raz, "Essay Review: The Morality of Obedience," 83 *Michigan Law Review* 732, 740–742 (1985).
94. Soper, *Theory of Law*, 121.
95. Ibid., 119–122.
96. See, for example, Burton, "Review Essay," 1976–1977; Raz, "Essay Review," 747–749; Note, "Book Review: *A Theory of Law*," 98 *Harvard Law Review* 1346, 1350–1351 (1985).
97. Fischer, "Book Review," 446.
98. Ibid., 447.
99. Ibid.
100. Ibid., 448.
101. Ibid., 449.

102. Ibid., 450.

103. Ibid. Fischer suggests a revision of the second condition to read: "The officials must believe that their directives are morally justified and do not impose severe or excessive burdens on any class." Although unsure whether Soper would accept such a revision or whether it adequately explains legal obligation, Fischer claims his revision is stronger than the weak formulation and weaker than the strong formulation (449–450).

104. This engages the entire issue of the justification, if any, of civil disobedience on the part of citizens and officials.

105. See, for example, Burton, "Review Essay," 1976–1977.

106. Thomas Morawetz, "Book Review: Addressing Sacred Texts," 80 *Northwestern University Law Review* 489, 497 (1985).

107. Soper, *Theory of Law*, 113–114.

108. Ibid., 118.

109. Ibid., 118–119.

110. See Chapter 3 generally.

111. Burton, "Review Essay," 1968–1969.

112. Ibid., 1969–1970.

## CHAPTER 3

1. Ronald Dworkin, *Taking Rights Seriously* (Cambridge, Mass.: Harvard University Press, 1977), 105–122.

2. Ibid., 82–84. The literature is replete with references to the principles and policies distinction. See, for example, Kent Greenawalt, "Policy, Rights, and Judicial Decision," 11 *Georgia Law Review* 991, 993–996 (1977); Joseph Raz, "Legal Principles and the Limits of Law," 81 *Yale Law Journal* 823, 848–851 (1972); Harry Wellington, "Common Law Rules and Constitutional Double Standards: Some Notes on Adjudication," 83 *Yale Law Journal* 221, 222–229 (1973). Dworkin states that things such as the subsidization of national defense are policy determinations, while antidiscrimination judgments are based on principles. He feels that even in hard cases where no settled rule dictates a decision, the determination should be made by principle and not policy. Dworkin notes, however, that policy and principles are not the only justifications for decisions. Ibid., 84–86.

3. Dworkin, *Taking Rights Seriously*, 23–31. Riggs v. Palmer, 115 NY 506, 22 NE 188 (1889); Henningsen v. Bloomfield Motors, Inc. 32 NJ 358, 161 A.2d 69 (1960).

4. Dworkin, *Taking Rights Seriously*, 23.

5. Ibid., 23–24. He further distinguishes principles by contrasting them with rules. Rules apply in an "all or nothing" way: if a rule is appropriate to apply to a given question then it determines the answer; if it is not appropriate to apply then it does not contribute anything to the answer. Thus, if two rules conflict then at least one must be invalid in the instant context. A principle, on the other hand, provides a reason for a decision but does not

necessarily provide the answer. Principles are relevant considerations that may conflict with one another and that must be "balanced out" or "weighted" by a judge arriving at a decision (24–27).

6. Ibid., 101–105. Dworkin further limits the rights to which judges may appeal by stating that institutional rights must be legal in nature and not of some other form (101).

7. Ibid.

8. Ibid., 28–31.

9. Ibid., 31–39.

10. Ibid., 117. Judgments on each scheme will often differ from judge to judge because each proceeds from her own philosophical and intellectual convictions (118). However, her subjective judgments will have no force because "they will not enter [her] calculations in such a way that different parts of the theory [she] constructs can be attributed to [her] independent convictions rather than the body of law [she] must justify" (117–118).

11. Ibid., 107–109.

12. Ibid.

13. Ibid., 111–115.

14. Ibid., 121–123. A theory of legislative supremacy, for example, ensures that any statute treated as a mistake will lose its gravitational force. Its specific authority, however, survives because the limitations of the statute must still be respected (121).

15. Ibid.

16. Ibid., 105, 106–123.

17. Ronald Dworkin, "Seven Critics," 11 *Georgia Law Review* 1201, 1252 (1977). Dworkin says that a jurisprudential question is raised when a theory based on one principle is a better fit with past doctrine and another theory with a contrary principle is morally advantageous. Although he admits his answer is "crude," Dworkin suggests that the theory that is a better fit, the one that characterizes less of past doctrine as mistakes, should prevail if the morally preferable theory stigmatizes past doctrine too much. When two theories each fit *adequately*, however, Dworkin contends that the theory that is morally preferable should prevail, even if it stigmatizes a greater amount of past doctrine as mistakes than does the other theory.

18. Dworkin, *Taking Rights Seriously*, 280–283.

19. Ibid., 160–162. The constructive model, says Dworkin, "does not assume . . . that principles of justice has some fixed, objective existence, so that descriptions of these principles must be true or false in some standard way" (160).

20. A Society retains certain common moral judgments that are fundamental to its use of the constructive model. Societies, however, are often quite diverse, and given the diversity of moral judgments, one society's construction of morality will not necessarily be applicable to another society. One commentator states that Dworkin's theory leaves open the possibility that the principles of different societies, and hence their law and morality,

may differ enormously. William T. Blackstone, "The Relationship of Law and Morality," 11 *Georgia Law Review* 1359, 1385 (1977).

21. See, for example, Greenawalt, "Policy, Rights, and Judicial Decision," 1037–1038.

22. See, for example, John Farago, "Judicial Cybernetics: The Effects of Self-Reference in Dworkin's Rights Thesis," 14 *Valpariso University Law Review* 371, 378 (1980); Greenawalt, "Policy, Rights, and Judicial Decision," 1037–1042.

23. Dworkin, *Taking Rights Seriously*, 284–285; Farago, "Judicial Cybernetics," 383–385.

24. A "tie" judgment results when the proposition on one side is just as strong as that supporting the other side. Dworkin conceives of a scale with a tie point as the single point in the center. Dworkin, *Taking Rights Seriously*, 285.

25. Raymond A. Belliotti, "Toward A Theory of Judicial Decisionmaking," 28 *The Catholic Lawyer* 215, 248–249 (1983).

26. See generally Part Two.

27. See generally Chapter 2.

28. Dworkin, "Seven Critics," 1202–1203.

29. Ibid., 1252.

30. Ronald Dworkin, *A Matter of Principle* (Cambridge, Mass.: Harvard University Press, 1985); Dworkin, *Law's Empire* (Cambridge, Mass.: Harvard University Press, 1986).

31. Dworkin, *Law's Empire*, 124.

32. Ibid., 95.

33. Ibid., 123–126.

34. Ibid., 130.

35. Ibid., 123.

36. Ibid., 124.

37. Ibid., 127–128.

38. In this vein, Stanley Fish writes, "To be sure, you can always cite a statute or a piece of the Constitution and declare roundly that you stand on it and will not go beyond it; but, in fact, you will *already* have gone beyond it, if by 'it' you understand a meaning that declares itself and repels interpretation. Meanings only become perspicacious against a background of interpretive assumptions in the absence of which reading and understanding would be impossible. A meaning that seems to leap off the page, propelled by its own self-sufficiency, is a meaning that flows from interpretive assumptions so deeply embedded that they have become invisible." Stanley Fish, "Still Wrong After All These Years," 6 *Law and Philosophy* 401, 403 (1987).

39. There are versions of jurisprudence that purport to be non-politicized: judicial decision making based on strict adherence to the plain meaning of constitutional provisions and legislative enactments ("textualism"), grounded on the intentions of the framers ("intentionalism"), or de-

rived from the rational or normative order immanent in the law ("formalism"). "Originalism" is a generic term that includes textualism and intentionalism. Edwin Meese and Robert Bork are two national figures who self-consciously embrace versions of originalism. See, for example, Raymond A. Belliotti, "Beyond Capitalism and Communism: Roberto Unger's Super-liberal Political Theory," 9 *Praxis International* 321, 328–331 (1989).

40. Dworkin, *Law's Empire*, 95.

41. Ibid., 154.

42. Ibid., 167.

43. Ibid., 189.

44. Ibid., 95.

45. Ibid.

46. Ibid., 155, 159. In the *Republic*, Plato introduces the Noble Lie—the falsehood told by the guardian class to the other classes that at birth the gods mix different kinds of metals into newborns—as a way of reinforcing citizens' willingness to accept their class status.

47. Ibid., 155.

48. Fish, "Still Wrong," 405–406. An interesting side consideration emerges here. Dworkin is tacitly admitting that the faith in right answers thesis is inadequate if right answers do not in fact exist. In other words, judges should not act *as if* there are right answers in the absence of right answers. Thus, to be consistent, he must argue for the right answer thesis and not merely the two weaker versions (faith in right answers thesis or judicial belief in right answers thesis) adumbrated previously.

49. "But where would one's sense of what was 'best' come from if not from that very history [of decisions, statutes, and invoking of precedents], which, because it formed the basis of the agent's education, would be the content of his judgment?" (ibid.).

50. Ibid.

51. Dworkin, *Law's Empire*.

52. Ibid., 46–48.

53. Ibid., 65–66.

54. Ibid., 52.

55. See note 17.

56. Dworkin, *Law's Empire*, 231, 242, 255.

57. Ibid., 242–244.

58. Ibid., 231, 257.

59. Ibid., 257.

60. Ibid., 168.

61. Ibid., 237–239.

62. Ibid., 52.

63. Ibid., 66.

64. Ibid., 52.

65. Ibid., 66–67.

66. Ibid., 225.

67. Ibid., 228–238.

68. Ibid., 231.

69. "Lawyers and judges cannot avoid politics in the broad sense of political theory. But law is not a matter of personal or partisan politics, and a critique of law that does not understand this difference will provide poor understanding and even poorer guidance" (Dworkin, *Matter of Principle*, 146).

70. Ibid.

71. See, for example, Dworkin, *Law's Empire*, 9–10.

72. Dworkin, *Matter of Principle*, 11, 12–19.

73. Ibid., 11, 16–18, 27–28.

74. Ibid., 12.

75. Ibid.

76. Ibid., 31.

77. Ibid., 16.

78. Ibid., 175–177; Dworkin, *Law's Empire*, 79–80.

79. Dworkin, *Law's Empire*, 78–86.

80. Ibid.

81. Ibid., 80–86.

82. "No problem of consistency arises for [the internal skeptic] because we are no longer dealing with the myth of two standpoints. . . . No one who says there is no answer to the question about Hamlet and Ophelia, because neither answer makes the play better or worse than the other, will go on to say that in his personal opinion they were lovers" (Dworkin, *Matter of Principle*, 176).

83. Ibid., 172.

84. Ibid., 171.

85. Ibid., 172–173.

86. Ibid., 172–174.

87. Ibid., 174.

88. See, for example, Dworkin, *Law's Empire*, 52–66.

89. Ibid., 46.

90. Ibid.

91. Ibid., 217–219.

92. Ibid., 225–226, 254–258; Dworkin, *Taking Rights Seriously*, 44–45; Larry Alexander and Michael Bayles, "Hercules or Proteus?: The Many Theses of Ronald Dworkin," 5 *Social Theory and Practice* 267, 280–283 (1980); Larry Alexander, "Striking Back at the Empire," 6 *Law and Philosophy* 419, 421–423 (1987).

93. George C. Christie, "Book Review: Dworkin's Empire," 1987 *Duke Law Journal* 157, 185 (1987).

94. James D. A. Boyle, "Review Essay: Legal Fiction," 38 *Hastings Law Journal* 1013, 1015 (1987).

95. Dworkin, *Law's Empire*, 273.

96. Ibid.

97. Ibid.

98. Ibid.

99. Ibid., 274.

100. Ibid.

101. Ibid.

102. Ibid., 274–275.

103. Ibid., 275.

104. Gerald J. Postema, "'Protestant' Interpretation and Social Practices," 6 *Law and Philosophy* 283, 301 (1987).

105. Ibid., 305.

106. Ibid., 313.

107. Ibid., 301.

108. Fish, "Still Wrong," 407–408.

109. Ibid., 407.

110. Ibid.

111. Ibid.

112. Ibid., 408.

113. Dworkin, *Law's Empire*, 274.

114. David Couzens Hoy, "Dworkin's Constructive Optimism v. Deconstructive Legal Nihilism," 6 *Law and Philosophy* 321, 349 (1987).

115. Dworkin, *Law's Empire*, 225.

116. See, for example, Roberto Unger, "The Critical Legal Studies Movement," 96 *Harvard Law Review* 561 (1983).

117. Boyle, "Review Essay," 1016.

118. Dworkin, *Taking Rights Seriously*, 76.

119. A. D. Woozley, "No Right Answer," in *Ronald Dworkin and Contemporary Jurisprudence*, ed. Marshall Cohen (Totowa, N.J.: Rowman and Littlefield, 1983), 173–181.

120. Ibid., 178–179.

121. Ronald M. Dworkin, "A Reply," in *Ronald Dworkin and Contemporary Jurisprudence*, ed. Cohen, 247, 276.

122. Ibid., 277.

123. Ibid.

124. Ibid., 278.

125. John Finnis, "On Reason and Authority in *Law's Empire*," 6 *Law and Philosophy* 357, 374 (1987).

126. Ibid.

127. Ibid.

128. Ibid.

129. Ibid., 376.

## CHAPTER 4

1. Gary S. Becker, *The Economics of Discrimination*, 2d ed. (Chicago: University of Chicago Press, 1971); Guido Calabresi, "Some Thoughts on Risk Distribution and the Law of Torts," 70 *Yale Law Journal* 499 (1960); Ronald H. Coase, "The Problem of Social Cost," 3 *Journal of Law & Economics* 1 (1960).

2. Coase, "Problem of Social Cost."

3. George Stigler, "The Law and Economics of Public Policy: A Plea to Scholars," 1 *Journal of Legal Studies* 1, 11–12 (1972).

4. Richard A. Posner, "The Economic Approach to Law," 53 *Texas Law Review* 757 (1975). Reprinted in *Readings in Jurisprudence and Legal Philosophy*, ed. Philip Shuchman (Boston: Little, Brown, 1979), 855–857.

5. Richard A. Posner, *Economic Analysis of Law* (Boston: Little, Brown, 1977), 4.

6. Lewis A. Kornhauser, "The Great Image of Authority," 36 *Stanford Law Review* 349, 353 (1984).

7. Ibid., 354.

8. Ibid.

9. Ibid., 355.

10. Ibid., 354.

11. Richard A. Posner, "Utilitarianism, Economics, and Legal Theory," 8 *The Journal of Legal Studies* 103, 119 (1979).

12. Ibid., 127.

13. Richard A. Posner, *The Economics of Justice* (Cambridge, Mass.: Harvard University Press, 1983), 60.

14. Ibid., 61.

15. Richard A. Posner, "The Ethical and Political Basis of the Efficiency Norm in Common Law Adjudication," 8 *Hofstra Law Review* 487, 488–491 (1980).

16. Ibid., 488–489.

17. Ibid., 489.

18. "Suppose some entrepreneur loses money because a competitor develops a superior product. Since the return to entrepreneurial activity will include a premium to cover the risk of losses due to competition, the entrepreneur is compensated for those losses ex ante" (ibid., 492).

19. Ibid., 492–493.

20. Ibid., 491–497.

21. Ronald M. Dworkin, "Why Efficiency?" 8 *Hofstra Law Review* 563, 575 (1980).

22. Ibid., 576–577.

23. Ibid., 580–581. "I was better off under the system of negligence before I was run down, at least on the reasonable assumption that I had no more chance of being run down than any one else. . . . But of course *after* the accident (if I have not in fact bought insurance) I would be better off under a system of strict liability. The difference can also be expressed . . . as a difference in expected welfare under different states of knowledge" (ibid.).

24. Posner, "Utilitarianism, Economics, and Legal Theory," 112.

25. Ibid., 113.

26. "The logic of utilitarianism seems to argue for pushing the boundary as far out as possible. . . . Since this goal seems attainable only by making lots of people miserable (those of us who would have to make room for all the foreigners, sheep, etc.), utilitarians are constantly seeking ways of con-

tracting the boundary. But to do so they must go outside of utilitarianism" (ibid.).

27. Ibid.

28. Ibid., 114.

29. Ibid., 116.

30. Ibid.

31. Ibid.

32. Ibid., 117.

33. Ibid., 118.

34. Posner, "Ethical and Political Basis of the Efficiency Norm," 496.

35. Posner, "Utilitarianism, Economics, and Legal Theory," 121–123, 130–131.

36. Ibid., 121. "The theft does not increase wealth. . . . In actual-market terms the thief's unwillingness (based on inability) to pay for the necklace shows that the necklace is worth less to him than to the owner. And resort to hypothetical-market analysis is unwarranted since there is no problem of high market transaction costs that would justify allowing the thief to circumvent the market."

37. Ibid., 123.

38. Ibid., 131–132.

39. Ibid., 135.

40. Ibid.

41. Ibid., 134.

42. Ibid.

43. "In a society where the ratio of people to resources was so high that the expected social cost of additional population exceeded the expected product, a case could be made for forcibly limiting the birthrate—depending, of course, on the costs of implementing such a policy by the inherently imperfect instruments of government" (ibid.).

44. Ibid.

45. Ibid., 133.

46. Ibid., 128.

47. Ibid.

48. Richard A. Posner, "A Reply to Some Recent Criticisms of the Efficiency Theory of the Common Law," 9 *Hofstra Law Review* 775, 791 (1981).

49. Posner, *Economics of Justice*, 76.

50. Ibid., 79n.58.

51. Peter J. Hammond, "The Economics of Justice and the Criterion of Wealth Maximization," 91 *Yale Law Journal* 1493, 1499 (1982).

52. Richard Schmalbeck, "The Justice Of Economics: An Analysis of Wealth Maximization as a Normative Goal," 83 *Columbia Law Review* 488, 504 (1983).

53. Ibid., 505.

54. Ibid.

55. Posner, *Economic Analysis of Law*, 11–12.

56. Ibid., 12.

57. Ibid., 11–12, 436.

58. Ibid., 439.

59. John J. Donohue III and Ian Ayres, "Posner's Symphony No. 3: Thinking About the Unthinkable," 39 *Stanford Law Review* 791, 799 (1987).

60. C. Edwin Baker, "The Ideology of the Economic Analysis of Law," 5 *Philosophy & Public Affairs* 3 (1975). Reprinted in *Readings in Jurisprudence*, ed. Schuchman, 874.

61. Ibid., 875.

62. Ibid.

63. Ibid.

64. Ibid.

65. Ibid., 876.

66. Ibid.

67. Ibid.

68. "Assume that a city is deciding whether to use an open space for high intensity recreation . . . favored by poor youth or for a fee-charging golf course favored by the rich. Assume that the total cost to the city of either use is the same and that there are no negotiation costs (or other transaction costs). Then if the rich were willing to offer the city $5,000 to make a golf course but that the poor youth could only scrape together $4,500 for their offer, would 'value' be increased by using the land as a golf course? Presumably, Posner would say yes. But if granted the right to have the land used for high intensity recreation, the poor youth might not give up the right for less than $7,000 while the rich . . . would be willing to sell the right for a little more than $5,000. Adopting the *situation post* perspective clearly favors the poor for whom the right constitutes a larger proportionate addition of wealth. . . . Posner's *situation ante* approach favors the rich" (ibid., 880–881).

69. Schmalbeck, "Justice of Economics," 502.

70. See, for example, Cento G. Veljanovski, "Wealth Maximization, Law, Ethics—On the Limits of Economic Efficiency," 1 *International Review of Law and Economics* 5 (1981). "Rights must be assigned before [WMP] can be used, and hence rights cannot be determined by it. If rights are to be assigned to mimic a perfect market outcome then we must know the rights structure on which that outcome was based" (20).

71. Warren J. Samuels, "Maximization of Wealth as Justice: An Essay on Posnerian Law and Economics as Policy Analysis," 60 *Texas Law Review* 147, 154 (1981).

72. Posner, "Utilitarianism, Economics, and Legal Theory," 135.

73. Samuels, "Maximization of Wealth," 154.

74. Laurence H. Tribe, "Policy Science: Analysis or Ideology," 2 *Philosophy & Public Affairs* 66 (1972). Reprinted in *Readings in Jurisprudence*, ed. Schuchman, 839–840.

75. Ibid., 847. "Talking of the . . . 'trade off between employment and

inflation' conceals the anguish of joblessness, or talking of the 'collapse mode in a world resource model' obscures what global starvation would mean."

76. Morton J. Horwitz, "Law and Economics: Science or Politics?" 8 *Hofstra Law Review* 905, 911–912 (1980).

77. Bruce Chapman, "Raising Johnny to Be Good: A Problematic Case for Economic Analysis of Law," 34 *University of Toronto Law Journal* 358, 373 (1984).

78. For an analysis of the dangers of the commodification of constitutive attributes, see Margaret Jane Radin, "Market Inalienability," 100 *Harvard Law Review* 1849 (1987). For an analysis that is partially critical of Radin's view see Raymond A. Belliotti, "Marxism, Feminism, and Surrogate Motherhood," 14 *Social Theory and Practice* 389 (1988).

79. Posner, *Economic Analysis of Law*, 10–13, 18, 42–44, 69.

80. Owen M. Fiss, "The Death of Law?" 72 *Cornell Law Review* 1, 8 (1986).

81. Posner, *Economics of Justice*, 198–199.

82. James B. White, "What Can a Lawyer Learn from Literature?" 102 *Harvard Law Review* 2014, 2047 (1989).

83. Kornhauser, "Great Image of Authority," 358.

84. Ibid., 361.

85. Richard A. Posner, "The Ethics of Wealth Maximization: Reply to Malloy," 36 *Kansas Law Review* 261, 263 (1988).

86. Ibid.

87. Ibid.

88. Posner, "Economic Approach to Law," 864–865.

89. Ibid., 868–869.

90. Ibid., 869.

91. Posner, "Ethics of Wealth Maximization," 264.

92. Posner, "Economic Approach to Law," 856.

93. Ibid.

94. Posner may be softening his position on the importance of WMP for judicial decision making. Rather than defending his former view that WMP is the only value promoted effectively by courts, he now seems to hold that certainty and formal accuracy are beyond possibility and thus courts should aspire to the most reasonable results given the totality of circumstances. See, for example, Richard A. Posner, "The Jurisprudence of Skepticism," 86 *Michigan Law Review* 827, 862 (1988). Thus, this chapter should be taken as an examination of WMP and not necessarily a critique of Posner's current position.

95. Gary Minda, "The Jurisprudential Movements of the 1980s," 50 *Ohio State Law Journal* 599, 607 n.32 (1989).

96. Ibid., 604–605 n.20.

## CHAPTER 5

1. See Chapter 3, note 39.

2. Owen M. Fiss, "Objectivity and Interpretation," in *Interpreting Law and Literature*, ed. Sanford Levinson and Steven Mailloux (Evanston, Ill.: Northwestern University Press, 1988), 232.

3. Ibid.

4. Ibid., 248.

5. Ibid.

6. Ibid.

7. Ibid., 240.

8. Ibid., 239.

9. Ibid., 238.

10. Ibid., 239.

11. Stanley Fish, "Fish vs. Fiss," in *Interpreting Law and Literature*, ed. Levinson and Mailloux, 252. Fish claims that Fiss's disciplining rules are themselves indeterminate and thus must be interpreted. Accordingly, Fish denies that disciplinary rules can stabilize the meaning of texts: "The problem with [a particular disciplinary rule is that it] . . . does not prevent—but provokes—disagreements about exactly what history is or about whether or not this piece of information counts as history, or (if it does count) about what its factual configurations are" (ibid.).

12. Robin L. West, "Adjudication Is Not Interpretation: Some Reservations About the Law-as-Literature Movement," 54 *Tennessee Law Review* 203, 215 n. 31 (1987).

13. See, for example, Sanford Levinson, "Law as Literature," in *Interpreting Law and Literature*, ed. Levinson and Mailloux, 171–172.

14. Fiss, "Objectivity and Interpretation," 233.

15. Ibid., 234.

16. Ibid. "The objective quality of interpretation . . . is bounded by the existence of a community that recognizes and adheres to the disciplining rules used by the interpreter and that is defined by its recognition of those rules. . . . Bounded objectivity is the only kind of objectivity to which the law—or any interpretive activity—ever aspires and the only one about which we care. To insist on more, to search for the brooding omnipresence in the sky, is to create a false issue." Ibid.

17. Stanley Fish, "Dennis Martinez and the Uses of Theory," 96 *Yale Law Journal* 1773, 1784 (1987).

18. Ibid., 1796 n. 60.

19. Ibid., 1796.

20. Stanley Fish, "Anti-Professionalism," 7 *Cardozo Law Review* 645, 658 (1986).

21. Ibid., 658–661.

22. Stanley Fish, "Interpretation and the Pluralist Vision," 60 *Texas Law Review* 495, 497 (1982).

23. Fish, "Fish vs. Fiss," 267–268.

24. Ibid., 256.

25. Fish, "Dennis Martinez," 1778.

26. Ibid., 1795.

27. Stanley Fish, *Is There a Text in This Class?* (Cambridge, Mass.: Harvard University Press, 1980), 327.

28. Fish, "Anti-Professionalism," 673–675.

29. See, for example, Fish, "Dennis Martinez," 1787–1788. "As a link in the chain [a judge] is a repository of the purposes, values, understood goals, forms of reasoning, modes of justification, etc., that the chain at once displays and enacts. It would follow then that an agent so embedded would not need anything external to what he already carried within him as a stimulus or guide to right—that is, responsible—action." Ibid.

30. See, for example, Fish, "Fish vs. Fiss," 260. "How are these [interpretive] conflicts to be settled? The answer . . . is that they are always in the process of being settled, and that no transcendent or algorithmic method . . . is required to settle them. The means of settling them are political, social, and institutional, in a mix, that is itself subject to modification and change" (ibid.).

31. See, for example, LisaMichelle Davis, "Epistemological Foundations and Meta-Hermeneutic Methods: The Search for a Theoretical Justification of the Coercive Force of Legal Interpretation," 68 *Boston University Law Review* 733, 768n.203 (1988).

32. See, for example, Martin P. Golding, "A Note on Discovery and Justification in Science and Law," 28 *Nomos* 124 (1986).

33. Fish, "Dennis Martinez," 1791.

34. Michael Moore, "The Interpretive Turn in Modern Theory: A Turn for the Worse?" 41 *Stanford Law Review* 871, 913–914 (1989).

35. Moore captures this point well: "If 'talking theory' is a practice—a rhetorical strategy for getting what we want, just like baseball pitching—then it too should be divorced from Fish's (or anyone else's) theorizing about how to carry on that practice. . . . If theorizing is just another doing, how (under Fish's psychology) can Fish tell us anything useful about how this doing is to be done?" (ibid., 914).

36. See, for example, ibid., 915. "Tacit knowledge (about judging, at least) is learned, just as the tacit knowledge exercised in playing the piano is learned. That knowledge comes from practice that is itself guided by a theory of how to play the piano well. . . . Sometimes the phenomenology may be as Fish describes: The decision just comes to a judge. Just as often, however, . . . judges think about how they should judge as they judge and direct their thoughts accordingly" (ibid.).

37. Fish, "Dennis Martinez," 1790.

38. See, for example, Moore, "Interpretive Turn," 916. "Fish slides from a correct observation—that giving justifying reasons in an opinion is not the same thing as describing the motivating reasons for an initial decision—to the incorrect conclusion that opinion writing is therefore mere rationalization of a decision already made on other grounds. In fact, however, judges sometimes change their tentative decisions precisely because they cannot find reasons that will produce a plausible opinion" (ibid.).

CHAPTER 6

1. See, for example, Karl Marx, *Economic and Philosophical Manuscripts* (1844); Karl Marx, "Excerpts from James Mill's Elements of Political Economy" (1844), in *Writings of the Young Marx on Philosophy and Society*, ed. L. D. Easton and K. Guddat, (Garden City, N.Y.: Doubleday, 1967); Richard Schmitt, *Marx and Engels: A Critical Reconstruction* (Boulder, Colo.: Westview Press, 1987), 151–159.

2. See, for example, Marx, *Economic and Philosophical Manuscripts* (1844); David Conway, *A Farewell to Marx* (Harmondsworth, England: Penguin, 1987), 34–41.

3. See, for example, Karl Marx and Friedrich Engels, *The German Ideology* (1845); Karl Marx, *Capital*, vol. 1 (1867); Peter Singer, *Marx* (Oxford: Oxford University Press, 1980), 25–34.

4. See note 3.

5. Marx, *Capital*, vol. 1; Schmitt, *Marx and Engels*, 74–85; Conway, *Farewell to Marx*, 98–105; Singer, *Marx*, 23–25, 50–54; and John Elster, *An Introduction to Karl Marx* (Cambridge: Cambridge University Press, 1986), 81–101.

6. See note 5.

7. See, for example, Conway, *Farewell to Marx*, 98–105; Allen Buchanan, *Marx and Justice* (Totowa, N.J.: Rowman and Littlefield, 1982), chap. 5; and Allen Wood, "The Marxian Critique of Justice," in *Marx, Justice, and History*, ed. M. Cohen, T. Nagel, and T. Scanlon (Princeton, N.J.: Princeton University Press, 1980), 3–41.

8. Schmitt, *Marx and Engels*, 30. Marx's clearest and best-known passage about the relationship is the following: "In the social production of their life, humans enter into definite relations that are indispensable and independent of their will, relations of production which correspond to a definite stage of development of their material productive forces. The sum total of these relations of production constitutes the economic structure of society, the real foundation, on which rises a legal and political superstructure and to which correspond definite forms of social consciousness. The mode of production of material life conditions the social, political, and intellectual life process in general. It is not the consciousness of humans that determines their being, but, on the contrary, their social being that determines their consciousness" (ibid.).

9. Ibid. "At a certain stage of their development, the material productive forces of society come in conflict with the existing relations of production. . . . Then begins the epoch of social revolution."

10. Ibid., 36–38.

11. Hugh Collins, *Marxism and Law* (Oxford: Oxford University Press, 1984), 78. "Plamenatz contends that is impossible for a set of relations of production to be described without reference to legal rules, and furthermore that many modes of production like capitalism are actually dependent upon the legal system for the creation of their basic economic relations."

12. Schmitt, *Marx and Engels*, 36; Jorge Larrain, "Base and Superstructure," in *A Dictionary of Marxist Thought*, ed. Tom Bottomore (Cambridge, Mass.: Harvard University Press, 1983), 44. " . . . political, legal, philosophical theories, religious ideas and their further development into systems of dogma—also exercise their influence upon the course of the historical struggles."

13. Larrain, "Base and Superstructure," 43. "If material production itself in not conceived in its specific historical form, it is impossible to understand what is specific in the spiritual production corresponding to it and the reciprocal influence of one on the other."

14. Schmitt, *Marx and Engels*, 35.

15. Ibid., 36. It seems clear that Marx and Engels aspired to more than the economic limitation view: "The ruling ideas are nothing more than the ideal expression of the dominant material relationships, the dominant material relationships grasped as ideas."

16. Ibid., 36–38.

17. Ibid., 36.

18. Ibid., 73.

19. Ibid., 37, 38.

20. Collins, *Marxism and Law*, 137. "[The] Marxist explanation of the form of modern law . . . [claims] that distinctive attributes such as formal justice and autonomy of legal reasoning depend upon complex legitimating ideologies, which are themselves derived from political practices within the relatively autonomous state not directly concerned with the capitalist relations of production."

21. *The German Ideology*; Schmitt, *Marx and Engels*, 54–56; Conway, *Farewell to Marx*, 170–177; and Elster, *Introduction to Marx*, 168–172. Engels explicitly used the term "false consciousness" in his letter to Franz Mehring, July 14, 1893, in Karl Marx and Friedrich Engels, *Selected Works* (Moscow: Progress Publishers, 1968), 690. "Ideology is a process accomplished by the so-called thinker consciously, it is true, but with a false consciousness. The real motive forces impelling him remain unknown to him; otherwise it simply would not be an ideological process. Hence he imagines false or seeming motive forces." Some theorists claim that Marx never explicitly used "false consciousness," but they admit that no substantive implications follow if they are correct. See, for example, Martin Seliger, *The Marxist Conception of Ideology* (Cambridge: Cambridge University Press, 1977), 30–31.

22. See, for example, Jorge Larrain, "Ideology," in *Dictionary of Marxist Thought*, ed. Bottomore, 218–220; Collins, *Marxism and Law*, 40; and R. G. Peffer, "Morality and the Marxist Concept of Ideology," in *Marx and Morality*, ed. K. Nielsen and S. C. Patten (Guelph, Ont.: Canadian Association for Publishing Philosophy, 1981), 67–91.

23. Schmitt, *Marx and Engels*, 58. Marxism is not committed to the simplistic position that all members of subordinate classes, or all subjects generally, are *necessarily* victims of the mystifying effects of ideological distortion. It should be obvious that at least some (and perhaps all) of the people some

of the time will be able to pierce through the smoke screen that is false consciousness.

24. In other words, Marxism cannot deny automatically the veracity of a perception or experience that does not support the conclusions of Marxism. On the other hand, critics of Marxism cannot accept automatically the veracity of such perceptions and experiences as evidence refuting Marxist conclusions.

25. Schmitt, *Marx and Engels*, 47. "When Marx and Engels use the term 'contradiction,' they are referring to oppositions, conflicts, and incoherences of all kinds but not to logical contradictions in the strict sense. . . . They are not accepting . . . irrationalism."

26. Collins, *Marxism and Law*, 11–12.

27. Ibid., 11.

28. Ibid.

29. Ibid., 13.

30. Ibid., 136. "[Marxists portray law] as a dialogue with the background dominant ideology on the basis of the formal constraints of coherence and consistency. . . . The judge's aim may be to treat like cases alike, but we can be sure that definitions of similarity and difference are determined by criteria supplied by that dominant ideology. Formal justice is not so much hollow justice but another style of class domination."

31. Ibid., 14.

32. Ibid., 48–49.

33. Ibid., 72–73. "Hard cases . . . occur when no legal expression of the dominant ideology has been established or during periods of ideological transition when there are competing background ideologies. Ultimately the material determination of the content of law in these hard cases is ensured because the dominant ideology is itself the source of the conflict between legal rules. . . . What can never be accepted by a Marxist is the view that each legal rule is not the product of a dialogue with the background ideology."

34. Ibid., 43. "There is no need . . . to suggest that the ruling class is aware of its class position and deliberately sets out to crush opposition. Instead, its perceptions of interest will appear to be the natural order of things since they are confirmed by everyday experience."

35. Ibid., 105.

36. Ibid., 106. "Law defined as an instrument of class oppression will disappear with the demise of the class system. Yet, both Engels and Lenin recognize that some norms will remain. There will be both rules for the administration of a planned economy and elementary rules of social life. They cannot be law, however, because they do not support a system of class oppression."

37. Ibid.

38. Ibid.

39. Ibid., 107.

40. Eugene Kamenka, "Law," in *A Dictionary of Marxist Thought*, ed. Bot-

tomore, 276. "Law is now seen as the regular, necessary, fair and efficient means of steering society in conditions of social ownership. Like the state, it is allegedly a fundamental element in human affairs, which has been captured and distorted in the class interest in class societies, but which will not wither away when class disappears and which has elements of a non-class nature within it."

41. Surya Sinha, *What is Law?* (New York: Paragon House, 1989), 218.

42. Mark V. Tushnet, "Marxism as Metaphor," 68 *Cornell Law Review* 281, 290 (1983).


CHAPTER 7

1. See, for example, Roberto M. Unger, "The Critical Legal Studies Movement," 96 *Harvard Law Review* 561 (1983); Unger, *Passion: An Essay on Personality* (New York: Free Press, 1984); Unger, *Social Theory: Its Situation and Its Task* (Cambridge: Cambridge University Press, 1987); Unger, *False Necessity: Anti-Necessitarian Social Theory in the Service of Radical Democracy* (Cambridge: Cambridge University Press, 1987); *Plasticity into Power* (Cambridge: Cambridge University Press, 1987); Morton Horwitz, *The Transformation of American Law, 1780–1860* (Cambridge, Mass.: Harvard University Press, 1977); Peter Gabel, "Intention and Structure in Contractual Conditions," 61 *Minnesota Law Review* 601 (1977); Paul Brest, "The Substance of Process," 42 *Ohio State Law Journal* 131 (1981); Mark V. Tushnet, "Truth, Justice, and the American Way," 57 *Texas Law Review* 1307 (1979); Duncan Kennedy, "Form and Substance in Private Law Adjudication," 89 *Harvard Law Review* 1685 (1976); Kennedy, "Legal Formality," 2 *Journal of Legal Studies* 351 (1977); Kennedy, "The Structure of Blackstone's *Commentaries*," 28 *Buffalo Law Review* 205 (1979); Mark Kelman, *A Guide to Critical Legal Studies* (Cambridge, Mass.: Harvard University Press, 1987); David Kairys, ed., *The Politics of Law* (New York: Pantheon, 1982); James Boyle, "The Politics of Reason," 133 *University of Pennsylvania Law Review* 685 (1985); Joseph W. Singer, "The Player and the Cards: Nihilism and Legal Theory," 94 *Yale Law Journal* 1 (1984); Gary Peller, "The Metaphysics of American Law," 73 *California Law Review* 1151 (1985); Critical Legal Studies symposiums are contained in 36 *Stanford Law Review* 1 (1984); 6 *Cardozo Law Review* 691 (1985); 52 *George Washington Law Review* 239 (1984); and 34 *American University Law Review* 939 (1985). See also, Duncan Kennedy and Karl Klare, "A Bibliography of Critical Legal Studies," 94 *Yale Law Journal* 461 (1984).

There are several different groups and strands of thought within CLS, including proponents of the Frankfurt School of Social Criticism (e.g., Kelman), Orthodox Marxists (e.g., Tushnet and some members of the National Lawyers Guild), Law and Social Science perspective (e.g., David Trubek), and those I have described elsewhere as neo-Nietzscheans (e.g., Boyle, Singer, Peller, and, arguably, Gabel and Kennedy). All these groups overlap in important areas of theory and practice. See Raymond A. Belliotti, "Radical Politics and Nonfoundational Morality," 29 *International Philosophical Quarterly* 33 (1989).

2. See, for example, Robert Gordon, "Historicism in Legal Scholarship," 90 *Yale Law Journal* 1017 (1981); Kairys, ed., *Politics of Law*; Kennedy, "Structure of Blackstone's *Commentaries*," and "Form and Substance."

3. Unger, "Critical Legal Studies Movement," 580.

4. See note 1.

5. See, for example, Kennedy, "Form and Substance."

6. See Unger, *Passion*, 53–64, 95–100; Kennedy, "Structure of Blackstone's *Commentaries*," 211–212. "The goal of individual freedom is at the same time dependent on and incompatible with the communal coercive action that is necessary to achieve it. Others . . . are necessary if we are to become persons at all—they provide us with the stuff of ourselves and protect us in crucial ways against destruction. . . . But at the same time . . . the universe of others . . . threatens us with annihilation" (212).

7. Kennedy, "Structure of Blackstone's *Commentaries*," 205.

8. See, for example, Kelman, *Critical Legal Studies*, chaps. 1 and 3.

9. See, for example, Unger, "Critical Legal Studies Movement"; Kennedy, "Form and Substance."

10. See note 9; Robert Gordon, "Critical Legal Histories," 36 *Stanford Law Review* 57, 114 (1984).

11. See, for example, Donald F. Brosnan, "Serious but Not Critical," 60 *Southern California Law Review* 259, 384–385 (1987); Christopher H. Schroeder, "Liberalism and the Objective Point of View," 28 *Nomos* 100, 108–109 (1986).

12. See note 10.

13. Ibid.

14. Unger, "Critical Legal Studies Movement," 667; Robert Gordon, "'Of Law and the River' and of Nihilism and Academic Freedom," 35 *Journal of Legal Education* 1, 4 (1985).

15. See, for example, Brosnan, "Serious but Not Critical," 354–357; Schroeder, "Liberalism," 109–111; Jeffrey H. Reiman, "Law, Rights, Community, and the Structure of Liberal Legal Justification," 28 *Nomos* 178, 189–192 (1986); Lawrence B. Solum, "On the Indeterminacy Crisis: Critiquing Critical Dogma," 54 *University of Chicago Law Review* 462, 472–484 (1987).

16. See note 10.

17. See, for example, Chapters 2 and 3.

18. See Chapters 2 and 3; Schroeder, "Liberalism," 110–112.

19. Gordon, "Critical Legal Histories," 114.

20. In fact, even those who label themselves Modern Formalists can accept certain aspects of the indeterminacy thesis. Thus, Ernest Weinrib writes, "Formalism does not rely on the antecedent determinacy for particular cases of the concepts entrenched in positive law, even when those concepts reflect the appropriate form of justice. . . . The distinctive feature of formalism is that it denies the primacy of the particular by claiming that particulars are intelligible only through conceptual categories. Particulars,

considered directly on their own as particulars, are regarded as unknow-able. . . . A function of positive law is to resolve such unavoidable indeter-minacy for particular cases." "Legal Formalism: On the Immanent Ra-tionality of Law," 97 *Yale Law Journal* 949, 1008–1009 (1988).

21. Charges that CLS is nihilistic have been raised often in the literature. See, for example, Paul Carrington, "Of Law and the River," 34 *Journal of Legal Education* 222, 227 (1984); Owen Fiss, "Objectivity and Interpretation," 34 *Stanford Law Review* 739 (1982); John Stick, "Can Nihilism Be Pragmatic?" 100 *Harvard Law Review* 332 (1986).

22. See, for example, Peller, "Metaphysics of American Law," 1159, 1165–1167, 1169–1170. In fact it is not clear what the world would look like if there were an objective moral order. Would there be more agreement on particular moral judgments? Perhaps, but it should be clear that the pres-ence of widespread agreement no more implies the existence of an objective moral order than does the absence of such agreement establish the lack of an objective moral order.

23. Raymond A. Belliotti, "Is Law a Sham?" 48 *Philosophy and Phenome-nological Research* 25, 39 (1987).

24. Belliotti, "Radical Politics and Nonfoundational Morality," 48–49.

25. Singer, "Player and the Cards," 52.

26. Ibid., 52–53.

27. Ibid., 62; James Boyle, "Modernist Social Theory," 98 *Harvard Law Review* 1066, 1081 (1985). "The conceptual grandiosity of abstract philosophy and social theory is but one style of thought about moral action, and not the most attractive style at that" (1081).

28. Singer, "Player and the Cards," 52–53.

29. Mark V. Tushnet, "Critical Legal Studies: An Introduction to Its Ori-gins and Underpinnings," 36 *Journal of Legal Education* 505, 515 (1986).

30. See, for example, Raymond A. Belliotti, "Critical Legal Studies: The Paradoxes of Indeterminacy and Nihilism," 113 *Philosophy and Social Criticism* 145, 150–151 (1987); Stick, "Can Nihilism Be Pragmatic?"; Brosnan, "Serious but Not Critical," 344–359.

31. See note 1. See also, Roberto Unger, *Knowledge and Politics* (New York: Free Press, 1975); Unger, *Law in Modern Society* (New York: Free Press, 1976).

32. Unger, *Passion*, 7–12.

33. Ibid., 100.

34. Ibid., 7–10.

35. Ibid., 86.

36. Ibid., 22–39, 53–55, 57–62, 65–67, 69–76. The "heroic ethic" attracts those who combine devotion to collective tasks with skepticism about the possibility of moral insight. Assuming a task at the margins of society and often in violation of some of its norms, the hero engages in limit-breaking activity. As he assigns unconditional value to a conditional task, he exalts pride at the expense of faith and disengages himself from ordinary con-

cerns. "Fusion with an impersonal absolute" accepts a contrast between our illusory phenomenal world, where the principle of individuation holds sway, and the plane of absolute reality, where distinctions between individuals and things vanish. Seen most clearly in Hinduism and Buddhism, adherents either take the path of the recluse or accept their social role while remaining aloof from it. "Confucianism" adheres to a particular list of social relations and ordering of the emotions. Viewing people as completely defined by fixed social roles and a particular political order, this ethic mistakes a specific system of social order as the solution to conflicting conduct and assertion. The "Christian-Romantic" ethic puts personal attachments up for grabs. Acknowledging that the qualities realized in faith, hope, and love override the claims of given social categories and that advances in self-understanding occur as we open ourselves to personal encounter, the ethic is beset by a deep ambivalence between a moralistic obsession with fixed rules and a fantasy of the super-individual who defies all obstacles while asserting his will.

37. Ibid., 32–39.

38. Boyle, "Modernist Social Theory," 1073–1074; Drucilla Cornell, "Toward a Modern/Postmodern Reconstruction of Ethics," 133 *University of Pennsylvania Law Review* 291, 296, 328, 356–358 (1985).

39. Cornell, "Toward a Modern/Postmodern Reconstruction," 356.

40. Unger, *Social Theory*, 9, 165–169. Unger identifies Foucault, Gramsci, and Dewey as ultra-theorists.

41. Ibid., 168–169.

42. See, for example, Bernard Yack, "Book Review: Toward a Free Marketplace of Social Institutions: Roberto Unger's 'Super-Liberal' Theory of Emancipation," 101 *Harvard Law Review* 1961, 1967–1970 (1988). For the view that CLS itself generally merely restates the problem of the fundamental contradiction, see Schroeder, "Liberalism," 108–109.

43. See, for example, Thomas Kuhn, *The Structure of Scientific Revolutions*, 2d ed. (Chicago: University of Chicago Press, 1970); Paul Feyerabend, *Against Method: Outline of an Anarchistic Theory of Knowledge* (London: New Left Books, 1975).

44. See, for example, Unger, *False Necessity*, 572.

45. Unger, *Plasticity*, chap. 3.

46. Unger, "Critical Legal Studies Movement," 584, 672–673.

47. Ibid., 577–578.

48. Ibid., 578–580.

49. Kelman, *Critical Legal Studies*, 215, 219; Paul Brest, "The Misconceived Quest for the Original Understanding," 60 *Boston University Law Review* 204, 225–226, 234–237 (1980).

50. Kelman, *Critical Legal Studies*, 215.

51. Ibid., 216–217; Brest, "Misconceived Quest," 209–217, 220–222. For a general analysis of the notion of "intentionality," see John Searle, *Intentionality* (Cambridge: Cambridge University Press, 1984).

52. Kelman, *Critical Legal Studies*, 219–221; Brest, "Misconceived Quest," 225–226, 234–237; and Hanna Pitkin, "Obligation and Consent," 59 *American Political Science Review* 990 (1965).

53. Kelman, *Critical Legal Studies*, 221; Brest, "Misconceived Quest," 229–231.

54. Unger, "Critical Legal Studies Movement," 580.

55. For example, the ideal of "democracy" is normally thought to be paramount in the sphere of "country," the ideal of "private community" in the sphere of "family," and the ideal of "contract and technological hierarchy" in the sphere of "work." Moreover, each of these ideals has certain institutional embodiments (three-branch representative government, nuclear family, management–workers, respectively). By developing new institutional embodiments for our abstract ideals we may efface their distinctive spheres of domain. For example, "democracy" may extend to "work," or "contract" may extend to "family." In the process, personal relations are emancipated from vested social hierarchy and division. Ibid., 578–581.

56. See, for example, Cornel West, "Between Dewey and Gramsci: Unger's Emancipatory Experimentalism," 81 *Northwestern University Law Review* 941, 942–943, 950–951 (1987); David E. Van Zandt, "Commonsense Reasoning, Social Change, and the Law," 81 *Northwestern University Law Review* 894, 938–940 (1987).

57. Law would reflect four kinds of rights: (1) Immunity rights would establish the nearly absolute claim of individuals to personal invasions. Such rights would include civic rights of political organization, expression, and participation; welfare entitlements; and options to withdraw functionally or physically from the established order. (2) Destabilization rights are collective entitlements that enable the disruption of established institutions and social practices to avoid the vesting of entrenched power. Their aim is the disruption of social hierarchy and division. (3) Market rights represent "conditional and provisional claims to divisible portions of social capital." In contrast to capitalist regimes, market rights will not be viewed as the paradigm of "rights," but will instead be a subcategory of rights. (4) Solidarity rights protect expectations that arise from the mutual reliance and vulnerability that characterize personal relations. The effect of such rights would be to ensure that good faith loyalty and reciprocity characterize the formation of contracts. "Critical Legal Studies Movement," 598–600, 612, 640.

58. The organization of government would be formed in light of three aspirations: (1) the branches of government should be multiplied to ensure that every feature of the social order is subject to destabilization and broadly based conflict; (2) conflicts among these increased branches of government should be resolved by principles of priority among the branches and by appeal to the electorate; and (3) the principles of priority would aim at resolving impasses clearly and quickly, permitting the political party in office a real opportunity to implement its programs. Ibid., 592–593, 596.

59. Ibid., 595.

60. See, for example, William A. Galston, "False Universality," 81 *Northwestern University Law Review* 751, 758–759, 761–762 (1987); Cass R. Sunstein, "Routine and Revolution," 81 *Northwestern University Law Review* 869, 890 (1987).

61. Belliotti, "Radical Politics," 50.

62. See also, Chapter 9.

## CHAPTER 8

1. Catharine A. MacKinnon, *Feminism Unmodified* (Cambridge, Mass.: Harvard University Press, 1987); MacKinnon, *Sexual Harassment of Working Women* (New Haven, Conn.: Yale University Press, 1979); MacKinnon, "Feminism, Marxism, Method and the State: An Agenda for Theory," 7 *Signs* 515 (1982) (hereinafter "Agenda for Theory"); MacKinnon, "Feminism, Marxism, Method and the State: Toward Feminist Jurisprudence," 8 *Signs* 635 (1983) (hereinafter "Toward Feminist Jurisprudence"); Ann C. Scales, "The Emergence of Feminist Jurisprudence: An Essay," 95 *Yale Law Journal* 1373 (1986).

2. Scales, "Emergence of Feminist Jurisprudence," 1377.

3. MacKinnon, "Agenda for Theory," 537.

4. MacKinnon, "Toward Feminist Jurisprudence," 645; ibid., 537.

5. MacKinnon, "Toward Feminist Jurisprudence," 658. "If objectivity is the epistemological stance of which women's sexual objectification is the social process, its imposition the paradigm of power in the male form, then the state will appear most relentless in imposing the male point of view when it comes closest to achieving its highest formal criterion of distanced aperspectivity. When it is most ruthlessly neutral, it will be most male."

6. MacKinnon, "Agenda for Theory," 516.

7. MacKinnon, "Toward Feminist Jurisprudence," 636n.3. Joan C. Williams calls such admissions "a standard disclaimer": "But the disclaimer does not solve the underlying problem. . . . [Authors of such disclaimers do not] explain why men and women whose behavior does not adhere to gender stereotypes should be denied the dignity of being 'real' men or 'real' women. . . . This insult reflects a gender system that (a) mandates correlation of behavior patterns with genitals and (b) consequently admits of only two, consistently dichotomous, behavior patterns." Williams, "Deconstructing Gender," 87 *Michigan Law Review*, 797, 813n.61 (1989).

8. MacKinnon, "Toward Feminist Jurisprudence," 636n.3.

9. Ibid., 646.

10. Ibid.

11. Ibid., 649.

12. Ibid.

13. Ibid., 650–651.

14. "But with rape, because sexuality defines gender, the only difference between assault and (what is socially considered) noninjury is the meaning

of the encounter to the woman. . . . Rape law . . . uniformly presumes a single underlying reality, not a reality split by divergent meanings, such as those inequality produces. . . . To attempt to solve [contested sexual encounters] by adopting the standard of reasonable belief without asking, on a substantive social basis, to whom the belief is reasonable and why—meaning, what conditions make it reasonable—is one-sided: male-sided" (ibid., 652, 654).

15. Scales, "Emergence of Feminist Jurisprudence," 1375. The differences approach that is the target of FU's attack here is suspicious of alleged differences between men and women, taking them to be invariably founded on inaccurate or merely partial data. Where differences are empirically established, advocates of this approach take them to be the pernicious results of nurture, not intrinsic nature. See, for example, Ruth Bader Ginsburg, "Sex Equality and the Constitution," 52 *Tulane Law Review* 451 (1978). The different voice approach is most closely associated with the work of Carol Gilligan. This approach castigates legal doctrine and moral theory for taking a partial perspective—the male vantage point—and presuming that it should be universally applied. In *In a Different Voice* (Cambridge, Mass.: Harvard University Press, 1982), Gilligan states that young girls and young boys deal with moral problems differently: boys are more legalistic ("the ethics of rights"); girls are more sensitive to preserving the relationships involved in given situations ("the ethics of care"). Gilligan argues that the ability to integrate the ethics of care with the ethics of rights indicates mature moral development. See Gilligan, ibid., 25–51, 151–174. FU criticizes the different voice approach. Scales is unconvinced that the required incorporation of the two voices can occur in our "current genderized realm": "By trying to make everything too nice, incorporationism represses contradictions. It usurps women's language in order to further define the world in the male image." "Emergence of Feminist Jurisprudence," 1383, 1385. MacKinnon pays lip service to the "strong and elegant sensitivity" in Gilligan's work but is firm in distancing herself from it: ("What is infuriating about [Gilligan's work] . . . is that it neglects the explanatory level. *Why* do women become these people, more than men, who represent *these* values? . . . The answer is clear: the answer is the subordination of women. . . . Calling [the ethics of care] hers is infuriating to me because we have never had the power to develop what ours really would be.") "Feminist Discourse, Moral Values, and the Law—A Conversation" (with Ellen C. DuBois, Mary C. Dunlap, Carol J. Gilligan, Catharine A. MacKinnon, Carrie J. Menkel-Meadow), 34 *Buffalo Law Review* 11, 73–75 (1985).

16. Scales, "Emergence of Feminist Jurisprudence," 1375.

17. Ibid., 1376.

18. Ibid.

19. MacKinnon, *Feminism Unmodified*, 34.

20. MacKinnon, "Feminist Discourse," 21.

21. Ibid., 24; Scales, "Emergence of Feminist Jurisprudence," 1385–1388, 1393–1399; Katherine O'Donovan, "Engendering Justice: Women's Perspec-

tives and the Rule of Law," 39 *University of Toronto Law Journal* 127, 147 (1989).

22. MacKinnon, "Agenda for Theory," 535.

23. Ibid.

24. Ibid., 536–537.

25. K. Lahey, "Implications of Feminist Theory for the Direction of Reform of the Criminal Code" (unpublished paper, 1984), 69, cited in Susan B. Boyd and Elizabeth Sheehy, "Canadian Feminist Perspectives on Law," 13 *Journal of Law and Society* 283, 296 (1986).

26. Scales, "Emergence of Feminist Jurisprudence," 1385.

27. Ibid.

28. Ibid., 1388.

29. Ibid., 1387.

30. Ibid.

31. Ibid.

32. Ibid.

33. Ibid., 1394; MacKinnon, *Sexual Harassment of Working Women*, 117.

34. Scales, "Emergence of Feminist Jurisprudence," 1398.

35. Ibid., 1400–1401.

36. Ibid., 1401.

37. Ibid.

38. Ibid., 1402–1403.

39. Justice Potter Stewart is widely remembered for a concurring opinion in which he stated that only "hard core" pornography could be banned but conceded the subjective nature of any definition: "I shall not today attempt to further define the kind of materials I understand to be embraced within that shorthand definition; and perhaps I could never succeed in intelligibly doing so. *But I know it when I see it*" (emphasis added). *Jacobellis v. Ohio*, 378 US 184, 197 (1964). Justice Stewart's observation is not generally considered the height of refined legal analysis or a helpful test for determining which material is pornographic.

40. MacKinnon, "Agenda for Theory," 542. MacKinnon is aware of the potential vacuity in claiming that women who oppose her views are victims of false consciousness: "Not all women agree with the feminist account of women's situation, nor do all feminists agree with any single rendition of feminism. . . . What is the point of view of the experience of all women? Most responses in the name of feminism . . . either (1) simply regard some women's views as 'false consciousness,' or (2) embrace any version of women's experience that a biological female claims as her own. The first approach treats women's views as unconscious conditioned reflections of their oppression, complicitous in it. . . . But if both feminism and antifeminism are responses to the condition of women, how is feminism exempt from devaluation by the same account? . . . The false consciousness approach begs this question by taking women's self-reflections as evidence of their stake in their own oppression, when the women whose self-reflections are at issue question whether their condition is oppressed at all. The second

response proceeds as if women are free. . . . So our problem is this: the false consciousness approach cannot explain experience as it is experienced by those who experience it. The alternative can only reiterate the terms of that experience." MacKinnon, "Toward Feminist Jurisprudence," 637n.5.

There is much in this quote that is perspicacious and that would be applauded by a mainstream analytic philosopher. The question is this: Does MacKinnon heed her own counsel? Or does she end up descending into the quagmire of "the first approach" when she rebukes her critics as "collaborators"? See, for example, MacKinnon, *Feminism Unmodified*, 198–205, 216–228.

41. MacKinnon, "Toward Feminist Jurisprudence," 637.

42. Ibid.

43. Ibid., 638.

44. Katharine T. Bartlett, "MacKinnon's Feminism: Power on Whose Terms?" 75 *California Law Review* 1559, 1562 (1987).

45. Ibid., 1563.

46. MacKinnon, *Feminism Unmodified*, 198–205, 216–228.

47. Bartlett, "MacKinnon's Feminism," 1563.

48. MacKinnon, "Toward Feminist Jurisprudence," 640.

49. Ibid., 638.

50. "MacKinnon's failure to acknowledge that not every fact related to women's experience neatly and unreservedly supports her thesis of male dominance not only reduces the persuasiveness of her work, but demonstrates an effort to control and objectify her subject that is characteristic of the male world she otherwise so firmly rejects. . . . She claims to speak for all women, yet dismisses in disgust as 'collaborators' those who don't think and act in accordance with her own views." Bartlett, "MacKinnon's Feminism," 1564.

51. "MacKinnon talked about how male domination is an *almost* metaphysically perfect system. It seems to me what she presents *is* a metaphysically perfect system and therefore one that is unreal. . . . It defines women as having no power, and if by definition women are those without power, then go home and lock the door because there is no possibility for change," Ellen C. DuBois, "Feminist Discourse," 70.

52. MacKinnon, *Feminism Unmodified*, 195. Although the criticism that MacKinnon tacitly relies on a notion of "authenticity" is recurrent, it is not clear that the charge is well founded. See, for example, Ruth Colker, "Feminism, Sexuality, and Self: A Preliminary Inquiry into the Politics of Authenticity," 68 *Boston University Law Review* 217, 220 n.8 (1988): "MacKinnon never takes a position on the concept of authenticity explicitly in her scholarship. However, when I asked her about the concept when she presented a paper . . . she responded that she found the concept unhelpful."

53. O'Donovan, "Engendering Justice," 139.

54. MacKinnon, "Agenda for Theory," 529–534, especially 532.

55. Williams, "Deconstructing Gender," 838. "Her inequality approach allows disadvantages produced by *gender* to be remedied by reference to *sex*.

This is in effect an acceptance and a reinforcement of the societal presumption that the social role of primary caretaker is necessarily correlated with possession of a vagina." However, given that MacKinnon uses "gender" and "sex" more loosely than Williams, it is not clear that her test would produce the deleterious effects that Williams fears. It is unclear whether MacKinnon's test is based on remedy by reference to "sex" in the way Williams assumes.

56. Although not clearly an exponent of FU, Robin West captures part of the contrast between feminist jurisprudence and "male" versions of legal theory: "Feminist legal scholars insist it is the heart and not the head, the ability to particularize, not generalize, one's *sensitivity* to context, and not one's ability to transcend it, the ability to connect . . . not the ability to 'see past' differences to some universal essence, which is the basis of . . . 'The Rule of Law.'" "Love, Rage, and Legal Theory," 1 *Yale Journal of Law and Feminism* 101, 102 (1989).

57. Richard Bernstein, "Pragmatism, Pluralism, and the Healing of Wounds," 63 *American Philosophical Society Proceedings* 5, 10 (No. 3, 1989).

58. Ibid., 16.

59. Ibid., 16–17.

60. Ibid., 15. "For there is a danger of *fragmenting* pluralism where . . . we are only able to communicate with the small group that already shares our own biases, and no longer even experience the need to talk with others outside of this circle. There is a *flabby* pluralism where our borrowings from different orientations are little more than glib superficial poaching. There is a *polemical* pluralism where the appeal to pluralism . . . becomes rather an ideological weapon to advance one's own orientation. There is a *defensive* pluralism, a form of tokenism, where we pay lip service to others 'doing their own thing' but are already convinced that there is nothing important to be learned from them."


CHAPTER 9

1. Epistemological Foundationalism is the view that our knowledge claims can ultimately be tested by certain foundational truths that themselves are immune to revision. Such foundational truths may be indubitable (incapable of consistently being doubted), self-evident (beyond and not in need of rational demonstration), or incorrigible, or they may be presuppositions of rationality itself. Metaphysical Realism is the view that reality is mind-independent, admits of one true description, and that humans arrive at truth insofar as their propositions about the world copy or correspond to reality. Metaphysical Realism often appeals to a notion of inherent essences—"things-in-themselves"—and sometimes appeals to a special human cognitive faculty (for example, intuition) by which we grasp these essences.

2. The inspiration for this section of the book is Pierre Schlag's "Missing Pieces: A Cognitive Approach to Law," 67 *Texas Law Review* 1195 (1989). Schlag posits four cognitive modes: prerationalism, rationalism, modernism, and postmodernism. I track these four closely, talk about rhetorical strategies rather than cognitive modes (because, among other reasons, it is not clear that deconstruction claims to be cognitive), and add a fifth strategy: the pragmatic.

3. See, for example, ibid., 1209–1210.

4. Ibid., 1211.

5. Richard Bernstein, "Pragmatism, Pluralism, and the Healing of Wounds," 63 *American Philosophical Society Proceedings* 5, 9 (No. 3, 1989).

6. Ibid. "[Pragmatists] were well aware of the danger of a type of fragmentation and hermetic isolation where only brute manipulative power rules. And they highlighted the ways in which all human life is shaped by social practices—practices which always present us with the challenge of practical reconstruction" (18).

7. Schlag, "Missing Pieces," 1213.

8. Ibid., 1216.

9. Ibid., 1241.

10. Ibid., 1217.

11. Ibid.

12. Ibid., 1241. David Hoy expresses the implications of deconstructionism for judicial decision making: "The hermeneutical search for the meaning of the literary, philosophical, or historical text, or the judge's attempt to interpret the legal text and to decide the case, would always be self-deception if all texts were in principle shot through with undecidability." Hoy, "Interpreting the Law: Hermeneutical and Poststructuralist Perspectives," in *Interpreting Law and Literature*, ed. Sanford Levinson and Steven Mailloux (Evanston, Ill.: Northwestern University Press, 1988), 331–332.

13. Schlag, "Missing Pieces," 1238.

14. See, for example, Thomas Kuhn, *The Structure of Scientific Revolutions*, 2d ed. (Chicago: University of Chicago Press, 1970).

15. Schlag, "Missing Pieces," 1241–1242.

16. Ibid., 1243. "The typical supposition within the legal community that intellectual endeavor can and must converge in 'points' or 'solutions' or 'ideas'—or 'conclusions'—has a real tendency to kill thought. . . . The systematic character of [analytic] misunderstanding [of the claims of other rhetorical strategies] turns out to be the very technique by which [the analytic mode] sustains itself as a viable cognitive orientation."

17. In fact, my analysis of rhetorical strategies can be viewed reflexively as predominantly analytic (the quest for classification and logical analysis), with significant pragmatic (appreciation for flux, pluralism, fallibalism, and a community of inquirers), intuitive (faith in progress of discourse, and commitment to standard methods of analysis), and substructural elements (the quest for an underlying substructure of discourse that can account for superstructural ideological phenomena).

18. Incommensurability often takes the following pattern: the analytic mode reveals the intuitive mode as based on prejudice and bias, the pragmatic mode reveals the analytic mode as partial and abstract, the substructural mode reveals the analytic mode as masking the workings of power and privilege and reveals the pragmatic mode as garnished conventionalism and expediency, and the deconstructive mode mocks the totalizing ambitions of the analytic and substructural modes. Each mode, especially the dominant analytic, has a tendency to recast the claims of other modes into its own mode as a first step toward undermining those claims.

19. See, for example, Schlag, "Missing Pieces," 1249–1250n.201. "It is simply not possible—so the argument goes—to claim both that the [rhetorical modes] are incommensurable and that there is a progression among them. . . . [Within the analytic mode] an assertion of incommensurability and progression really is a tension or a contradiction. But this tension or contradiction . . . is a function of the [analytic] attempt to maintain the meanings of incommensurability and progression at once constant and determining throughout the text. . . . On the other hand, [that analytic mode] has already been shown to be suspect—it is a cognitive framework whose claims to universal status have already been severely shaken. These statements, of course, will probably not persuade the [advocate of the analytic]. But then again—which way does that cut? Is it evidence that the [analytic] objection is right—or is it evidence that [the analytic mode] is rather limited as a stock cognitive mode?"

## CHAPTER 10

1. Lon Fuller claimed that the Rule of Law comprised a morality internal and necessary to law. He thought that the following eight elements captured the Rule of Law: generality, notice, prospectivity, clarity, noncontradictoriness, conformability, stability, and congruence. See *The Morality of Law*, rev. ed. (New Haven, Conn.: Yale University Press, 1969), 33–94.

2. See, for example, John Rawls, *A Theory of Justice* (Cambridge, Mass.: Harvard University Press, 1971), 235–240 and pt. 1.

3. Margaret Jane Radin, "Reconsidering the Rule of Law," 69 *Boston University Law Review* 781, 790 (1989).

4. Ibid., 791.

5. Ibid., 797.

6. Ibid.

7. Ibid., 798, 800.

8. See, for example, Jerold S. Auerbach, *Justice Without Law?* (New York: Oxford University Press, 1983), 4–5.

9. See, for example, M. P. Baumgartner, "Law and Social Status in Colonial New Haven, 1639–1665," 1 *Research in Law and Sociology* 153 (1978); Herbert Harley, "Justice or Litigation," 6 *Virginia Law Review* 143, 150 (1919); Jerome A. Cohen, "Chinese Mediation on the Eve of Modernization," 54

California Law Review 1201 (1966); Auerbach, *Justice Without Law?* 20, 47–60, 76–86, 119–120.

10. See, for example, Auerbach, *Justice Without Law?* 135, 144–146; J. Edward Thornton, "Resolving Disputes Without Law," 40 *The Alabama Lawyer* 104, 106 (1979).

11. Radin, "Reconsidering the Rule of Law," 783.

12. Ibid., 815.

13. Ibid., 819.

14. Ibid.

15. Ibid., 817.

16. Ibid., 813.

17. Ibid., 813–814.

18. Ibid., 817.

19. Ibid.

20. If God is taken to be a necessary intermediary between the standard of Good and human understanding, a related question remains: How can we be sure that God is accurately echoing the standard of Good when we have no independent point from which to compare God's reports and the standard itself?

21. See, for example, the work of Ronald Dworkin discussed in Chapter 3.

22. See, for example, Duncan Kennedy, "Form and Substance in Private Law Adjudication," 89 *Harvard Law Review* 1685, 1710–1713 (1976). The historical "experience of unresolvable conflict among . . . values" will not disappear.

23. Ronald Dworkin, *A Matter of Principle* (Cambridge, Mass.: Harvard University Press, 1985), 168.

24. Ibid., 167.

25. Ibid., 171. "I think that the problem of objectivity . . . is a fake because the distinction that might give it meaning, the distinction between substantive arguments within and skeptical arguments about social practices, is itself a fake" (ibid., 173–174).

26. Hilary Putnam, *The Many Faces of Realism* (LaSalle, Ill.: Open Court, 1987), 86.

27. See, for example, Chapter 6; Jürgen Habermas, "Between Philosophy and Science: Marxism as Critique," in *Theory and Practice* (Boston: Beacon Press, 1973); Karl Korsch, *Three Essays on Marxism* (London: Pluto Press, 1971).

28. Cornel West, *The American Evasion of Philosophy* (Madison: University of Wisconsin Press, 1989), 197; Richard Rorty, "The World Well Lost," 69 *Journal of Philosophy* 665 (October 26, 1972).

29. Wilfred Sellars, "Empiricism and the Philosophy of Mind," in *Minnesota Studies in the Philosophy of Science*, vol. 1, ed. Herbert Fiegl and Michael Scriven (Minneapolis: University of Minnesota Press, 1956), 289.

30. Putnam, *Many Faces of Realism*, 70.

31. Ibid., 77.

32. Dworkin, *Matter of Principle*, 169.

33. Putnam, *Many Faces of Realism*, 67.

34. Ludwig Wittgenstein, *On Certainty*, ed. G.E.M. Anscombe and G.H. von Wright, trans. Denis Paul and G.E.M. Anscombe (Oxford: Basil Blackwell, 1969), sect. 200.

35. Throughout this work, "ideology" is not used as a pejorative. It is used as a general term to describe one's descriptive and prescriptive world vision, or political philosophy.

36. Ronald Dworkin, *Taking Rights Seriously* (Cambridge, Mass.: Harvard University Press, 1977), 105.

37. Richard Posner talks about various stabilizing mechanisms embodied in law in "The Jurisprudence of Skepticism," 86 *Michigan Law Review* 827, 864 (1988). "These include the principle of judicial self-restraint . . . rules defining and limiting the circumstances in which judges consider themselves free to overrule previous cases, and the conversion of multifactored tests to formulas or algorithms. . . . Still other auxiliary principles . . . include strict construction, rigid adherence to stare decisis, favoring the underdog in close cases. . . . None of them, however, can be derived by the methods of legal reasoning. All depend on a judgment of political theory" (864).

38. "There is no choice without reflection nor reflection without knowledge, including self-knowledge . . . no knowledge without language, no language without categories. . . . Adjudication would, it seems, have to be a process of conversation (argument) and recognition, hence of reason, as much as of choice." Frank I. Michelman, "Justification (and Justifiability) of Law in a Contradictory World," 28 *Nomos* 71, 89–90 (1986).

39. Martin P. Golding, "A Note on Discovery and Justification in Science and Law," 28 *Nomos* 124, 137 (1986).

40. I am not using "injustice" in its narrow political sense. Instead, I am using it broadly to mean "moral inadequacy."

41. David Luban offers a virtually identical pragmatic justification of the adversary system in "The Adversary System Excuse," in *The Good Lawyer* (Totowa, N.J.: Rowman and Allanheld, 1983), 111–113.

42. Luban, however, claims that his pragmatic justification is "nonideological." See ibid., 112. I dispute Luban's claim in "Our Adversary System: In Search of a Foundation," 1 *Canadian Journal of Law and Jurisprudence* 19, 33 (1988).

# INDEX